AMERICA'S
FAMILY RECIPES

The Best Home Cooking Across the Country   2006

Editor: Beth Wittlinger
Art Director: Lori Arndt
Executive Editor/Books: Heidi Reuter Lloyd
Graphic Art Associates: Ellen Lloyd, Catherine Fletcher
Proofreader: Linne Bruskewitz
Editorial Assistant: Barb Czysz

Food Editor: Janaan Cunningham
Senior Recipe Editor: Sue A. Jurack
Recipe Editor: Janet Briggs

Food Photographers: Rob Hagen, Dan Roberts, Jim Wieland
Associate Photographer: Lori Foy
Set Stylists: Sue Myers, Jennifer Bradley Vent
Associate Set Stylist: Melissa Haberman
Food Stylists: Sarah Thompson, Joylyn Trickel

Creative Director: Ardyth Cope
Senior Vice President/Editor in Chief: Catherine Cassidy
President: Barbara Newton
Founder: Roy Reiman

For additional copies of this book or information on other books, write *Taste of Home* Books, P.O. Box 908, Greendale WI 53129, call toll-free 1-800/344-2560 to order with a credit card or visit our Web site at ***www.reimanpub.com***.

PICTURED ABOVE AND ON FRONT COVER. From top left: Raspberry Peach Pie (p. 106), Tangy Potato Salad (p. 29), Jalapeno Corn Bread (p. 187) and Best-Ever Fried Chicken (p. 194).

Discover 340 New Family Favorites!

ALL OF THE BEST RECIPES can be found in *America's Family Recipes 2006*, which serves up 340 favorites. Delicious recipes are paired with beautiful photography to bring you the best of North America!

This giant collection includes the very best recipes from a year's worth of recent issues of *Country Woman*, *Country*, *Country EXTRA*, *Reminisce* and *Reminisce EXTRA* magazines. All the recipes you'll find are hearty, wholesome and proven favorites of a family just like yours.

Each recipe comes directly from the personal recipe files of hundreds of everyday cooks across the country. And every dish has been sampled and approved by the toughest critic around—a hungry family! Then our Test Kitchen staff (and some lucky taste-testers) tried out every recipe in this book, too. So you can be doubly confident each dish is one for the files because it is already a winner.

This book begins with an appealing assortment of 23 Breakfast & Brunch items. Whether you host a special holiday gathering or just want something different for a weekend treat, this chapter has some of the best recipes your family will ever taste.

Next up you'll find 17 Snacks & Beverages. So the next time you have family, friends or coworkers clamoring for one of your homemade treats, look to this chapter. For example, Susan Kruspe's prize-winning Orange Fruit Dip (p. 21) is perfect for picnics, showers and family events.

In addition, this tried-and-true treasury contains a savory selection of 37 Soups, Salads & Sandwiches. This chapter even features a special section on the pressure cooker, which offers recipes for putting this time-saving kitchen tool to delicious use!

You can also take your pick of this beautiful book's 49 recipes included in the Main Dishes chapter. It's filled with wonderful comfort foods like Vicky Reinhold's very favorite recipe for Super Swiss Steak (p. 60) that cooks up in the skillet for a wonderful meal. Or, try Rebecca Baird's recipe for Beef Stroganoff; your family will never guess it's lighter! Plus, we highlight sausage on pages 68 through 71 with eight useful hints on page 70.

There is also a Side Dishes chapter filled with 16 family-pleasing complements. Larkspur, Colorado cook Ruth Beers shares her recipe for Sweet Potato Pineapple Bake, which is certain to be a hit for your next holiday meal.

A Breads & Rolls chapter is complete with 16 recipes for yeast breads, quick breads and muffins to tempt the taste buds and delight the senses with wonderful aromas and flavors of fresh-baked goodies.

Everyone will save room for a sweet treat when you select any of this book's 54 scrumptious cakes, pies, cookies and more that span two entire chapters. Plus, in addition to the chapters for main dishes and desserts, you can find even more within our special meal chapters. That includes:

Cooking for Two—A separate chapter with 6 complete meals plus individual recipes (65 in all) properly proportioned to serve two people.

Thirty-Minute Meals—Six complete meals (18 recipes in all) that are ready to eat in less than half an hour.

Most Memorable Meals—Six complete meals featuring 24 favorite recipes from home cooks.

Want more? *America's Family Recipes 2006* offers trips to Wyoming, New York and North Dakota to discover lamb, corn and sugar beets!

As you page through *America's Family Recipes 2006*, watch for the special symbol at right. It signifies a "best of the best" recipe representing a winner of a coast-to-coast cooking contest sponsored by one of our magazines.

Finally, throughout this colorful collection are helpful kitchen tips from everyday cooks plus dozens of "restricted diet" recipes marked with this check ☑ that use less fat, sugar or salt.

Welcome to *America's Family Recipes 2006*!

Contents

For special family gatherings or to **liven up an ordinary morning,** try a selection of this chapter's recipes.

Breakfast & Brunch

BRUNCH PLEASERS. Pictured above from top left: Cream Cheese Coils (p. 6), Cream Cheese Coffee Cake (p. 7) and Blueberry Buttermilk Pancakes (p. 9).

These are my absolute favorite sweet rolls! They never last long around my family. They're easy to make but look like you spent a lot of time on them.

~Susan Peck
REPUBLIC, MISSOURI

Cream Cheese Coils

(Pictured on page 4)

3-3/4 to 4-1/4 cups all-purpose flour
3/4 cup sugar, *divided*
2 packages (1/4 ounce *each*) active dry yeast
1-1/2 teaspoons salt
3/4 cup milk
1/2 cup water
1/2 cup butter, cubed
1 egg
1 package (8 ounces) cream cheese, softened
1 egg yolk
1/2 teaspoon vanilla extract

GLAZE:
1 cup confectioners' sugar
1/2 teaspoon vanilla extract
3 to 4 teaspoons water

In a large mixing bowl, combine 1 cup flour, 1/2 cup sugar, yeast and salt. In a saucepan, heat the milk, water and butter to 120°-130°. Add to dry ingredients; beat on medium speed for 2 minutes. Add egg and 1/2 cup flour; beat on high for 2 minutes. Stir in enough remaining flour to form a stiff dough. Cover and refrigerate for 2 hours.

Turn dough onto a lightly floured surface; divide into 18 pieces. Shape each piece into a ball; roll each into a 15-in. rope. Holding one end of rope, loosely wrap dough around, forming a coil. Tuck end under; pinch to seal. Place coils 2 in. apart on greased baking sheets. Cover and let rise until doubled, about 1 hour.

In a small mixing bowl, combine the cream cheese, egg yolk, vanilla and remaining sugar; beat until smooth. Using the back of a spoon, make a 1-in.-wide indentation in the center of each coil; spoon a rounded tablespoon of the cream cheese mixture into each indentation.

Bake at 400° for 10-12 minutes or until lightly browned. Remove from pans to wire racks to cool.

In a small bowl, combine the confectioners' sugar, vanilla and enough water to achieve drizzling consistency. Drizzle over cooled rolls. Store in the refrigerator. **Yield:** 1-1/2 dozen.

This is a great recipe for a brunch as well as breakfast. I serve it with fresh stir-fried asparagus, a fruit salad and croissants.

~Marilyn Moores
INDIANAPOLIS, INDIANA

Artichoke Egg Casserole

4 jars (6-1/2 ounces *each*) marinated artichoke hearts
1/2 cup chopped green onions
2 to 3 garlic cloves, minced
1 tablespoon vegetable oil
8 eggs
1 jar (4-1/2 ounces) sliced mushrooms, drained
3 cups (12 ounces) shredded sharp cheddar cheese
1 cup butter-flavored cracker crumbs (about 25 crackers)

Drain artichokes, reserving 1/2 cup marinade. Set aside. Cut artichokes into slices. In a skillet, saute green onions and garlic in oil until tender. Remove from the heat.

In a large bowl, beat eggs well. Stir in the artichokes, mushrooms, cheese, cracker crumbs, onion mixture and the reserved marinade.

Transfer to a greased 13-in. x 9-in. x 2-in. baking dish. Bake, uncovered, at 350° for 35-40 minutes or until a knife inserted near the center comes out clean. **Yield:** 9 servings.

Bacon buns are a family tradition, handed down two generations from Lithuania. You can also fill them with ground cooked ham.
~Mary Ann Simkus
HAMPSHIRE, ILLINOIS

Bacon Buns

10 bacon strips, diced
1/3 cup chopped onion
1 package (16 ounces) hot roll mix
1 egg, lightly beaten

In a skillet, cook bacon and onion over medium heat until bacon is crisp and onion is tender; drain on paper towels.

Prepare hot roll mix according to package directions. Turn dough onto a floured surface; knead until smooth and elastic, about 5 minutes. Place in a greased bowl, turning once to grease top. Cover and let rise in a warm place until doubled, about 40 minutes.

Divide dough into 18 pieces. On a floured surface, roll out each piece in-to a 5-in. circle. Top each with 1 table-spoon of bacon filling. Fold dough around filling, shaping each piece into a small loaf; pinch edges to seal.

Place seam side down on greased baking sheets. Cover loosely with plastic wrap coated with nonstick cooking spray. Let rise in a warm place for 20-30 minutes.

Brush egg over buns. Bake at 350° for 20-25 minutes or until golden brown. Remove from pans to wire racks. Serve warm. Refrigerate left-overs. **Yield:** 1-1/2 dozen.

A good friend gave me this recipe a few years back. I've made it often, and everyone who has tried it loves it.
~Judy Coffey
KESWICK RIDGE, NEW BRUNSWICK

Cream Cheese Coffee Cake

(Also pictured on page 5)

1/2 cup butter, softened
1 cup sugar
3 eggs
1 teaspoon vanilla extract
2 cups all-purpose flour
1 teaspoon baking powder
1 teaspoon baking soda
1/4 teaspoon salt
1 cup (8 ounces) sour cream

FILLING:
2 packages (3 ounces *each*) cream cheese
2 tablespoons confectioners' sugar
2 tablespoons lemon juice

CINNAMON-NUT TOPPING:
1/4 cup finely chopped pecans
2 tablespoons sugar
1/2 teaspoon ground cinnamon

In a large mixing bowl, cream butter and sugar. Add eggs and vanilla; beat well. Combine the flour, baking powder, baking soda and salt; add to creamed mixture alternately with sour cream. Set batter aside.

In a small mixing bowl, beat cream cheese, confectioners' sugar and lemon juice until smooth. Spoon half of the batter into a greased and floured 10-in. tube pan. Top with filling and remaining batter. Combine topping ingredients; sprinkle over batter.

Bake at 350° for 30-35 minutes or until a toothpick inserted near the center of cake comes out clean. Cool for 10 minutes before removing from pan to a wire rack. **Yield:** 12 servings.

A friend shared this recipe with me. It has homemade flavor without the time or fuss it takes to make from-scratch yeast rolls.
~Barbara Strohbehn
GLADBROOK, IOWA

No-Fuss Caramel Rolls

    1 cup packed brown sugar
1/2 cup heavy whipping cream
    8 frozen unbaked cinnamon rolls, thawed

In a bowl, combine the brown sugar and cream; pour into a greased 13-in. x 9-in. x 2-in. baking dish. Place rolls cut side up in the dish. Cover and let rise until doubled, about 1 hour.

    Bake at 350° for 20-22 minutes or until light brown. Cool for 5 minutes before inverting onto a serving platter. **Yield:** 8 servings.

Bacon Bake-Off

Helpful Hint

If you like bacon, buy several pounds when it's on sale. Then put the strips in a single layer on jelly roll pans and pop them in the oven to bake at 350° for 30-45 minutes or until they're crisp. Place the strips on paper towels to drain before storing them in a freezer container. This makes it easy to remove only the number of strips needed for a quick breakfast or sandwich. A short time in the microwave reheats the bacon.

Our family raised chickens, making my mother naturally creative with eggs. Since Dad didn't care for eggs alone but did like fish, she often mixed eggs with salmon. I still prepare this wholesome omelet today.
    ~Ruth Chasteen
WOODVILLE, FLORIDA

Fresh Salmon Omelet

    1 salmon fillet (1 inch thick, about 10 ounces)
1/4 cup finely chopped onion
1/4 cup finely chopped green pepper
    2 tablespoons butter, *divided*
    6 eggs
1/4 cup shredded cheddar cheese
1/4 teaspoon pepper
    1 medium tomato, optional
1/4 medium green pepper, optional

Remove the skin and bones from the salmon; cut into 1/2-in. chunks. In a 10-in. skillet, saute the salmon, onion and green pepper in 1 tablespoon butter. Remove and set aside.

    In a small bowl, beat eggs. Melt remaining butter in same skillet over medium heat; add eggs. As eggs set, lift edges, letting uncooked portion flow underneath.

    When the eggs are set, spoon salmon mixture over one side, then sprinkle with cheese and pepper; fold omelet over filling. Cover and let stand for 1-1/2 minutes or until the cheese is melted.

    If desired, make a tomato rose. With a small sharp knife, peel the skin in a thin continuous strip, starting from the base of the tomato. Roll up tightly, skin side out, from the stem end. Tuck end of strip under rose and place on omelet. From green pepper, cut out two leaves. Arrange on each side of tomato rose. **Yield:** 3 servings.

My husband and I have three active sons, so I'm always busy in the kitchen. This rich quick bread is a favorite. I like to cover loaves with colored plastic wrap to give as gifts.

~Sharon Walker
HUNTINGTON STATION, NEW YORK

Country Cinnamon Swirl Bread

1/4 cup butter, softened
1-1/3 cups sugar, *divided*
1 egg
2 cups all-purpose flour
1 teaspoon baking powder
1/2 teaspoon baking soda
1/2 teaspoon salt
1 cup buttermilk
1 tablespoon ground cinnamon

In a large mixing bowl, beat butter, 1 cup sugar and egg until blended. Combine the flour, baking powder, baking soda and salt; add to egg mixture alternately with buttermilk. In a small bowl, combine the cinnamon and remaining sugar.

Pour a third of the batter into a greased 8-in. x 4-in. x 2-in. loaf pan; sprinkle with a third of the cinnamon-sugar. Repeat layers twice. Bake at 350° for 45-50 minutes or until a toothpick inserted near the center comes out clean. Cool for 10 minutes before removing from pan to a wire rack to cool completely. **Yield:** 1 loaf.

For years, I made these pancakes plain. Then my husband and I started growing blueberries. What a delicious addition!

~Marlene Jackson
LOWELL, ARKANSAS

Blueberry Buttermilk Pancakes

(Also pictured on page 5)

BLUEBERRY SYRUP:
2 cups fresh *or* frozen blueberries
1 cup sugar
1/2 cup water
1 tablespoon lemon juice

PANCAKES:
1 package (1/4 ounce) active dry yeast
2 tablespoons warm water (110° to 115°)
2 cups all-purpose flour
1 tablespoon sugar
1 teaspoon baking soda
1/2 teaspoon salt
2 cups buttermilk
2 tablespoons vegetable oil
3 eggs
1/2 cup heavy whipping cream
1-1/4 cups fresh *or* frozen blueberries

In a small saucepan, combine blueberries, sugar and water. Bring to a boil. Reduce heat; simmer, uncovered, for 15 minutes or until slightly thickened. Remove from heat. Stir in lemon juice; keep warm.

In a small bowl, dissolve yeast in warm water. In a large bowl, combine flour, sugar, baking soda and salt. Gradually stir in buttermilk, yeast mixture and oil until smooth. In a small bowl, beat eggs and cream; stir into the batter.

Pour batter by 1/4 cupfuls onto a greased hot griddle. Sprinkle each pancake with about 1 tablespoon blueberries. Turn when bubbles form on top of pancake; cook until second side is golden brown. Serve with warm blueberry syrup. **Yield:** 6 servings.

Editor's Note: If using frozen blueberries, do not thaw before adding to batter.

I'm in my 80s and still enjoy making all my old recipes. These crispy twists bake up nice and sweet! ~Lois Heffelfinger
HAMILTON, OHIO

Cinnamon Twists

1 tablespoon plus 1-1/2 cups sugar, *divided*
1/4 cup warm water (110° to 115°)
1 package (1/4 ounce) quick-rise yeast
3-1/2 cups all-purpose flour
1-1/2 teaspoons salt
1/2 cup cold butter, cubed
1/2 cup shortening
1/2 cup sour cream
2 eggs, lightly beaten
1 teaspoon vanilla extract
2 teaspoons ground cinnamon

In a small bowl, dissolve 1 tablespoon sugar in warm water. Add yeast; let stand for 5 minutes. In a large bowl, combine flour and salt. Cut in butter and shortening until crumbly.

Combine the sour cream, eggs and vanilla; stir into flour mixture. Stir in yeast mixture until well blended (do not knead). Divide dough into four sections. Wrap each section in plastic wrap; refrigerate for at least 2 hours.

Combine cinnamon and remaining sugar; sprinkle 3-4 tablespoons on a work surface. Place one portion of the dough on cinnamon-sugar. Roll out to a 9-in. x 6-in. rectangle.

Sprinkle center third of dough with 1 tablespoon cinnamon-sugar. Fold one unsugared section over center. Sprinkle top of dough with 1 tablespoon cinnamon-sugar.

Bring remaining section of dough over cinnamon-sugar and sprinkle with 1 tablespoon cinnamon-sugar. Roll dough into a 12-in. x 8-in. rectangle. Cut into twelve 1-in. strips. Twist each strip several times. Repeat with the remaining dough.

Place strips on ungreased baking sheets. Bake at 350° for 15-20 minutes or until golden brown. Cool for 1 minute before removing to wire racks to cool completely. **Yield:** 4 dozen.

This German classic is such a part of our reunions, we designate a special place to serve it. Five generations flock to the "Kuchen Room" for this coffee cake. ~Stephanie Schentzel
NORTHVILLE, SOUTH DAKOTA

Rich Fruit Kuchens

1-1/8 teaspoons active dry yeast
1/2 cup warm water (110° to 115°)
1/2 cup warm milk (110° to 115°)
1/2 cup sugar
1/2 teaspoon salt
1/2 cup vegetable oil
1 egg, lightly beaten
3-1/2 cups all-purpose flour

CUSTARD:
4 eggs, lightly beaten
2 cups heavy whipping cream
1-1/2 cups sugar
8 to 10 cups sliced peeled tart apples *or* canned sliced peaches, drained *or* combination of fruit

TOPPING:
1/2 cup sugar
1/2 cup all-purpose flour
1 teaspoon ground cinnamon
1/4 cup cold butter

In a large mixing bowl, dissolve yeast in warm water. Add the milk, sugar, salt, oil and egg; mix well. Gradually add flour, beating until smooth (dough will be soft). Place in a greased bowl, turning once to grease top. Do not knead. Cover and refrigerate overnight.

The next day, for custard, whisk the eggs, cream and sugar in a large bowl until combined. Set aside. Divide dough into four portions. On a lightly floured surface, roll each portion into a 10-in. circle. Press each circle onto the bottom and up the sides of an ungreased 9-in. pie plate. Arrange 2 to 2-1/2 cups of fruit in each crust. Pour 1 cup custard over fruit.

For topping, combine the sugar, flour and cinnamon in a small bowl. Cut in butter until mixture resembles coarse crumbs. Sprinkle 1/3 cup over each coffee cake. Cover edges of dough with foil. Bake at 350° for 35-40 minutes or until golden brown and custard reaches 160°. **Yield:** 4 coffee cakes (6-8 servings each).

We love to hold potluck meals at our church, and this is the dish I often make for those get-togethers. It always gets rave reviews.
~Ilene Harrington
NIPOMO, CALIFORNIA

Cheese 'n' Ham Strata

5 cups cubed bread, *divided*
2 cups cubed fully cooked ham
1/4 cup chopped green pepper
2 tablespoons chopped onion
2 cups (8 ounces) shredded cheddar cheese
1 cup (4 ounces) shredded pepper Jack cheese
1 can (10-3/4 ounces) condensed cream of chicken soup, undiluted
1-1/3 cups milk
4 eggs
1 cup mayonnaise
1/2 teaspoon pepper
Dash cayenne pepper
2 tablespoons butter, melted
2 tablespoons minced fresh parsley

Place 3-1/2 cups bread cubes in a greased 13-in. x 9-in. x 2-in. baking dish. Top with ham, green pepper and onion; sprinkle with cheeses. In a large bowl, combine soup and milk. Stir in the eggs, mayonnaise, pepper and cayenne. Pour over cheeses. Toss remaining bread cubes with butter. Sprinkle over soup mixture. Cover and refrigerate for 8 hours or overnight.

Remove from the refrigerator 30 minutes before baking. Bake, uncovered, at 350° for 40-50 minutes or until a knife inserted near the center comes out clean. Sprinkle with parsley. Let stand for 5 minutes before serving. **Yield:** 8-10 servings.

Editor's Note: Reduced-fat or fat-free mayonnaise is not recommended for this recipe.

I make this moist and tangy coffee cake for small gatherings with family or to give to a friend in need of a little cheer.
~Cathy Clemons
NARROWS, VIRGINIA

Almond-Apple Coffee Cake

1-1/2 cups thinly sliced peeled tart apples
3 tablespoons brown sugar
1 tablespoon lemon juice
3/4 teaspoon apple pie spice
2 tablespoons butter, softened
1/3 cup sugar
1 egg
1 teaspoon vanilla extract
1 cup all-purpose flour
1/2 teaspoon baking soda
1/8 teaspoon salt
1/2 cup buttermilk
1 tablespoon sliced almonds

GLAZE:
1/4 cup confectioners' sugar
1 teaspoon buttermilk
1/4 teaspoon vanilla extract

In a large saucepan, combine the apples, brown sugar, lemon juice and apple pie spice. Cook over medium-high heat for 5 minutes or until syrup is thickened and apples are tender, stirring occasionally.

In a small mixing bowl, cream butter and sugar. Beat in egg and vanilla. Combine flour, baking soda and salt; add to creamed mixture alternately with buttermilk. Spoon batter into a greased 9-in. springform pan. Arrange apple mixture over top; sprinkle with almonds.

Bake at 350° for 20-25 minutes or until a toothpick inserted near the center comes out clean. Cool on wire rack. Remove sides of pan. Combine the glaze ingredients; drizzle over top. **Yield:** 8 servings.

We grow wheat, and I bake a lot of bread using our own flour. This is one of my family's favorite recipes. I like it because it's fast and easy to make.
~Jonita Williams
STOCKTON, KANSAS

Apple Sticky Buns

3-1/4 cups all-purpose flour
2 packages (1/4 ounce *each*) active dry yeast
1/4 cup sugar
1 teaspoon salt
3/4 cup milk
1/4 cup water
1/4 cup butter, cubed
1 egg
1-1/2 cups finely chopped peeled apples

TOPPING:
1 cup packed brown sugar
3/4 cup butter, cubed
3/4 cup chopped walnuts *or* pecans
1 tablespoon water
1 tablespoon corn syrup
1 teaspoon ground cinnamon

In a large mixing bowl, combine 1-1/2 cups flour, yeast, sugar and salt. In a saucepan, heat the milk, water and butter to 120° to 130°. Add to dry ingredients; beat just until moistened. Add egg; beat until smooth. Stir in remaining flour and apples. Do not knead. Cover and let rise in a warm place for 30 minutes.

Meanwhile, in a saucepan, combine the topping ingredients. Bring to a boil, stirring until blended. Pour into an ungreased 13-in. x 9-in. x 2-in. baking dish. Stir dough down. Spoon walnut-size pieces of dough over nut mixture. Cover and let rise for 30 minutes.

Bake at 375° for 30-35 minutes or until golden brown. Let stand for 1 minute before inverting onto a large serving platter. **Yield:** 12-16 servings.

I make this simple meat and veggie bake often because it provides plenty of delicious left-overs for later. My fiance and I love broccoli, so this hearty recipe pleases us both. It would go over big as a featured entree for a brunch buffet.
~Robin Moherman
ASHLAND, OHIO

🎀 Sausage and Broccoli Bake

1 package (10 ounces) frozen chopped broccoli
1 pound bulk Italian sausage
3 cups seasoned salad croutons
2 cups (8 ounces) shredded sharp cheddar cheese
4 eggs, beaten
1 can (10-3/4 ounces) condensed cream of broccoli soup, undiluted
1-1/3 cups milk
1 can (2.8 ounces) french-fried onions

Cook broccoli according to package directions; drain and set aside. In a large skillet, cook sausage over medium heat until the meat is no longer pink; drain.

Combine the broccoli, sausage, croutons and cheese. Transfer to a greased 2-qt. baking dish. In a bowl, combine the eggs, soup and milk. Pour over sausage mixture. Bake, uncovered, at 375° for 25 minutes.

Sprinkle with french-fried onions. Bake for 3-5 minutes or until knife inserted near center comes out clean. **Yield:** 6-8 servings.

When I was a girl, we had a lot of pear trees. This recipe was one that my mother made often for us. I still remember how good those pears tasted.
~Isabel Shurtleff
LITTLE COMPTON, RHODE ISLAND

Gingered Pears

4 medium ripe pears, peeled, quartered and cored
1 cup water
1/4 cup sugar
1/2 teaspoon ground ginger

In a large skillet, place pears in water. Cover and cook over medium heat for 25-30 minutes or until tender. Turn the pears over.

Combine sugar and ginger; sprinkle over pears. Cover and cook 5-10 minutes longer. Serve warm. **Yield:** 4 servings.

Besides cranberries, I've filled these with cooked pitted prunes, apricots, pie filling and even jam or jelly.
~Shirley Dehler
COLUMBUS, WISCONSIN

🏵 Cranberry Kolaches

4 to 4-1/2 cups all-purpose flour
1/4 cup sugar
1 package (1/4 ounce) active dry yeast
1 teaspoon salt
3/4 cup milk
1/2 cup water
1/4 cup butter, cubed
1 egg

FILLING:
1 cup whole-berry cranberry sauce
1 cup grated peeled tart apple
1/2 teaspoon ground cinnamon

GLAZE (optional):
1 cup confectioners' sugar
1/4 teaspoon vanilla *or* orange extract
1 to 2 tablespoons milk

In a large mixing bowl, combine 2 cups flour, sugar, yeast and salt. In a saucepan, heat the milk, water and butter to 120°-130°. Add to dry ingredients; beat just until moistened. Add egg; beat until smooth. Stir in enough remaining flour to form a soft dough (dough will be sticky). Do not knead. Cover and let rest for 20 minutes.

Turn dough onto a floured surface; roll to 1/2-in. thickness. Cut with a floured 2-1/2-in. biscuit cutter. Place 2 in. apart on lightly greased baking sheets. Cover and let rise in a warm place until doubled, about 1 hour.

Using the back of a spoon, make a 1-1/2-in.-wide well in the center of each roll. Combine filling ingredients; spoon into each well. Bake at 350° for 15-20 minutes or until golden brown. Remove from pans to wire racks to cool.

If glaze is desired, combine confectioners' sugar, extract and enough milk to achieve drizzling consistency. Drizzle over rolls. Store in the refrigerator. **Yield:** 1-1/2 dozen.

Bursting with Bountiful *Blueberries*

Blueberries are a wonderful treat on their own, and they're a delightful ingredient in cakes, desserts, muffins and more! To keep blueberries from sinking to the bottom of cakes or quick breads, gently toss them with a little flour before stirring into the batter. Remember to pick fresh blueberries when they're dry; any dew or rain can make them soft and spoil faster. Deep-blue berries will have the best flavor.

Here's a versatile dumpling recipe that's excellent as a sweet breakfast sprinkled with whole grain cereal or for dessert. Blueberries are one of my favorite fruits, and this dish is a fantastic way to enjoy them.

~Melissa Radulovich
LITTLETON, COLORADO

Blueberries 'n' Dumplings

(Pictured above)

    3 cups apple cider *or* juice
1/4 cup quick-cooking tapioca
    4 cups fresh blueberries
1/3 cup packed brown sugar
1/2 teaspoon almond extract

DUMPLINGS:
    1 cup all-purpose flour
    1 tablespoon sugar
1-1/2 teaspoons baking powder
1/2 teaspoon salt
1/4 teaspoon ground nutmeg
    1 egg
    6 tablespoons milk
    1 tablespoon vegetable oil
3/4 cup cold heavy whipping cream
    1 tablespoon maple syrup

In a Dutch oven, combine the cider and tapioca; let stand for 5 minutes. Add the blueberries and brown sugar. Bring to a boil. Reduce heat to medium-low; simmer, uncovered, until tapioca is transparent, stirring occasionally. Stir in almond extract; continue simmering.

For dumplings, in a large bowl, combine the flour, sugar, baking powder, salt and nutmeg. In a small bowl, beat the egg, milk and oil; stir into dry ingredients just until moistened (batter will be stiff).

Drop batter by 1/4 cupfuls onto simmering blueberry mixture. Cover and simmer for 25 minutes or until a toothpick inserted in dumplings comes out clean (do not lift lid while simmering).

In a small mixing bowl, beat cream and syrup until soft peaks form. Spoon blueberry mixture into serving bowls; top with the dumplings. Serve with maple cream. **Yield:** 4 servings.

With their refreshing blend of citrus and blueberry flavors, these tender muffins are perfect for breakfast or a snack. My mother and husband really enjoy the sweet nut topping on these treats.

~Janice Baker
LONDON, KENTUCKY

Orange Blueberry Muffins

(Pictured at left)

1 cup quick-cooking oats
1 cup orange juice
3 cups all-purpose flour
1 cup sugar
2-1/2 teaspoons baking powder
1 teaspoon salt
1/2 teaspoon baking soda
1 cup vegetable oil
3 eggs, beaten
1-1/2 cups fresh *or* frozen blueberries
1-1/2 teaspoons grated orange peel

TOPPING:
1/2 cup chopped walnuts
1/3 cup sugar
1 teaspoon ground cinnamon

In a small bowl, combine the oats and orange juice. In a large bowl, combine the flour, sugar, baking powder, salt and baking soda. Combine the oil, eggs and oat mixture; stir into dry ingredients just until moistened. Fold in blueberries and orange peel.

Fill paper-lined muffin cups two-thirds full. Combine the topping ingredients; sprinkle over batter. Bake at 400° for 15-20 minutes or until a toothpick comes out clean. Cool for 5 minutes before removing from pans to wire racks. **Yield:** 1-1/2 dozen.

Editor's Note: If using frozen blueberries, do not thaw before adding to batter.

Every time I have company for dinner or go to someone's house for a meal, I'm asked to make this.

~Leslie Palmer
SWAMPSCOTT, MASSACHUSETTS

Blueberry Coffee Cake

☑ **Uses less fat, sugar or salt. Includes Nutrition Facts and Diabetic Exchanges.**

1/3 cup butter, softened
3/4 cup sugar
1 egg
1/4 cup egg substitute
1 teaspoon vanilla extract
2 cups all-purpose flour
1 teaspoon baking powder
1 teaspoon baking soda
1/4 teaspoon salt
1 cup (8 ounces) reduced-fat sour cream
1 cup fresh *or* frozen blueberries

TOPPING:
3 tablespoons sugar
2 teaspoons ground cinnamon
2 teaspoons confectioners' sugar

In a large mixing bowl, beat the butter and sugar until crumbly, about 2 minutes. Beat in the egg, egg substitute and vanilla. Combine the flour, baking powder, baking soda and salt; add to the egg mixture alternately with the sour cream. Fold in the blueberries.

Coat a 10-in. fluted tube pan with nonstick cooking spray and dust with flour. Spoon half of the batter into prepared pan. Combine sugar and cinnamon; sprinkle half over batter. Repeat layers.

Bake at 350° for 40-50 minutes or until a toothpick inserted near the center comes out clean. Cool for 10 minutes before removing from pan to a wire rack to cool completely. Dust with confectioners' sugar. **Yield:** 14 servings.

Nutrition Facts: One piece equals 191 calories, 7 g fat (4 g saturated fat), 32 mg cholesterol, 218 mg sodium, 30 g carbohydrate, 1 g fiber, 4 g protein. **Diabetic Exchanges:** 1-1/2 starch, 1 fat, 1/2 fruit.

Editor's Note: If using frozen blueberries, do not thaw before adding to batter.

Everyone will gobble up these light and airy rolls—the caramel flavor is wonderful. Pretty as well as tasty, they will brighten breakfast or snacktime. ~Frances Amundson
GILBY, NORTH DAKOTA

Caramel Cinnamon Rolls

2 packages (1/4 ounce *each*) active dry yeast
1-1/2 cups warm water (110° to 115°)
1 cup warm milk (110° to 115°)
1/3 cup sugar
1/3 cup vegetable oil
1 egg
3 teaspoons baking powder
2 teaspoons salt
6 to 7 cups all-purpose flour

FILLING:
1/4 cup butter, softened
1-1/2 cups sugar
4 teaspoons ground cinnamon

TOPPING:
1 cup packed brown sugar
1 cup vanilla ice cream
1/2 cup butter

In a large mixing bowl, dissolve yeast in warm water. Add the milk, sugar, oil, egg, baking powder, salt and 3 cups flour; beat until smooth. Stir in enough remaining flour to form a soft dough. Turn dough onto a floured surface; knead until smooth and elastic, about 6-8 minutes. Place in a greased bowl, turning once to grease top. Cover and let rise in a warm place until doubled, about 1-1/2 hours.

Punch dough down. Turn onto a lightly floured surface; divide in half. Roll each portion into a 12-in. x 10-in. rectangle. Spread each with 2 tablespoons butter.

Combine the sugar and cinnamon; sprinkle over butter to within 1/2 in. of edges. Roll up jelly-roll style, starting with a long side; pinch seam to seal.

Cut each into 12 slices. Place cut side down in two greased 13-in. x 9-in. x 2-in. baking pans. Cover and refrigerate for up to 24 hours.

To bake, remove rolls from the refrigerator and let stand for 30 minutes. In a saucepan, combine topping ingredients. Bring to a boil; boil and stir for 1 minute. Pour over dough. Bake at 350° for 30-35 minutes or until golden brown. Immediately invert onto serving plates. **Yield:** 2 dozen.

We live on a remote side of an island in southeastern Alaska where blueberries are abundant. I use these and other berries as many ways as possible all summer long. These smoothies are scrumptious. ~Bonnie Roher
WRANGELL, ALASKA

Very Berry Smoothies

☑ Uses less fat, sugar or salt. Includes Nutrition Facts and Diabetic Exchanges.

2 cartons (6 ounces *each*) blueberry yogurt
1/4 cup grape juice
1-1/2 cups frozen blueberries
1 cup frozen blackberries
Sugar substitute equivalent to 2 tablespoons sugar

In a blender, place all ingredients in the order listed; cover and process until blended. Pour into chilled glasses; serve immediately. **Yield:** 4 servings.

Nutrition Facts: One serving (3/4 cup) equals 149 calories, 1 g fat (trace saturated fat), 4 mg cholesterol, 80 mg sodium, 31 g carbohydrate, 4 g fiber, 4 g protein. **Diabetic Exchanges:** 1 reduced-fat milk, 1 fruit.

Editor's Note: This recipe was tested with Splenda No Calorie Sweetener.

This roll recipe, from my husband's family, is one I always prepare for our church conferences. Serve them with scrambled eggs, and you have a filling breakfast. As a variation, you can replace the cinnamon filling with a mixture of raisins and pecans.

~Shenai Fisher
TOPEKA, KANSAS

Frosted Cinnamon Rolls

1 package (1/4 ounce) active dry yeast
1 cup warm milk (110° to 115°)
1/2 cup sugar
1/3 cup butter, melted
2 eggs
1 teaspoon salt
4 to 4-1/2 cups all-purpose flour

FILLING:
1/4 cup butter, melted
3/4 cup packed brown sugar
2 tablespoons ground cinnamon

CREAM CHEESE FROSTING:
1/2 cup butter, softened
1-1/2 cups confectioners' sugar
1/4 cup cream cheese, softened
1/2 teaspoon vanilla extract
1/8 teaspoon salt

In a large mixing bowl, dissolve yeast in warm milk. Add the sugar, butter, eggs, salt and 2 cups flour; beat until smooth. Stir in enough remaining flour to form a soft dough (dough will be sticky).

Turn onto a floured surface; knead until smooth and elastic, about 6-8 minutes. Place in a greased bowl, turning once to grease top. Cover and let rise in a warm place until doubled, about 1 hour.

Punch the dough down. Turn onto a floured surface; divide in half. Roll each portion into an 11-in. x 8-in. rectangle; brush with butter. Combine brown sugar and cinnamon; sprinkle over dough to within 1/2 in. of edges. Roll up jelly-roll style, starting from a long side; pinch seam to seal.

Cut each into eight slices. Place cut side down in two greased 13-in. x 9-in. x 2-in. baking pans. Cover and let rise until nearly doubled, about 1 hour.

Bake at 350° for 20-25 minutes or until golden brown. Cool in pans on wire racks. In a small mixing bowl, combine frosting ingredients until smooth. Frost rolls. Store in the refrigerator. **Yield:** 16 rolls.

When you're in the mood for some good finger food, turn to this recipe. Fans of mustard, dill and vinegar flavors, my family says these eggs are the best. I like them because they are a cinch to fill and make a popular contribution to a brunch. ~Carrie Long
SILVER LAKE, WISCONSIN

Savory Deviled Eggs

6 hard-cooked eggs
1/4 cup mayonnaise
1 teaspoon white wine vinegar
1 teaspoon Dijon mustard
1/2 teaspoon dill weed
1/4 teaspoon garlic powder
1/8 teaspoon salt
Fresh dill sprigs, optional

Slice eggs in half lengthwise; remove yolks and set whites aside. In a small bowl, mash yolks. Add mayonnaise, vinegar, mustard, dill, garlic powder and salt.

Spoon into egg whites. Garnish with dill sprigs if desired. Refrigerate until serving. **Yield:** 1 dozen.

Great for **company** or just plain **snacking,** this chapter is filled with **recipes** you and your family are **sure** to enjoy.

Snacks & Beverages

DELIGHTFUL TREATS. From left to right: Crabmeat Appetizer Cheesecake (p. 20), Cornmeal Onion Rings (p. 22) and Orange Fruit Dip (p. 21).

Crabmeat Appetizer Cheesecake

(Pictured on page 19)

1/2 cup seasoned bread crumbs
1/2 cup grated Parmesan cheese
1/4 cup butter, melted

FILLING:

1/4 cup *each* chopped sweet red, yellow and green pepper
1/4 cup chopped onion
1/4 cup butter
4 packages (three 8 ounces, one 3 ounces) cream cheese, softened
3 eggs, lightly beaten
2 cups heavy whipping cream
2 cups canned crabmeat, drained, flaked and cartilage removed
2 cups (8 ounces) shredded Swiss cheese
1/2 teaspoon salt

In a bowl, combine the bread crumbs, Parmesan cheese and butter. Press onto the bottom of a 10-in. springform pan; set aside. In a skillet, saute the peppers and onion in butter until tender; set aside.

In a mixing bowl, beat cream cheese until smooth. Add eggs; beat on low speed just until combined. Stir in the cream, crab, Swiss cheese, pepper mixture and salt. Pour over crust. Place pan on a baking sheet.

Bake at 325° for 60-65 minutes or until center is almost set. Cool on a wire rack for 10 minutes. Carefully run a knife around the edge of pan to loosen. Cool 1 hour longer.

Refrigerate overnight. Remove sides of pan. Let stand at room temperature for 30 minutes before serving. **Yield:** 16-18 servings.

Freezer Salsa

3/4 cup chopped onion
1/2 cup finely chopped celery
1/3 cup finely chopped sweet red *or* green pepper
1 to 2 jalapeno peppers, seeded and finely chopped
3 garlic cloves, minced
1/4 cup olive oil
12 plum tomatoes, peeled, seeded and chopped (about 6 cups)
3 cans (6 ounces *each*) tomato paste
1/3 cup lime juice
1/3 cup white vinegar
1 tablespoon honey
1 tablespoon sugar
1-1/2 teaspoons salt
1 teaspoon dried basil

In a large saucepan, saute the onion, celery, peppers and garlic in oil for 5 minutes or until tender.

Stir in the remaining ingredients; bring to a boil. Reduce heat; cover and simmer for 20 minutes, stirring occasionally. Cool completely. Spoon into freezer containers. Cover and freeze for up to 3 months. Stir before serving. **Yield:** about 6 cups.

Editor's Note: When cutting or seeding hot peppers, use rubber or plastic gloves to protect your hands. Avoid touching your face.

This is one of my family's favorite recipes for cold winter nights. We also make it on camping trips.
~Lorene Goodwin
BELLE FOURCHE, SOUTH DAKOTA

Jalapeno Bean Dip

2 pounds ground beef
1 medium onion, chopped
1 garlic clove, minced
2 cans (8 ounces *each*) tomato sauce
1 can (15-1/2 ounces) chili beans, undrained
1 can (8 ounces) kidney beans, rinsed and drained
2 medium jalapeno peppers, chopped
1/2 teaspoon salt
1/8 teaspoon cayenne pepper
1 package (16 ounces) corn chips
1 cup (4 ounces) shredded cheddar cheese
1 cup (8 ounces) sour cream

In a large skillet, cook the beef, onion and garlic over medium heat until meat is no longer pink; drain. Stir in the tomato sauce, beans and jalapeno peppers; mix well. Bring to a boil.

Add salt and cayenne. Reduce heat; cover and simmer for 20 minutes. To serve, spoon beef mixture over chips; sprinkle with cheese. Top with sour cream. **Yield:** 12 servings.

Editor's Note: When cutting or seeding hot peppers, use rubber or plastic gloves to protect your hands. Avoid touching your face.

I often take a platter of fruit and this dip to picnics, bridal showers and family events. Depending on the season, I'll have strawberries, cantaloupe, apples and other fresh fruits.
~Susan Kruspe
SHORTSVILLE, NEW YORK

Orange Fruit Dip

(Pictured on page 19)

1-1/2 cups cold milk
1 can (6 ounces) frozen orange juice concentrate, thawed
1 package (3.4 ounces) instant vanilla pudding mix
1/4 cup sour cream
Assorted fresh fruit

In a bowl, whisk milk, orange juice concentrate and pudding mix for 2 minutes. Let stand for 2 minutes or until soft-set. Whisk in sour cream.

Cover and refrigerate for at least 4 hours. Serve with fresh fruit. **Yield:** 2-3/4 cups.

When neighbors or friends visit us on a chilly evening, I'll serve this warm beverage with ham sandwiches and deviled eggs.
~Bernice Morris
MARSHFIELD, MISSOURI

Mulled Dr. Pepper

8 cups Dr. Pepper
1/4 cup packed brown sugar
1/4 cup lemon juice
1/2 teaspoon ground allspice
1/2 teaspoon whole cloves
1/4 teaspoon salt
1/4 teaspoon ground nutmeg
3 cinnamon sticks (3 inches)

In a 3-qt. slow cooker, combine all ingredients; mix well. Cover and cook on low for 2 hours or until desired temperature is reached.

Discard cloves and cinnamon sticks before serving. **Yield:** 8-10 servings.

My husband says these onion rings are the best he's ever eaten. The cornmeal and pecans give them a special crunch that we both really enjoy.

~Mila Bryning
ALEXANDRIA, VIRGINIA

Cornmeal Onion Rings

(Also pictured on page 19)

2 pounds onions
2 eggs
1 cup buttermilk
2 cups all-purpose flour
1 cup cornmeal
1/2 cup finely chopped pecans
1 to 1-1/2 teaspoons salt
1/2 teaspoon pepper
Oil for deep-fat frying

Cut onions into 1/2-in. slices; separate into rings. In a shallow bowl, whisk eggs and buttermilk until blended. In another shallow bowl, combine the flour, cornmeal, pecans, salt and pepper. Dip onion rings in egg mixture, then coat with flour mixture.

In an electric skillet or deep-fat fryer, heat 1 in. of oil to 375°. Fry the onion rings, a few at a time, for 1 to 1-1/2 minutes on each side or until golden brown. Drain on paper towels. **Yield:** 8 servings.

This is a lovely dip to serve at get-togethers. It is quick and easy to make, and guests always enjoy it. A friend was kind enough to share the recipe with me.

~Dorothy Pritchett
WILLS POINT, TEXAS

Spinach Onion Dip

☑ **Uses less fat, sugar or salt. Includes Nutrition Facts and Diabetic Exchanges.**

1 cup (8 ounces) 1% cottage cheese
1 tablespoon lemon juice
1 package (10 ounces) frozen chopped spinach, thawed and squeezed dry
1 cup reduced-fat sour cream
1/2 cup minced fresh parsley
1/4 cup chopped green onions
3/4 teaspoon garlic salt
1/2 teaspoon hot pepper sauce

In a blender or food processor, combine cottage cheese and lemon juice; cover and process until smooth. Add remaining ingredients; process just until combined. Refrigerate for at least 4 hours. **Yield:** 2-1/2 cups.

Nutrition Facts: One serving (2 tablespoons) equals 29 calories, 1 g fat (1 g saturated fat), 4 mg cholesterol, 105 mg sodium, 2 g carbohydrate, 1 g fiber, 3 g protein. **Diabetic Exchange:** 1 vegetable.

I acquired this recipe after attending a holiday cooking school years ago. It's still a favorite with my family and friends for New Year's Day.

~Agnes Anderson
SEDRO-WOOLLEY, WASHINGTON

Cocktail Sausages in Orange Sauce

1/2 cup sugar
4-1/2 teaspoons cornstarch
1/4 teaspoon ground cloves
1/8 teaspoon ground cinnamon
3/4 cup orange juice
2 tablespoons cider vinegar
1 package (16 ounces) miniature smoked sausage links

In a large saucepan, combine the sugar, cornstarch, cloves and cinnamon. Gradually stir in the orange juice until smooth. Stir in vinegar.

Bring to a boil; cook and stir for 1 minute or until thickened. Add sausages. Cook and stir until heated through. **Yield:** 8 servings.

The first time I tried this dip was at a reunion. I hunted down the person who prepared it, acquired the recipe and have been making it ever since. Our daughter served it at our surprise 50th wedding anniversary party, and it was a hit. ~Betty Claycomb
ALVERTON, PENNSYLVANIA

Dilly Corned Beef Dip

1 can (12 ounces) corned beef
2 cups (16 ounces) sour cream
2 cups mayonnaise
1/3 cup minced fresh parsley
2 tablespoons finely chopped onion
2 tablespoons snipped fresh dill *or* 2 teaspoons dill weed
1/2 teaspoon seasoned salt
Assorted crackers *or* vegetables

Crumble corned beef into a large bowl. Add the sour cream, mayonnaise, parsley, onion, dill and seasoned salt; mix well. Serve with crackers or vegetables. **Yield:** 6 cups.

Here's a refreshing beverage that goes with any meal. Carbonated ginger ale makes it a wonderful alternative to ordinary iced tea or other soft drinks. This thirst-quencher appeals to all ages. ~Brenda Jeffers
OTTUMWA, IOWA

Ginger Iced Tea

1 cup iced tea mix with lemon and sugar
4 cups water
2 liters ginger ale, chilled
Ice cubes

In a pitcher, combine the iced tea mix and water; refrigerate until chilled. Just before serving, add ginger ale. Serve over ice. **Yield:** 3 quarts.

Capped with tomatoes, these tasty morsels always delight family and friends. They couldn't be easier to make, and my kids get the biggest kick out of them. They gobble the toadstools up—and even eat the spinach "grass" I display them on. ~Sue Cravatta
ELMWOOD PARK, ILLINOIS

Fairy-Tale Mushrooms

2 plum tomatoes
4 hard-cooked eggs, peeled
1/3 cup mayonnaise
1 package (10 ounces) fresh baby spinach

Cut tomatoes in half widthwise; scoop out and discard pulp. Invert onto paper towels to drain. Carefully push each tomato half onto the narrow end of an egg.

Cut a small hole in the corner of a small plastic bag; fill with mayonnaise. Pipe dots onto tomato tops. Place on a spinach-lined serving plate. **Yield:** 4 servings.

After my mother and sister described the hot crab sandwiches they had eaten at a San Francisco restaurant, I developed this recipe for dip. It's become a family favorite, especially during vacations to the Oregon coast, where we can catch fresh crabs.

~Christine Woody
COTTAGE GROVE, OREGON

Hot Crab Spread

1-1/2 cups chopped green onions
6 garlic cloves, minced
1 tablespoon butter
1 tablespoon mayonnaise
8 cups (32 ounces) shredded Monterey Jack cheese
4 cans (6 ounces *each*) crabmeat, drained, flaked and cartilage removed
Assorted crackers

In a skillet, saute onions and garlic in butter until tender. Transfer to a 3-qt. slow cooker; add mayonnaise. Stir in cheese. Cover and cook on low for 30 minutes or until cheese is melted, stirring occasionally.

Stir in crab; cover and cook 1 hour longer or until heated through. Serve spread warm with crackers. **Yield:** 6 cups.

Editor's Note: Reduced-fat or fat-free mayonnaise may not be substituted for regular mayonnaise.

I have made many different kinds of candied nuts over the years, but we like these best. The buttermilk prevents them from becoming too sweet.

~Betty Claycomb
ALVERTON, PENNSYLVANIA

Sugared Mixed Nuts

1 tablespoon plus 1/4 cup butter, *divided*
2 cups sugar
1 cup buttermilk
1 teaspoon baking soda
4 cups mixed nuts

Line two 15-in. x 10-in. x 1-in. baking pans with foil; butter the foil with 1 tablespoon butter and set aside. In a large heavy saucepan, combine the sugar, buttermilk and baking soda.

Cook over medium heat until a candy thermometer reads 236° (soft-ball stage), stirring constantly. Remove from the heat. Stir in nuts and remaining butter. Spread in a single layer in prepared pans. Cool; break apart. **Yield:** 8 cups.

Editor's Note: We recommend that you test your candy thermometer before each use by bringing water to a boil; the thermometer should read 212°. Adjust your recipe temperature up or down based on your test.

The crust is crispy, and the peppers give this dish a nice zesty flavor. ~Peggy Campbell
WELCH, TEXAS

Armadillo Eggs

2 jars (16 ounces *each*) whole pickled jalapeno peppers
4 cups (16 ounces) shredded cheddar cheese, *divided*
1 pound bulk pork sausage
1-1/2 cups biscuit/baking mix
3 eggs, lightly beaten
2 envelopes pork-flavored seasoned coating mix

Cut each jalapeno in half lengthwise; remove seeds and stems. Stuff each pepper half with about 1 tablespoon cheddar cheese. In a bowl, combine the uncooked sausage, biscuit mix and remaining cheese; mix well. Shape about 2 tablespoonfuls around each pepper.

Dip into eggs, then roll in coating mix. Place on a baking sheet coated with nonstick cooking spray. Bake at 350° for 35-40 minutes or until golden brown. **Yield:** about 3 dozen.

Editor's Note: When cutting or seeding hot peppers, use rubber or plastic gloves to protect your hands. Avoid touching your face.

Years ago, I found a version of this recipe in a cookbook. At first taste, my family judged it a keeper. The tangy, saucy meatballs are requested by our friends whenever I host card night. We also take the yummy dish on camping trips.
~Marybell Lintott
VERNON, BRITISH COLUMBIA

Cranberry Meatballs And Sausages

1 egg, beaten
1 small onion, finely chopped
3/4 cup dry bread crumbs
1 tablespoon dried parsley flakes
1 tablespoon Worcestershire sauce
1/4 teaspoon salt
1 pound bulk pork sausage
1 can (16 ounces) jellied cranberry sauce
3 tablespoons cider vinegar
2 tablespoons brown sugar
1 tablespoon prepared mustard
1 package (1 pound) miniature smoked sausage links

In a large bowl, combine the first six ingredients. Crumble bulk sausage over the mixture and mix well. Shape into 1-in. balls. In a large skillet, cook meatballs over medium heat until browned; drain.

In a large saucepan, combine the cranberry sauce, vinegar, brown sugar and mustard. Cook and stir over medium heat until cranberry sauce is melted. Add the meatballs and sausage links. Bring to a boil.

Reduce heat; simmer, uncovered, for 10-15 minutes or until meatballs are no longer pink and sauce is slightly thickened. **Yield:** 14-16 servings.

I was served this dip when I was on a visit to Key West. I was able to copy the recipe at home. Now my husband and sons love to eat it for any occasion but especially while watching football games.
~Deana Bennett
FARMVILLE, VIRGINIA

Party Cheese Dip

1 can (15-1/2 ounces) black beans, rinsed and drained
1 can (15-1/4 ounces) whole kernel corn, drained
1 can (10 ounces) tomatoes with green chilies, drained
1 pound process cheese (Velveeta), cubed
Tortilla chips

In an ungreased 1-1/2-qt. microwave-safe bowl, combine beans, corn, tomatoes and cheese. Cover and microwave on high for 5 minutes. Carefully uncover; stir. Microwave 1-2 minutes longer or until the cheese is melted. Serve warm with tortilla chips. **Yield:** 4 cups.

Editor's Note: This recipe was tested in a 1,100-watt microwave.

I like to garnish this iced tea with some of our sweet Hawaiian pineapple. It's so refreshing!
~Beverly Toomey
HONOLULU, HAWAII

Fruity Iced Tea

1 gallon water
24 individual tea bags
6 fresh mint sprigs
3-1/3 cups sugar
3 cups unsweetened pineapple juice
1 cup lemon juice

In a Dutch oven, bring water to boil. Remove from the heat. Add tea bags; steep for 10 minutes. Discard tea bags; add mint. Steep 5 minutes longer; discard mint.

Stir in the sugar, pineapple juice and lemon juice until sugar is dissolved. Cover and refrigerate until chilled. **Yield:** 4 quarts.

Bring delight to the table with fresh-tasting salads, steaming soups or satisfying sandwiches.

Soups, Salads & Sandwiches

MEAL STARTERS. From left: Savory Sandwich Ring (p. 28) and Tangy Potato Salad (p. 29).

I first made this alternative to a submarine sandwich for a party. Now it's a mainstay on my menu plan for gatherings or when my family is tired of ordinary meat-and-cheese sandwiches.

~Susanne Ebersol
BIRD-IN-HAND, PENNSYLVANIA

Savory Sandwich Ring

(Pictured on page 27)

2 tubes (11 ounces *each*) refrigerated crusty French bread dough
2 teaspoons olive oil
3 garlic cloves, pressed
1/2 teaspoon Italian seasoning
1/3 cup Italian salad dressing
1/2 pound thinly sliced deli ham
1/4 pound sliced process American *or* Swiss cheese, halved
1/4 to 1/2 pound thinly sliced deli roast beef *or* turkey
2 cups shredded lettuce
1 medium red onion, thinly sliced
1 medium green pepper, thinly sliced
1 medium tomato, thinly sliced

Place both loaves of dough seam side down on a greased 14-in. pizza pan, forming one large ring; pinch ends to seal. With a sharp knife, make eight 1/2-in.-deep slashes across the top of dough; lightly brush with oil.

Spread garlic over oil; sprinkle with Italian seasoning. Bake at 350° for 25-30 minutes or until golden. Cool 10 minutes before removing from pan to a wire rack to cool completely.

To assemble, cut bread in half horizontally. Brush salad dressing over cut sides. Layer the bottom half with ham, cheese, beef, lettuce, onion, green pepper and tomato; replace top. Serve immediately. Refrigerate leftovers. **Yield:** 8-10 servings.

This is a light, colorful and tasty salad for the holidays and during "veggie season." It travels well and is an expected dish at family reunions.

~Joanne Neuendorf
POTOSI, WISCONSIN

Calico Salad

☑ **Uses less fat, sugar or salt. Includes Nutrition Facts and Diabetic Exchanges.**

2 cups fresh broccoli florets
2 cups fresh cauliflowerets
1 cup halved cherry *or* grape tomatoes
1/2 cup chopped red onion
1/2 cup chopped celery
1/4 cup chopped sweet red pepper
1/4 cup chopped green pepper
1/2 cup fat-free sour cream
2 tablespoons fat-free milk
1 tablespoon ranch salad dressing mix
1/4 cup unsalted sunflower kernels
3 bacon strips, cooked and crumbled

In a large bowl, combine the first seven ingredients. In another bowl, combine the sour cream, milk and salad dressing mix. Pour over vegetables; toss to coat. Refrigerate until serving. Stir in sunflower kernels and bacon. **Yield:** 8 servings.

Nutrition Facts: One serving (3/4 cup) equals 86 calories, 5 g fat (1 g saturated fat), 4 mg cholesterol, 86 mg sodium, 8 g carbohydrate, 2 g fiber, 4 g protein. **Diabetic Exchanges:** 2 vegetable, 1 fat.

My mother gave this recipe to me, and it's one of my family's favorites. It's popular at church suppers, too.
~Precious Owens
ELIZABETHTOWN, KENTUCKY

Turnip Slaw

3 cups shredded peeled turnips
3 tablespoons sour cream
1 tablespoon sugar
1 tablespoon minced fresh parsley
1 tablespoon cider vinegar
1 tablespoon mayonnaise
1/4 teaspoon salt

Place turnips in a large bowl. In a small bowl, combine the sour cream, sugar, parsley, vinegar, mayonnaise and salt; mix well. Pour over turnips; toss to coat. Cover and refrigerate for 1 hour. **Yield:** 6 servings.

My potato salad is so easy, I can quickly put it together in the small kitchen of our home on the lake. I've shared the recipe with our three daughters, and it's become a signature dish with all of them.
~Marilyn VanScyoc
CARTHAGE, INDIANA

Tangy Potato Salad

(Pictured on page 27 and on front cover)

8 cups cubed peeled cooked potatoes (about 11 medium)
10 bacon strips, cooked and crumbled
3 hard-cooked eggs, chopped
1 carton (8 ounces) French onion dip
1/2 cup dill pickle relish
1/2 teaspoon salt
1/2 teaspoon pepper
Leaf lettuce, optional

In a large bowl, combine the potatoes, bacon and eggs. In a small bowl, combine the dip, pickle relish, salt and pepper. Stir into potato mixture. Cover and refrigerate for at least 2 hours. Serve in a lettuce-lined bowl if desired. **Yield:** 10-12 servings.

This salad is a complete meal, or it can be served as a side dish. When I was young, this was the only salad dressing my mother ever made.
~Naomi Richards
CEDAR RAPIDS, IOWA

Everything Salad

6 eggs, beaten
1/3 cup sugar
1/3 cup cider vinegar
1 teaspoon salt
4 cups cooked elbow macaroni
3 hard-cooked eggs, chopped
1-1/4 cups cubed fully cooked ham
1 cup (4 ounces) cubed process cheese (Velveeta)
2 celery ribs, thinly sliced
1 medium onion, chopped
3/4 cup sweet pickle relish
3/4 cup sliced stuffed olives
1/3 cup mayonnaise

In a saucepan, combine eggs, sugar, vinegar and salt; cook and stir over low heat for 10 minutes or until mixture is thickened and a thermometer reads 160°. Cool completely, stirring several times.

In a bowl, combine the macaroni, hard-cooked eggs, ham, cheese, celery, onion, pickle relish and olives. Stir mayonnaise into cooled egg mixture; pour over macaroni mixture. Stir to coat. Cover and refrigerate for at least 2 hours. **Yield:** 6-8 servings.

No matter where I take this attractive salad, I'm asked to share the recipe. With its red and green layers, it dresses up any holiday buffet. I'm a retired teacher who loves to cook—especially dishes I can make ahead, like this one.
~Bonnie Bredenberg
BEMIDJI, MINNESOTA

Holiday Gelatin Mold

1 can (8 ounces) sliced pineapple
1 package (3 ounces) lime gelatin
4 cups boiling water, *divided*
2 tablespoons lemon juice
1 package (3 ounces) lemon gelatin
2 packages (3 ounces *each*) cream cheese, softened
1/3 cup mayonnaise
1 package (3 ounces) raspberry gelatin
2 medium firm bananas

Drain pineapple, juice. In a bowl, dissolve lime gelatin in 1 cup boiling water. Combine the pineapple juice, lemon juice and enough cold water to measure 1 cup; add to dissolved gelatin. Cut pineapple slices in half; arrange on the bottom of a 12-cup ring mold coated with nonstick cooking spray.

Pour a small amount of lime gelatin over the pineapple; refrigerate until set. Add remaining lime gelatin; refrigerate until firm.

In a small mixing bowl, dissolve lemon gelatin in 1 cup boiling water. Refrigerate until partially set. Beat until light and fluffy.

In another small mixing bowl, beat cream cheese until fluffy. Add mayonnaise; mix well. Fold in whipped gelatin; pour over lime layer. Refrigerate until firm.

Dissolve raspberry gelatin in remaining boiling water. Slice bananas; place over lemon layer. Carefully spoon raspberry gelatin over bananas. Refrigerate until firm or overnight. **Yield:** 16 servings.

A friend gave me this cherished soup recipe over 25 years ago. At the time, she was in her 60s and working as a cook on a riverboat barge.
~Sherry Smith
SALEM, MISSOURI

Creamy Split Pea Soup

1/2 pound sliced bacon, diced
1 large onion, chopped
2 ribs celery, sliced
1 pound dried green split peas
2 quarts water
2 medium potatoes, peeled and diced
2 cups diced fully cooked ham
2 teaspoons salt
1 bay leaf
1/4 teaspoon pepper
1 cup heavy whipping cream

In a Dutch oven or soup kettle, cook bacon over medium heat until crisp. Using a slotted spoon, remove bacon to paper towels; drain, reserving drippings. Add onion and celery to drippings. Saute until vegetables are tender; drain. Add the peas, water, potatoes, ham, salt, bay leaf and pepper. Bring to a boil. Reduce heat; cover and simmer for 45 minutes or until peas are very tender, stirring occasionally. Discard bay leaf.

Cool slightly. Process in small batches in a blender until smooth. Return to Dutch oven; stir in cream. Heat through (do not boil). Garnish with reserved bacon. **Yield:** 12 servings (3 quarts).

An impromptu picnic inspired me to put together this dressed-up chicken salad sandwich. The sauce gives leftover grilled poultry a scrumptious punch. An instant summertime favorite, these sandwiches have become a mainstay at our house. ~Linda Orme

BATTLEGROUND, WASHINGTON

Barbecued Chicken Salad Sandwiches

1-1/2 pounds boneless skinless chicken breasts
1/2 cup barbecue sauce
1 cup mayonnaise
1/2 cup finely chopped onion
1/2 cup finely chopped celery
1/4 teaspoon salt
1/4 teaspoon crushed red pepper flakes
8 kaiser rolls, split
8 tomato slices
8 lettuce leaves

Place the chicken in a large resealable plastic bag; add barbecue sauce. Seal the bag and turn to coat. Refrigerate overnight.

Grill chicken, covered, over medium-hot heat for 6-8 minutes on each side or until juices run clear. Cool; cover and refrigerate chicken until chilled.

Chop chicken; place in a bowl. Stir in the mayonnaise, onion, celery, salt and pepper flakes. Serve on rolls with tomato and lettuce. **Yield:** 8 servings.

Helpful Hint

Make Ahead Chicken

To make cubed cooked chicken for recipes, simmer some boneless chicken breasts in a little water seasoned with salt, pepper and your favorite herbs. Cool and dice; keep in the freezer for later.

This salad is especially satisfying with oranges from our own trees. ~Margaret Pache

MESA, ARIZONA

Orange Crab Salad

2 medium navel oranges, peeled and sectioned
1 medium grapefruit, peeled and sectioned
4 green onions, chopped
1/2 cup chopped celery
1/2 cup chopped pecans
1 can (6 ounces) lump crabmeat, drained and flaked
4 cups mixed salad greens
1 can (3 ounces) chow mein noodles

GINGER SALAD DRESSING:
1/2 cup mayonnaise
2 teaspoons sugar
2 teaspoons lemon juice
2 teaspoons prepared horseradish
1 teaspoon minced fresh gingerroot

In a bowl, combine the first six ingredients. Divide the salad greens among four salad plates. Sprinkle with the chow mein noodles. Top each with about 3/4 cup crab mixture.

In a small bowl, whisk together the dressing ingredients. Serve with crab salad. **Yield:** 4 servings.

The salad dressing is a light and pleasant complement to the two fruits. And preparation is a snap!

~Sue Broyles
CHEROKEE, TEXAS

Grapefruit Avocado Salad

1/2 cup sugar
1/3 cup white vinegar
1-1/2 teaspoons finely chopped onion
1 teaspoon prepared mustard
1/2 teaspoon salt
1 cup vegetable oil
1-1/2 teaspoons poppy seeds
4 medium pink *or* red grapefruit, peeled and sectioned
4 medium avocados, peeled and cut into wedges
Bibb lettuce

In a mixing bowl, combine the sugar, vinegar, onion, mustard and salt; stir until sugar is dissolved. Gradually whisk in oil. Stir in poppy seeds. Cover and refrigerate until serving.

Just before serving, stir salad dressing. Arrange grapefruit and avocados on lettuce-lined plates; drizzle with desired amount of dressing. Refrigerate leftovers. **Yield:** 8-10 servings.

At least a triple batch of my chicken salad is needed to satisfy hungry relatives at our summer get-togethers. It's the most requested recipe I make. This salad is so versatile, it can be scooped onto a bed of lettuce or stuffed into a pita.

~Donna Cooper
RISING SUN, INDIANA

Flavorful Chicken Salad Sandwiches

3 cups pineapple juice
1/3 cup soy sauce
3 pounds boneless skinless chicken breasts
2 cups water
1/2 cup *each* chopped green pepper, red onion and celery
1-1/2 cups mayonnaise
1/2 teaspoon garlic salt
1/2 teaspoon pepper
1/2 teaspoon Italian seasoning
1/2 teaspoon dried basil
1/4 teaspoon seasoned salt
10 lettuce leaves
10 sandwich rolls, split

In a bowl, combine pineapple juice and soy sauce; mix well. Pour 1-1/2 cups into a large resealable plastic bag; add chicken. Seal bag and turn to coat; refrigerate overnight. Cover and refrigerate remaining marinade.

Drain and discard marinade from chicken. In a large saucepan, combine the chicken, water and reserved marinade. Bring to a boil. Reduce heat; cover and simmer for 10-15 minutes or until chicken juices run clear. Drain; cool slightly. Shred chicken.

In a large bowl, combine the chicken, green pepper, onion and celery. In a small bowl, combine the mayonnaise and seasonings. Spoon over chicken mixture; gently stir to coat. Refrigerate until serving. Serve on lettuce-lined rolls. **Yield:** 10 servings.

When I misplaced my recipe for cranberry salad, I created my own. My daughter likes it so much and asks me to make it frequently.
~Gayle Durfee
SAN CLEMENTE, CALIFORNIA

Cran-Raspberry Gelatin Salad

2 packages (3 ounces *each*) cranberry gelatin
1 cup boiling water
1 package (8 ounces) cream cheese, softened
1 package (12 ounces) frozen raspberries, thawed and drained
1 cup ginger ale
1 can (8 ounces) crushed pineapple, drained
1/3 cup chopped pecans
1/2 teaspoon vanilla extract
1 carton (8 ounces) frozen whipped topping, thawed
1-1/2 cups miniature marshmallows
Additional whipped topping

In a small bowl, dissolve gelatin in boiling water. In a mixing bowl, beat cream cheese until smooth. Gradually add hot gelatin mixture and beat until smooth. Stir in the berries, ginger ale, pineapple, pecans and vanilla. Refrigerate for 30 minutes or until partially set.

Fold in whipped topping and marshmallows. Transfer to a 13-in. x 9-in. x 2-in. dish coated with nonstick cooking spray. Cover and refrigerate for 4 hours or until firm. Spread with additional whipped topping. **Yield:** 12-16 servings.

My husband, Frank, a former Army cook, adapted this nourishing chowder from my mother's homemade potato soup. We've developed recipes as a team for over 50 years. Our motto is, "The couple who cooks together, stays together."
~JoAnn Hilliard
EAST LIVERPOOL, OHIO

Bratwurst Potato Soup

1 pound fully cooked bratwurst links, cut into 1/2-inch slices
2 medium potatoes, peeled and chopped
2 cups water
1 medium onion, chopped
1/2 teaspoon salt
Dash pepper
4 cups shredded cabbage
3 cups milk, *divided*
2 tablespoons all-purpose flour
1 cup (4 ounces) shredded Swiss cheese

In a Dutch oven or soup kettle, combine the bratwurst, potatoes, water, onion, salt and pepper. Bring to a boil. Reduce heat; cover and simmer for 10 minutes. Add the cabbage. Cover and simmer for 10-15 minutes or until vegetables are tender.

Stir in 2-1/2 cups milk. Combine flour and remaining milk until smooth. Stir into soup. Bring to a boil; cook and stir for 2 minutes or until thickened. Remove from the heat. Stir in cheese until melted. **Yield:** 8-10 servings.

The addition of barley makes this both a flavorful and hearty broccoli soup. It's a delicious way to warm up on a cold day.

~Cindy Sutton
HOLBEIN, SASKATCHEWAN

Broccoli Barley Soup

2 medium onions, chopped

2 garlic cloves, minced

4 ounces sliced fresh mushrooms

3 tablespoons butter

3 cups chicken broth

3 cups vegetable broth

3/4 cup uncooked medium pearl barley

1/4 to 1/2 teaspoon dried rosemary, crushed

1 pound fresh broccoli, cut into florets

2 tablespoons cornstarch

1/4 cup cold water

2 cups half-and-half cream

Salt and pepper

Grated Parmesan cheese

In a large saucepan or Dutch oven, saute the first three ingredients in butter until tender. Add the broths, barley and rosemary. Bring to a boil. Reduce heat; cover and simmer for 30 minutes or until barley is tender. Add broccoli; cover and cook for 10 minutes or until broccoli is tender.

In a small bowl, combine cornstarch and cold water until smooth; stir into the soup. Bring to a boil; cook and stir for 2 minutes or until thickened. Reduce heat; stir in the cream, salt and pepper (do not boil). Sprinkle with Parmesan cheese. **Yield:** 8 servings (about 2 quarts).

Living in Wisconsin, I like to make dishes featuring cheese. This chowder is one of my best. It makes a great meal served with salad greens and rye rolls.

~Ruth Protz
OSHKOSH, WISCONSIN

Ham Cheddar Chowder

3 cups water

3 cups diced peeled potatoes

1 cup diced carrots

1 cup diced celery

1 medium onion, chopped

2 teaspoons salt

1/2 teaspoon pepper

6 tablespoons butter

6 tablespoons all-purpose flour

4 cups milk

3 cups (12 ounces) shredded cheddar cheese

1 cup cubed fully cooked ham

In a large saucepan or Dutch oven, bring water to a boil. Add the potatoes, carrots, celery, onion, salt and pepper. Reduce heat. Cover and simmer for 20 minutes or until vegetables are tender; drain and set vegetables aside.

In same pan, melt butter. Stir in flour until smooth. Gradually add milk. Bring to a boil; cook and stir for 2 minutes or until thickened. Remove from the heat; stir in cheese until melted. Add ham and reserved vegetables. Cook on low until heated through. Do not boil. **Yield:** 8 servings (about 2 quarts).

Blueberries combine nicely with oranges, onion and a tangy dressing to make this green salad really special. I like to take it when we go on family picnics. My grandson always wants a second helping.

~Ellen Irene Smith
WOODLAND, WASHINGTON

Blueberry-Orange Onion Salad

3 cups torn salad greens

2 medium navel oranges, peeled and sliced

4 sweet onion slices, separated into rings

2 cups fresh blueberries

BLUEBERRY SOUR CREAM DRESSING:

1/2 cup sour cream

1 tablespoon white wine vinegar

1 tablespoon crushed blueberries

1-1/2 teaspoons sugar

1-1/2 teaspoons lemon juice

1/4 teaspoon salt

Arrange greens on four salad plates. Top with the orange slices and onion rings. Sprinkle with blueberries.

In a small bowl, combine dressing ingredients; stir until blended. Drizzle over salads. Serve immediately. **Yield:** 4 servings.

Savory slices of this bread make a popular Saturday night meal for my family. Just like pizza, it can be eaten as a fun finger food. Guests can't stop nibbling when I serve it at parties. Plus, it's good warm or cold.

~Pat Coon
ULSTER, PENNSYLVANIA

Sausage Pizza Loaf

1 pound bulk Italian sausage

1/4 cup *each* chopped onion, sweet red pepper and green pepper

2 packages (6-1/2 ounces *each*) pizza crust mix

1 cup (4 ounces) shredded mozzarella cheese

1/2 cup chopped pepperoni

1 egg, lightly beaten

2 tablespoons grated Parmesan cheese

1 teaspoon dried oregano

1/4 teaspoon garlic powder

In a large skillet, cook the sausage, onion and peppers over medium heat until the meat is no longer pink; drain.

Combine crust mixes; prepare according to package directions. With greased fingers, press onto the bottom of a greased 15-in. x 10-in. x 1-in. baking pan. Combine the sausage mixture, mozzarella cheese, pepperoni and egg; spread over dough to within 1/2 in. of the edges.

Sprinkle with the Parmesan cheese, oregano and garlic powder. Roll up jelly-roll style, starting with a long side; pinch seams to seal. Arrange seam side down on pan and shape into a crescent. Bake at 400° for 30 minutes or until golden brown. **Yield:** 15 servings.

Attend Schmeckfest!

Freeman, South Dakota celebrates the ethnic foods, crafts and traditions of the Germans-from-Russia Mennonites who settled there in the 1870s. Held every year in March or early April, Schmeckfest is a "festival of eating."

South Dakota

So many people seek out this salad at get-togethers, I always have a couple of giant bowls waiting. A guest who said she didn't like salads tried this one and ended up taking the leftovers home.

~Gloria Jarrett
LOVELAND, OHIO

Poppy Seed Tossed Salad

1/3 cup cider vinegar
3/4 cup sugar
　1 small onion, cut into wedges
1/2 teaspoon salt
1/2 teaspoon ground mustard
　1 cup vegetable oil
　4 teaspoons poppy seeds
　1 package (3 ounces) ramen noodles
　2 packages (5 ounces *each*) spring mix salad greens
　1 head iceberg lettuce, torn

　1 can (15 ounces) mandarin oranges, drained
1/2 cup slivered almonds, toasted

In a blender, combine the first five ingredients; cover and process until smooth. While processing, gradually add oil in a steady stream. Stir in poppy seeds. Crush the ramen noodles; discard seasoning packet.

In a large salad bowl, toss the greens, lettuce, noodles, oranges and almonds. Drizzle with poppy seed dressing; toss to coat. **Yield:** 26 servings (1-3/4 cups dressing).

My kids aren't excited about vegetables, but they love them in this soup. It's an easy recipe to make.

~Linda Korte
NEW LISKEARD, ONTARIO

Family Vegetable Beef Soup

　2 pounds ground beef
　1 medium onion, chopped
　1 can (46 ounces) tomato juice
　1 can (28 ounces) diced tomatoes, undrained
　1 jar (4-1/2 ounces) sliced mushrooms, drained
　2 cups frozen cut green beans
　2 cups *each* finely chopped celery, cabbage and carrots
　2 teaspoons dried oregano
　1 teaspoon dried basil

1/2 teaspoon garlic powder
　1 teaspoon salt
1/2 teaspoon pepper

In a Dutch oven or soup kettle, cook the beef and onion over medium heat until meat is no longer pink; drain. Stir in the remaining ingredients. Bring to a boil. Reduce the heat; cover and simmer for 2 hours. **Yield:** 14 servings (3-1/2 quarts).

This dish is a pleasure to serve because it's attractive as well as tasty.

~Becky Armstrong
CANTON, GEORGIA

Crawfish Etouffee

1/3 cup all-purpose flour
1/2 cup vegetable oil
  1 large green pepper, chopped
  1 large onion, chopped
  1 cup chopped celery
  1 can (15 ounces) tomato sauce
  1 cup water
  1 tablespoon Worcestershire sauce
  1 teaspoon garlic powder
  1 teaspoon paprika
  1 teaspoon lemon juice
3/4 teaspoon Creole seasoning
  2 pounds frozen cooked crawfish tails, thawed
Hot cooked rice

In a heavy Dutch oven, whisk the flour and oil until smooth. Cook over medium-high heat for 5 minutes, whisking constantly. Reduce heat to medium; cook and stir 10 minutes longer or until mixture is reddish-brown.

Add the green pepper, onion and celery; cook and stir for 5 minutes. Add tomato sauce, water, Worcestershire sauce, garlic powder, paprika, lemon juice and Creole seasoning. Bring to a boil. Reduce heat; cover and simmer for 45 minutes. Add crawfish and heat through. Serve with hot cooked rice. **Yield:** 8 servings.

I serve these sandwiches for a special party treat. The red and green peppers add color along with flavor.

~Judy Long
EFFINGHAM, ILLINOIS

Italian Sub Sandwiches

1-1/2 pounds Italian sausage links, cut into 1/2-inch pieces
  2 medium red onions, thinly sliced
  2 medium sweet red peppers, thinly sliced
  2 medium green peppers, thinly sliced
  1 garlic clove, minced
  3 medium tomatoes, chopped
  1 teaspoon dried oregano
Salt and pepper to taste
  8 submarine sandwich buns (about 10 inches), split

In a large skillet, cook sausage over medium heat just until no longer pink; drain. Add the onions, peppers and garlic. Cover and cook for 25 minutes or until vegetables are tender, stirring occasionally. Add tomatoes and oregano. Cover and simmer for 5-6 minutes or until tomatoes are cooked. Season with salt and pepper.

Meanwhile, hollow out bottom of roll, leaving 1/2-in. shell. (Discard removed bread or save for another use.) Toast rolls. Fill with sausage mixture. **Yield:** 8 servings.

Stress-Free *Pressure Cooker Recipes*

Busy cooks are taking the pressure off dinner. What's their secret? Pressure cooking! Today's new models are safer and more user-friendly, but they still help you fix filling foods with slow-cooked flavor…flat-out fast! We hope you enjoy these recipes from our Test Kitchen staff.

Brimming with meat and vegetables, this full-bodied soup is sure to take the chill off frosty weather. Vary the veggies to make the most of your garden plenty.

Beef Vegetable Soup

(Pictured above)

1-1/2 pounds beef shanks *or* meaty beef soup bones
    1 tablespoon vegetable oil
    6 cups water
    2 medium carrots, sliced
    2 celery ribs, diced
    1 medium red potato, cut into 1/2-inch cubes
    1 small onion, chopped
    1 garlic clove, minced
    1 bay leaf
    1 teaspoon salt
    1 teaspoon dried basil
    1 teaspoon dried thyme
  1/4 teaspoon pepper
    1 can (16 ounces) kidney beans, rinsed and drained
    1 can (14-1/2 ounces) diced tomatoes, undrained
    1 medium zucchini, diced
  1/2 cup uncooked elbow macaroni

In a pressure cooker over medium-high heat, brown beef on both sides in oil. Add water, carrots, celery, potato, onion, garlic and seasonings. Close cover securely; place pressure regulator on vent pipe. Bring cooker to full pressure over high heat. Reduce heat to medium-high and cook for 15 minutes. (Pressure regulator should maintain a slow steady rocking motion; adjust heat if needed.)

Remove from the heat. Immediately cool according to manufacturer's directions until pressure is completely reduced. Discard bay leaf. Remove beef with a slotted spoon; when cool enough to handle, remove meat from bones. Discard bones and dice the meat.

Return meat to the pan. Add beans, tomatoes and zucchini. Bring soup to a simmer. Stir in macaroni. Cook, uncovered, for 8-10 minutes or until macaroni and zucchini are tender. **Yield:** 10 servings (2-1/2 quarts).

Editor's Note: This recipe was tested at 15 pounds of pressure (psi).

Beef chuck roast gives this sandwich and its broth a hearty flavor. This is also a great "do-ahead" recipe.

French Dip Sandwiches

1 boneless beef chuck roast
   (about 3 pounds)
1 teaspoon dried oregano
1 teaspoon dried rosemary,
   crushed
1/2 teaspoon seasoned salt
1/4 teaspoon pepper
3 cups beef broth
1 bay leaf
1 garlic clove, peeled
Sliced French bread

Place roast on a rack in a pressure cooker; sprinkle with oregano, rosemary, seasoned salt and pepper. Add broth, bay leaf and garlic. Close cover securely; place pressure regulator on vent pipe.

Bring cooker to full pressure over high heat. Reduce heat to medium-high and cook for 1 hour. (Pressure regulator should maintain a slow steady rocking motion; adjust heat if needed.)

Remove from the heat. Immediately cool according to manufacturer's directions until pressure is completely reduced. Remove beef; shred with two forks. Discard bay leaf and garlic from broth. Serve shredded beef on French bread with broth for dipping. **Yield:** 8-10 servings.

Editor's Note: This recipe was tested at 15 pounds of pressure (psi).

Your family will love the zesty but mild flavor of this hefty stew. But you'll appreciate the change-of-pace flavor—and the extra change you'll pocket using less expensive pork cuts! Serve it over rice, noodles or mashed potatoes.

Green Chili Stew

1/4 cup all-purpose flour
1/2 teaspoon salt
1/4 teaspoon pepper
2 pounds boneless pork, cut
   into 1-1/2-inch cubes
2 tablespoons vegetable oil
1 large onion, chopped
2 garlic cloves, minced
1 can (14-1/2 ounces) diced
   tomatoes, undrained
1 cup water
2 cans (4 ounces *each*) chopped
   green chilies
Minced fresh cilantro, optional

In a large resealable plastic bag, combine the flour, salt and pepper. Add pork, a few pieces at a time, and shake to coat. In a pressure cooker over medium heat, brown pork in oil. Add onion and garlic; cook and stir for 3 minutes. Add the tomatoes, water and chilies.

Close cover securely; place pressure regulator on vent pipe. Bring cooker to full pressure over high heat. Reduce heat to medium-high and cook for 8 minutes. (Pressure regulator should maintain a slow steady rocking motion; adjust heat if needed.)

Remove from the heat. Immediately cool according to manufacturer's directions until pressure is completely reduced. Garnish with cilantro if desired. **Yield:** 6 servings.

Editor's Note: This recipe was tested at 15 pounds of pressure (psi).

Flavors of tart tomatoes and cloves shine in this good-for-you soup. Having to cut down on sodium, I often experiment with spices to replace the salt.
~Carol Foiles
CLARK, SOUTH DAKOTA

Spiced Tomato Soup

1 can (14-1/2 ounces) diced tomatoes, undrained
1 teaspoon low-sodium beef bouillon granules
1 cup hot water
1 tablespoon finely chopped onion
1 tablespoon sugar
1/8 teaspoon ground cloves
1/8 teaspoon dried marjoram
1/8 teaspoon dried thyme
1 bay leaf

In a blender or food processor, cover and process tomatoes until pureed. In a saucepan, dissolve bouillon in water. Add tomatoes and remaining ingredients. Bring to a boil, stirring occasionally. Reduce the heat; simmer, covered, for 20-25 minutes. Discard bay leaf. **Yield:** 2 servings.

Cream cheese, horseradish and Dijon mustard are a nice complement to the spinach in this sandwich. It also slices easily to make tasty appetizers.
~Barbara Nowakowski
MESA, ARIZONA

Horseradish Beef Roll-Ups

☑ Uses less fat, sugar or salt. Includes Nutrition Facts and Diabetic Exchanges.

1 package (8 ounces) reduced-fat cream cheese
1 tablespoon prepared horseradish
1 tablespoon Dijon mustard
5 fat-free flour tortillas (8 inches)
30 fresh spinach leaves, stems removed
5 thin slices deli roast beef (about 1/3 pound)
1 cup (4 ounces) reduced-fat shredded cheddar cheese

In a mixing bowl, beat cream cheese, horseradish and mustard until smooth. Spread about 3 tablespoons over each tortilla. Top each with six spinach leaves and a slice of beef.

Sprinkle each with about 3 tablespoons cheese; roll up tightly. Wrap in plastic wrap. Refrigerate for 4 hours before serving. **Yield:** 5 servings.

Nutrition Facts: One serving equals 308 calories, 13 g fat (8 g saturated fat), 54 mg cholesterol, 952 mg sodium, 27 g carbohydrate, 1 g fiber, 19 g protein. **Diabetic Exchanges:** 3 lean meat, 2 starch.

I first tried balsamic vinegar when I made this salad. Now I can't resist any recipe that features the ingredient. This pasta dish is not only ideal for summer picnics; it makes a great side salad or vegetarian entree.
~Elizabeth Kohnen
ALGONQUIN, ILLINOIS

Roasted Pepper Pasta Salad

1 package (12 ounces) tricolor spiral pasta
1 cup sliced green onions
1 jar (7 ounces) roasted sweet red peppers, drained and thinly sliced
4 ounces crumbled feta cheese
1 envelope Italian salad dressing mix
1/2 cup chicken broth
3 tablespoons balsamic vinegar

Cook pasta according to package directions; drain and rinse with cold water. In a large bowl, combine pasta, onions, red peppers and cheese.

In a small bowl, whisk salad dressing mix, broth and vinegar. Pour over pasta mixture; toss to coat. Cover and refrigerate for at least 1 hour. **Yield:** 8 servings.

For a change of pace, I'll use this marinade to give my hamburgers a unique Asian-inspired flavor.
~Myra Innes
AUBURN, KANSAS

Asian-Style Hamburgers

1-1/2 pounds ground beef
1/4 cup vegetable oil
1/4 cup soy sauce
2 tablespoons ketchup
1 tablespoon white vinegar
2 garlic cloves, minced
1/4 teaspoon pepper
6 hamburger buns, split
Leaf lettuce and tomato slices, optional

Shape meat into six patties; place in a shallow dish. In a bowl, whisk together the oil, soy sauce, ketchup, vinegar, garlic and pepper. Set aside 1/4 cup for basting; cover and refrigerate. Pour remaining marinade over the patties. Cover and refrigerate for at least 3 hours.

Grill burgers, uncovered, over medium heat for 5-6 minutes on each side until meat juices run clear, basting occasionally with reserved marinade. Serve on hamburger buns with lettuce leaves and tomato slices if desired. **Yield:** 6 servings.

We find many ways to prepare the abundance of fresh seafood available in our area, and this "fish chowdy" is a hearty favorite. Featuring a flavorful combination of haddock, shrimp and scallops, the chowder is great to serve a group.
~Kristine Lowell
SOUTHBOROUGH, MASSACHUSETTS

New England Seafood Chowder

4 pounds haddock fillets, cut into 3/4-inch pieces
1/4 pound uncooked medium shrimp, peeled and deveined
1/4 pound bay scallops
4 bacon strips, diced
3 medium onions, quartered and thinly sliced
2 tablespoons all-purpose flour
2 cups diced peeled potatoes
4 cups milk
2 tablespoons butter
1 tablespoon minced fresh parsley
2 teaspoons salt
1/2 teaspoon lemon-pepper seasoning
1/4 teaspoon pepper

Place haddock in a Dutch oven; cover with water. Bring to a boil over medium heat. Reduce heat; simmer, uncovered, for 20 minutes. Add the shrimp and scallops; simmer 10 minutes longer. Drain, reserving 2 cups cooking liquid; set liquid and seafood aside.

In a soup kettle, cook bacon over medium heat until crisp; drain on paper towels. In the drippings, saute onions until tender. Stir in flour until blended. Gradually stir in reserved cooking liquid. Bring to a boil; cook and stir for 2 minutes or until thickened. Reduce heat. Add potatoes; cover and cook for 15-20 minutes or until potatoes are tender.

Add the milk, seafood, butter, parsley, salt, lemon-pepper and pepper; heat through. Sprinkle with bacon. **Yield:** 15 servings (3-3/4 quarts).

This colorful salad complements any festive menu. Served alone, it's a complete meal when you want to eat light.
~Suzanne McKinley
LYONS, GEORGIA

Warm Ham 'n' Spinach Salad

- 1 package (10 ounces) fresh spinach, torn
- 1 cup sliced fresh mushrooms
- 2 hard-cooked eggs, coarsely chopped
- 1 cup diced fully cooked ham
- 3/4 cup sweet-and-sour salad dressing

In a large salad bowl, combine the spinach, mushrooms and eggs. In a small skillet coated with nonstick cooking spray, cook ham over medium heat for 5 minutes or until lightly browned. Add to the spinach mixture.

In a small saucepan, bring the salad dressing to a boil. Pour over salad and toss to coat. Serve immediately. **Yield:** 8-10 servings.

This is a pretty salad with a nice variety of flavors and textures. It's a "meal in a bowl" for lighter eating on a warm day.
~Dorothy Smith
EL DORADO, ARKANSAS

Hearty Layer Salad

- 6 cups mixed salad greens
- 1 can (15 ounces) garbanzo beans or chickpeas, rinsed and drained
- 1 cup sliced fresh mushrooms
- 1 cup cherry tomatoes, halved
- 1 small cucumber, thinly sliced
- 1 cup thinly sliced red onion, cut in half and separated
- 3 hard-cooked eggs, sliced
- 1/2 cup chopped walnuts, toasted

DRESSING:
- 1 large ripe avocado, peeled and sliced
- 1 cup (8 ounces) sour cream
- 2 tablespoons lemon juice
- 2 garlic cloves, minced
- 1/2 teaspoon ground cumin
- 1/4 to 1/2 teaspoon salt
- 1/8 teaspoon cayenne pepper

In a large glass bowl, layer first eight ingredients. In a blender, combine the dressing ingredients; cover and process until smooth. Serve with the salad. **Yield:** 10 servings.

Crab 'n' Shrimp Gumbo

6 bacon strips, diced

2 large onions, chopped

2 garlic cloves, minced

2 cans (one 28 ounces, one 14-1/2 ounces) diced tomatoes

3 cans (10-1/2 ounces *each*) condensed beef consomme, undiluted

2 cups water

4 medium leeks, cut into 1/4-inch slices

1 medium carrot, peeled and diced

2 pounds fresh *or* frozen okra, cut into 1/2-inch slices

1-1/2 pounds uncooked medium shrimp, peeled and deveined

1 pound fresh *or* frozen crabmeat, flaked and cartilage removed

1/2 teaspoon salt

1/2 teaspoon cayenne pepper

1/3 cup all-purpose flour

1/3 cup cold water

3 tablespoons minced fresh parsley

Hot cooked rice

In a large skillet, cook bacon over medium heat until crisp. Using a slotted spoon, remove to paper towels to drain, reserving 1 tablespoon drippings. In same skillet, saute onions and garlic in drippings until tender.

Pour into a Dutch oven or soup kettle. Add the tomatoes, consomme and water. Cover and bring to a boil; add leeks and carrot. Reduce heat; simmer, uncovered, for 30 minutes. Add okra and simmer, uncovered, for 25 minutes, stirring occasionally. Add the shrimp, crab, salt and cayenne; simmer, uncovered, for 5 minutes.

In a small bowl, combine flour and cold water until smooth. Stir into gumbo mixture. Bring to a boil; cook and stir for 2 minutes or until slightly thickened. Stir in parsley and reserved bacon. Serve immediately with rice. **Yield:** 16-20 servings (about 5 quarts).

Roast Beef Potato Salad

1-1/2 pounds small red potatoes

2 cups julienned cooked roast beef

1 cup thinly sliced red onion

1/2 to 3/4 cup julienned sweet red pepper

1/4 cup olive oil

2 tablespoons red wine vinegar

1 to 2 tablespoons minced fresh thyme *or* 1 to 2 teaspoons dried thyme

1 teaspoon salt

1/4 to 1/2 teaspoon cayenne pepper

8 cups torn leaf lettuce

In a large saucepan, cook potatoes in boiling salted water until tender, about 15 minutes. Cool slightly; cut into quarters. In a bowl, combine the warm potatoes, beef, onion and red pepper.

In a small bowl, whisk the oil, vinegar, thyme, salt and cayenne. Pour over potato mixture and toss to coat. Refrigerate for at least 2 hours. Serve over lettuce. **Yield:** 6-8 servings.

No time to make a homemade soup? Think again! You'll be ladling out steaming bowls of this satisfying chowder in no time. Canned corn and crab blend beautifully in the creamy, colorful soup. It's truly one of the best I've ever tasted.

~Sarah McClanahan
RALEIGH, NORTH CAROLINA

Crab Corn Chowder

3 teaspoons chicken bouillon granules
2 cups boiling water
6 bacon strips, diced
1/3 cup *each* diced sweet red, yellow and orange peppers
1/2 cup chopped onion
1/4 cup all-purpose flour
3 cups half-and-half cream
2 cans (14-3/4 ounces *each*) cream-style corn
1-1/2 teaspoons seasoned salt
1/2 teaspoon dried basil
1/4 to 1/2 teaspoon cayenne pepper
2 cans (6 ounces *each*) crabmeat, drained, flaked and cartilage removed *or* 2 cups imitation crabmeat, flaked
1/2 cup minced chives

Dissolve bouillon in water; set aside. In a Dutch oven or soup kettle, cook bacon over medium heat until crisp. Remove bacon to paper towels to drain, reserving drippings. In the same pan, saute peppers and onion in drippings until tender. Stir in flour. Gradually stir in bouillon. Bring to a boil; cook and stir for 2 minutes or until thickened.

Reduce heat; gradually stir in cream and corn. Add the seasoned salt, basil and cayenne. Cook for 8-10 minutes or until heated through, stirring occasionally (do not boil). Stir in the crab. Garnish each bowl with bacon and chives. **Yield:** 8 servings.

When made with tricolor pasta, this is a colorful and tasty salad to take to any summer gathering.

~Marcia Buchanan
PHILADELPHIA, PENNSYLVANIA

Hearty Pasta Salad

2 cups uncooked spiral pasta
1 cup cooked cubed pastrami, turkey *or* roast beef
1/4 cup *each* chopped carrot, celery and onion
3/4 cup mayonnaise
1/4 cup grated Parmesan cheese
1/4 teaspoon salt
1/4 teaspoon pepper
1/4 teaspoon lemon juice

Cook pasta according to package directions; drain and rinse with cold water. In a large bowl, combine the pasta, pastrami, carrot, celery and onion. Combine the mayonnaise, Parmesan cheese, salt, pepper and lemon juice. Add to the pasta mixture; toss to coat. Cover and refrigerate for 1 hour or until serving. **Yield:** 4 servings.

A friend brought samples of this recipe to a soup-tasting class sponsored by our extension homemakers club. It was a great hit with my family. The mix of sausage, apples and vegetables makes a different and flavorful combination.
~Marcia Wolff
ROLLING PRAIRIE, INDIANA

🎀 Kielbasa Cabbage Soup

3 cups coleslaw mix
2 medium carrots, chopped
1/2 cup chopped onion
1/2 cup chopped celery
1/2 teaspoon caraway seeds
2 tablespoons butter
1 carton (32 ounces) chicken broth
3/4 to 1 pound fully cooked kielbasa *or* Polish sausage, cut into 1/2-inch pieces
2 medium unpeeled Golden Delicious apples, chopped
1/4 teaspoon pepper
1/8 teaspoon salt

In a large saucepan, saute the coleslaw mix, carrots, onion, celery and caraway seeds in butter for 5-8 minutes or until the vegetables are crisp-tender. Stir in the remaining ingredients.

Bring to a boil. Reduce heat; simmer, uncovered, for 20-30 minutes, stirring occasionally. **Yield:** 6 servings (2 quarts).

My husband loves his mom's endive dressing, so I asked her to share the recipe with me. I usually serve this with boiled potatoes and sliced smoked ham.
~Angela Degler
GREENVILLE, GEORGIA

🎀 Warm Bacon Endive Dressing

1/2 pound bacon strips, diced
1 medium onion, chopped
2 tablespoons sugar
1-1/2 teaspoons cornstarch
1/2 teaspoon salt
2 tablespoons cider vinegar
1 cup milk
1 egg, lightly beaten
3 bunches curly endive, torn (about 12 cups)
3 hard-cooked eggs, sliced

In a skillet, cook bacon over medium heat until crisp. Remove to paper towels; drain, reserving 1 tablespoon drippings. Set bacon aside. Saute onion in the drippings until tender. Add sugar, cornstarch, salt and vinegar; stir until smooth. Gradually stir in the milk. Bring to a boil; cook and stir for 2 minutes or until thickened. Reduce heat.

Add a small amount of hot mixture into the beaten egg; return all to the pan, stirring constantly. Bring to a gentle boil; cook and stir 2 minutes longer. Remove from the heat.

In a large salad bowl, combine the endive, hard-cooked eggs and reserved bacon. Add desired amount of warm dressing; toss to coat. Refrigerate leftover dressing. **Yield:** 10-12 servings.

Get ready to roll out **mouth-watering** main dishes ranging from **skillet suppers** and **oven entrees** to cookout classics.

Main Dishes

HEARTY FAVORITES. From left: Spicy Spaghetti Sauce (p. 48) and South Carolina-Style Ribs (p. 49).

Vine-ripened tomatoes roast up into a versatile sauce that's excellent over pasta, grilled chicken and fish or on toasted French bread for bruschetta. I often double or triple the recipe, and my husband still can't get enough.

~Amanda Cerza
WILMINGTON, ILLINOIS

Chunky Roasted Tomatoes

2 pounds plum tomatoes
2 tablespoons olive oil
1 small onion, chopped
1 garlic clove, minced
1 teaspoon salt
1 teaspoon sugar
1/2 teaspoon dried basil
1/2 teaspoon dried oregano
1/4 teaspoon pepper
Hot cooked pasta
Shredded Parmesan cheese

Cut tomatoes into wedges; discard seeds. Place the tomatoes in a greased 13-in. x 9-in. x 2-in. baking dish. Drizzle with oil. Sprinkle with onion, garlic and seasonings; toss to coat. Spread in a single layer.

Bake, uncovered, at 350° for 50-60 minutes or until heated through, stirring twice. Toss with hot cooked pasta and sprinkle with Parmesan cheese. **Yield:** 3-4 servings.

I appreciate that this hearty pasta sauce is quick to assemble and cooks in just a few hours. My husband and I have our hands full raising two children and 25,000 game birds on our farm.

~Jennifer Mai
PIERCEVILLE, KANSAS

Spicy Spaghetti Sauce

(Pictured on page 47)

1 pound ground beef
1 large onion, chopped
1 can (46 ounces) tomato juice
1 can (12 ounces) tomato paste
1 can (4 ounces) mushroom stems and pieces, drained
2 tablespoons minced fresh parsley
1 tablespoon garlic salt
1 tablespoon dried basil
2 teaspoons sugar

2 teaspoons dried oregano
1/4 to 1/2 teaspoon crushed red pepper flakes
3 bay leaves
Hot cooked spaghetti

In a Dutch oven, cook the beef and onion over medium heat until meat is no longer pink; drain. Stir in the tomato juice, tomato paste, mushrooms and seasonings; bring to a boil.

Reduce heat; simmer, uncovered, for 2-1/2 hours, stirring occasionally. Discard bay leaves. Serve over spaghetti. **Yield:** 6-1/2 cups.

These enchiladas bake up soft, tender and saucy. It's a nice meatless main dish that's also quick and easy.   ~Lois Hansen
PINEDALE, CALIFORNIA

Sour Cream Enchiladas

4 cups (16 ounces) shredded cheddar cheese, *divided*
2 cups (16 ounces) sour cream
2 cans (2-1/4 ounces *each*) sliced ripe olives, drained
1 bunch green onions, thinly sliced
8 flour tortillas (8 inches), warmed
1 can (19 ounces) enchilada sauce

In a large bowl, combine 3 cups shredded cheddar cheese and sour cream. Set aside 2 tablespoons olives

and 2 tablespoons onions. Add remaining olives and onions to cheese mixture; mix well. Spoon 1/2 cup down the center of each tortilla. Roll up and place seam side down in a greased 13-in. x 9-in. x 2-in. baking dish. Pour enchilada sauce over the top. Sprinkle with remaining cheese.

Cover and bake at 325° for 25-30 minutes or until heated through and cheese is melted. Sprinkle with reserved olives and onions. **Yield:** 4 servings.

This recipe makes some of the best country-style pork ribs you'll ever eat, especially when cooked on a grill. We use the same sauce on barbecued chicken, too. ~Karen Conklin
SANTEE, SOUTH CAROLINA

South Carolina-Style Ribs

(Also pictured on page 47)

    4 pounds baby-back pork ribs
1/2 cup red wine vinegar
1/2 cup honey
1/2 cup prepared mustard
    2 tablespoons vegetable oil
    4 teaspoons Worcestershire sauce
    2 teaspoons butter
    2 teaspoons coarsely ground pepper
    1 teaspoon salt
    1 teaspoon hot pepper sauce

Cut ribs into serving-size pieces. Place ribs meat side up in a roasting pan.

Bake, uncovered, at 325° for 2 hours; drain.

Meanwhile, combine the vinegar, honey, mustard, oil, Worcestershire sauce, butter, pepper, salt and hot pepper sauce in a saucepan. Bring to a boil over medium heat. Reduce heat; simmer, uncovered, for about 30 minutes or until slightly reduced. Remove from the heat; cool at room temperature for 1 hour.

Brush sauce over ribs. Bake, uncovered, for 1 to 1-1/4 hours longer or until ribs are tender, basting occasionally. **Yield:** 6-8 servings.

Helpful Hint

Tomato Tips

To save time, I always process whole, fresh tomatoes in a blender until smooth. Then I cook them to the desired thickness for tomato or spaghetti sauce. The blender comes in handy for making salsa, too. I use it to cut up garlic and hot peppers with about 1 cup tomatoes. Not only is it fast, but using the blender ensures the ingredients are well chopped and uniform in size.

~Karen Sawatzky, MacGregor, Manitoba

I made several of these hearty pies for a branding bee on our cattle ranch. Everybody had to have the recipe. With mashed potatoes, ground beef, beans and fresh vegetables, it's truly a meal in itself. ~Betty Jorsvick
OLDS, ALBERTA

Taco Potato Pie

    2 cups cold mashed potatoes (prepared with milk and butter)
    1 envelope taco seasoning, *divided*
    1 pound ground beef
1/2 cup chopped onion
    1 can (16 ounces) refried beans
1/2 cup barbecue sauce
1/4 cup water
    1 cup shredded lettuce
    1 medium tomato, seeded and chopped
    1 cup (4 ounces) shredded cheddar cheese
    Sour cream

Combine the potatoes and 2 tablespoons taco seasoning. Press into a greased 9-in. deep-dish pie plate; set aside.

In a skillet, cook beef and onion over medium heat until meat is no longer pink; drain. Stir in the beans, barbecue sauce, water and remaining taco seasoning. Cook and stir until hot and bubbly. Spoon into potato crust.

Bake at 350° for 30-35 minutes or until heated through. Top with lettuce, tomato, cheese and sour cream. **Yield:** 4-6 servings.

This is a great way to use ground beef, and I often double the recipe because it's so easy. Whenever I make this dish, I receive so many compliments.

~Phyllis Stewart
GOODWOOD, ONTARIO

Mediterranean Beef Toss

☑ Uses less fat, sugar or salt. Includes Nutrition Facts and Diabetic Exchanges.

1/2 pound lean ground beef
4 garlic cloves, minced
3/4 teaspoon salt, *divided*
1/4 teaspoon pepper
3 teaspoons olive oil, *divided*
1 medium red onion, sliced
2 medium zucchini, sliced
1 medium green pepper, cut into 1-inch pieces
1 can (**28** ounces) diced tomatoes, undrained
1 teaspoon red wine vinegar
1 teaspoon dried basil
1 teaspoon dried thyme
Hot cooked spaghetti, optional

In a nonstick skillet, cook the beef, garlic, 1/4 teaspoon salt and pepper in 1 teaspoon oil over medium heat until meat is no longer pink; drain. Remove and keep warm. In the same skillet, saute onion in remaining oil for 2 minutes. Add zucchini and green pepper; cook and stir for 4-6 minutes or until vegetables are crisp-tender.

Stir in the tomatoes, vinegar, basil, thyme and remaining salt. Add beef mixture; heat through. Serve over spaghetti if desired. **Yield:** 4 servings.

Nutrition Facts: One serving (1-1/2 cups beef mixture, calculated without spaghetti) equals 204 calories, 9 g fat (3 g saturated fat), 21 mg cholesterol, 739 mg sodium, 18 g carbohydrate, 6 g fiber, 15 g protein. **Diabetic Exchanges:** 2 lean meat, 1 starch, 1/2 fat.

I like to serve this colorful vegetable and rice dish when I'm hosting a buffet luncheon.

~Jennifer Blakely
AURORA, COLORADO

Chickpea Cauliflower Curry

1 cup uncooked brown rice
4 cups cauliflowerets
1 medium onion, chopped
1 large carrot, diced
2 garlic cloves, minced
2 teaspoons vegetable oil
2 teaspoons minced fresh gingerroot
1-1/2 teaspoons curry powder
1/2 teaspoon salt
1/8 teaspoon ground cloves, optional
1 can (**15** ounces) chickpeas *or* garbanzo beans, rinsed and drained
1 can (**14-1/2** ounces) diced tomatoes, undrained
1 cup fresh *or* frozen peas

Cook the rice according to package directions. Set aside and keep warm. Place cauliflower in a saucepan; cover with water. Bring to a boil; cook for 5 minutes. Drain and set aside.

In a large skillet, saute onion, carrot and garlic in oil until tender. Stir in the ginger, curry, salt and cloves if desired. Add the beans, tomatoes, peas and cauliflower. Cook and stir for 5 minutes or until heated through. Remove from heat. Serve over the rice. **Yield:** 8-10 servings.

My mother passed down this recipe to me, and I use it often to make fajitas. The lemon juice and soy sauce give it some zing.

~Traci Yokoo
LA MIRADA, CALIFORNIA

Peppered Flank Steak

2 tablespoons chopped green onions
2 tablespoons lemon juice
2 tablespoons soy sauce
2 tablespoons vegetable oil
1 garlic clove, minced
1 teaspoon pepper
1/2 teaspoon celery salt
1 beef flank steak (1-1/2 pounds)

In a large resealable plastic bag, combine the first seven ingredients; add steak. Seal bag and turn to coat; refrigerate overnight.

If grilling the steak, coat grill rack with nonstick cooking spray before starting the grill. Drain and discard marinade.

Grill steak, covered, over medium-hot heat or broil 4 in. from the heat for 6-8 minutes on each side or until meat reaches desired doneness (for medium-rare, a meat thermometer should read 145°; medium, 160°; well-done, 170°). Thinly slice across the grain. **Yield:** 6 servings.

My family loves pizza and chicken, so I knew when I found this recipe that it would be a hit. We make it often because we get so many requests.

~Debby Bitner
MASON CITY, ILLINOIS

Chicken Fajita Pizza

1 tube (10 ounces) refrigerated pizza crust
1 pound boneless skinless chicken breasts, cut into 2-inch strips
1 tablespoon vegetable oil
1 cup sliced green pepper
1 cup thinly sliced onion
2 teaspoons chili powder
1 garlic clove, minced
1/2 teaspoon ground cumin
1/2 teaspoon salt
1/2 cup salsa
2 cups (8 ounces) shredded Monterey Jack cheese

Unroll the pizza crust onto a greased 15-in. x 10-in. x 1-in. baking pan; flatten dough and build up edges slightly. Prick dough several times with a fork. Bake at 425° for 10-15 minutes or until lightly browned.

Meanwhile, in a skillet, saute chicken in oil for 5 minutes. Add the green pepper, onion, chili powder, garlic, cumin and salt; cook 3 minutes longer or until vegetables are crisp-tender. Spoon over crust; top with salsa and cheese. Bake for 12-15 minutes or until crust is golden brown and cheese is melted. **Yield:** 8-10 slices.

A dear friend shared the recipe for this tender ham with me. I've taken it to reunions, weddings, graduations, baptisms, holiday gatherings and more. It's a delicious way to please a crowd. The cranberry sauce adds flavor and color. ~Susan Seymour
VALATIE, NEW YORK

Cranberry-Glazed Ham

- 1 can (16 ounces) whole-berry cranberry sauce
- 1/2 cup orange juice
- 3 tablespoons steak sauce
- 1 tablespoon vegetable oil
- 1 tablespoon prepared mustard
- 1 tablespoon brown sugar
- 1/2 bone-in fully cooked ham (about 8 pounds)

In a bowl, combine the cranberry sauce, orange juice, steak sauce, oil, mustard and brown sugar. Score the surface of the ham with shallow diagonal cuts, making diamond shapes.

Place ham in a large resealable plastic bag. Add cranberry mixture; seal bag and turn to coat. Cover and refrigerate for at least 8 hours or overnight, turning several times. Drain and reserve marinade. Place ham on a rack in a foil-lined roasting pan; cover with foil. Bake at 325° for 1-3/4 hours.

Place reserved marinade in a saucepan. Bring to a rolling boil; boil for 1-2 minutes. Brush some of the marinade over ham. Bake, uncovered, for 45-60 minutes or until a meat thermometer reads 140°, brushing with marinade every 15 minutes. Warm remaining marinade; serve with ham.
Yield: 16-20 servings.

You'd never guess this creamy, full-flavored Stroganoff is actually light! It's very meaty and features a thick tomato sauce that makes it look so impressive. ~Rebecca Baird
SALT LAKE CITY, UTAH

Beef Stroganoff

☑ Uses less fat, sugar or salt. Includes Nutrition Facts and Diabetic Exchanges.

- 1 pound beef tenderloin, cut into 1/4-inch strips
- 4 teaspoons canola oil, *divided*
- 1/2 pound sliced fresh mushrooms
- 1 large onion, thinly sliced
- 2 garlic cloves, minced
- 1/3 cup all-purpose flour
- 1/2 teaspoon dried basil
- 1/4 teaspoon salt
- 1/8 teaspoon pepper
- 1 can (14 ounces) beef broth
- 3 tablespoons apple juice
- 1 tablespoon tomato paste
- 1/2 teaspoon Worcestershire sauce
- 1/2 cup fat-free sour cream
Dash ground nutmeg
Hot cooked yolk-free noodles

In a large nonstick skillet or Dutch oven, brown beef in batches in 2 teaspoons oil over medium heat. Remove and keep warm. In the same skillet, saute the mushrooms, onion and garlic in remaining oil until tender.

Return meat to the pan. Sprinkle with flour, basil, salt and pepper; stir until blended. Add the broth, apple juice, tomato paste and Worcestershire sauce. Cook and stir over medium-low heat for 8-10 minutes or until meat is tender. Stir in sour cream and nutmeg until blended (do not boil). Serve over noodles. **Yield:** 4 servings.

Nutrition Facts: One serving (1 cup beef mixture; calculated without noodles) equals 343 calories, 14 g fat (4 g saturated fat), 73 mg cholesterol, 583 mg sodium, 22 g carbohydrate, 2 g fiber, 30 g protein. **Diabetic Exchanges:** 3 lean meat, 1 vegetable, 1 fat, 1/2 starch, 1/2 fat-free milk.

Marinated Chicken Breasts

1 cup sugar
1 cup water
1 cup soy sauce
1/4 cup pineapple juice
1/4 cup vegetable oil
1 teaspoon garlic powder
1 teaspoon ground ginger
8 boneless skinless chicken breast halves (about 2-1/2 pounds)

In a bowl, combine the first seven ingredients; remove 3/4 cup for basting; cover and refrigerate. In a large resealable plastic bag, place the chicken and remaining marinade. Seal bag and turn to coat; refrigerate for 4 hours or overnight.

Drain and discard marinade. Grill chicken, covered, over medium heat for 3 minutes on each side. Baste with reserved marinade. Grill 3-4 minutes longer on each side or until juices run clear, basting several times. **Yield:** 8 servings.

🎗Creamy Chicken Lasagna

12 uncooked lasagna noodles
2 tablespoons cornstarch
1 can (12 ounces) evaporated milk
2 cups chicken broth
1 can (8 ounces) tomato sauce
1/2 cup grated Parmesan cheese
2 garlic cloves, minced
2 teaspoons Dijon mustard
1/2 teaspoon dried basil
1/4 teaspoon ground nutmeg
1/8 teaspoon cayenne pepper
2 cups cooked chicken strips (12 ounces)
24 cherry tomatoes, thinly sliced
1 cup (4 ounces) shredded cheddar cheese
Paprika and minced fresh parsley

Cook noodles according to package directions. Meanwhile, in a large saucepan, combine the cornstarch and milk until smooth. Whisk in the broth, tomato sauce, Parmesan cheese, garlic, mustard, basil, nutmeg and cayenne. Bring to a boil over medium heat; cook and stir for 2 minutes or until thickened. Remove from the heat.

Drain noodles. Spread 1/4 cup sauce into a greased 13-in. x 9-in. x 2-in. baking dish. Set aside 1 cup sauce. Stir chicken and tomatoes into the remaining sauce. Layer four noodles and half of the chicken mixture in baking dish. Repeat layers. Top with remaining noodles; spread with reserved sauce. Sprinkle with cheddar cheese and paprika.

Cover and bake at 350° for 45-50 minutes or until bubbly. Let stand for 15 minutes before cutting. Sprinkle with parsley. **Yield:** 9-12 servings.

Tomato Baked Haddock

☑ Uses less fat, sugar or salt. Includes Nutrition Facts and Diabetic Exchanges.

1 medium green pepper, chopped
1 small onion, chopped
1 tablespoon butter
1 tablespoon all-purpose flour
1 can (14-1/2 ounces) diced tomatoes, undrained
1 pound fresh *or* frozen haddock fillets, thawed
1/2 teaspoon salt
Pepper to taste
1/2 cup shredded part-skim mozzarella cheese

In a nonstick skillet, saute the green pepper and onion in butter until tender. Stir in the flour until blended. Add tomatoes; cook and stir until thickened, about 3 minutes.

Place the fillets skin side down in an 11-in. x 7-in. x 2-in. baking dish coated with nonstick cooking spray. Sprinkle with salt and pepper; top with tomato mixture. Bake, uncovered, at 350° for 20-25 minutes or until fish flakes easily with a fork. Sprinkle with cheese. Bake 2 minutes longer or until the cheese is melted. **Yield:** 4 servings.

Nutrition Facts: One serving equals 204 calories, 6 g fat (4 g saturated fat), 80 mg cholesterol, 625 mg sodium, 10 g carbohydrate, 2 g fiber, 27 g protein. **Diabetic Exchanges:** 3 very lean meat, 2 vegetable, 1 fat.

Beef Spinach Hot Dish

1 pound ground beef
1 medium onion, chopped
2 garlic cloves, minced
1 can (4 ounces) mushroom stems and pieces, drained
1 teaspoon salt
1 teaspoon dried oregano
1/4 teaspoon pepper
2 packages (10 ounces *each*) frozen chopped spinach, thawed and squeezed dry
1 can (10-3/4 ounces) condensed cream of celery soup, undiluted
1 cup (8 ounces) sour cream
2 cups (8 ounces) shredded mozzarella cheese, *divided*

In a large skillet, cook beef, onion and garlic over medium heat until the meat is no longer pink; drain. Stir in the mushrooms, salt, oregano and pepper. Add the spinach, soup and sour cream. Stir in half of the mozzarella cheese.

Transfer to a greased 2-qt. baking dish. Bake, uncovered, at 350° for 15 minutes. Sprinkle with the remaining cheese; bake 5 minutes longer or until cheese is melted. **Yield:** 6-8 servings.

Our son, a restaurant owner, showed me how to make this quick shrimp and noodle dish zipped up with garlic and cayenne. It's also tasty served over rice. ~Gertraud Casbarro
SUMMERVILLE, SOUTH CAROLINA

Garlic Lime Shrimp

1 pound uncooked large shrimp, peeled and deveined
5 garlic cloves, minced
1/2 teaspoon salt
1/4 to 1/2 teaspoon cayenne pepper
1/2 cup butter
3 tablespoons lime juice

1 tablespoon minced fresh parsley
Hot cooked pasta

In a large skillet, saute the shrimp, garlic, salt and cayenne in butter until the shrimp turn pink, about 5 minutes. Stir in lime juice and parsley. Serve over pasta. **Yield:** 4 servings.

Here's a meal on a skewer with a unique twist. The pineapple, cantaloupe and peppers complement the sausage perfectly. I frequently fire up the grill for these simple kabobs in summer. ~Patricia Eggemeyer
ELLIS GROVE, ILLINOIS

Polynesian Sausage Kabobs

1/2 cup lemon juice
1/2 cup soy sauce
1/3 cup water
1/3 cup honey
1/4 teaspoon salt
1-1/2 pounds fully cooked kielbasa or Polish sausage, cut into 1-1/2-inch slices
1 small pineapple, cut into 1-inch cubes
1 small cantaloupe, cut into 1-inch cubes
2 medium green peppers, cut into 1-inch pieces

In a large bowl, combine the first five ingredients; mix well. Set aside half of the marinade for basting; cover and refrigerate. Pour remaining marinade into a large resealable plastic bag; add sausage. Seal bag and turn to coat. Refrigerate for 3 hours.

Drain and discard the marinade from sausage. On metal or soaked wooden skewers, alternate the sausage, pineapple, cantaloupe and green peppers. Grill, uncovered, over medium heat for 10 minutes or until sausage is browned, turning and basting frequently with reserved marinade. **Yield:** 5 servings.

This is a flavorful seafood dish that draws compliments each time I serve it to family and friends.

~Cora Robin
ST. BERNARD, LOUISIANA

Creamy Shrimp Noodle Skillet

- 1 package (16 ounces) medium egg noodles
- 2 medium onions, chopped
- 1 medium green pepper, chopped
- 2 celery ribs, chopped
- 3 garlic cloves, minced
- 3/4 cup butter
- 1 tablespoon all-purpose flour
- 3 cups half-and-half cream
- 1-1/2 pounds uncooked medium shrimp, peeled and deveined
- 1 jalapeno pepper, seeded and chopped
- 2 tablespoons minced fresh parsley
- 8 ounces process cheese (Velveeta), cubed

Cook noodles according to package directions; drain and set aside. In a large saucepan or Dutch oven, saute the onions, green pepper, celery and garlic in butter until tender. Stir in flour until blended. Gradually stir in cream. Bring to a boil; cook and stir for 2 minutes or until thickened.

Reduce heat; add shrimp, jalapeno pepper and parsley. Simmer, uncovered, for 3 minutes. Stir in cheese; cook 3 minutes longer or until cheese is melted. Stir in the noodles; heat through. **Yield:** 6-8 servings.

Editor's Note: When cutting or seeding hot peppers, use rubber or plastic gloves to protect your hands. Avoid touching your face.

This recipe from my husband's grandmother is my favorite way to use home-canned tomatoes. The bacon-flavored tomato mixture and tender dumplings are a delicious main dish or a side with roasted or grilled meats...and the leftovers are great!

~Paulette Wilhelmi
MINNESOTA LAKE, MINNESOTA

Parsley Dumplings With Tomatoes

- 1/2 pound sliced bacon, diced
- 2 cups chopped onions
- 2 tablespoons butter
- 2 cans (28 ounces *each*) diced tomatoes, undrained
- 1 tablespoon sugar
- 1/2 teaspoon salt

DUMPLINGS:
- 2 cups all-purpose flour
- 3 teaspoons baking powder
- 1 teaspoon salt
- 1/4 cup cold butter
- 1/4 cup minced fresh parsley
- 1 cup milk

In a large skillet, cook bacon over medium heat until crisp. Remove to paper towels with a slotted spoon. Drain drippings. In the same skillet, saute onions in butter until tender. Stir in the tomatoes, sugar, salt and bacon; bring to a boil. Reduce heat; cover and simmer while preparing dumplings.

In a bowl, combine the flour, baking powder and salt; cut in butter until mixture is crumbly. Add parsley. Stir in milk just until moistened.

Drop by tablespoonfuls onto simmering tomato mixture. Cover and simmer for 20-25 minutes or until a toothpick inserted into dumplings comes out clean (do not lift cover while simmering). Serve immediately. **Yield:** 8-10 servings.

If you know anything about Texans, you know we love our black-eyed peas. But you don't have to be from here to enjoy this recipe.

~Sue Wilhite
ODESSA, TEXAS

Black-Eyed Pea Jambalaya

2 cans (15-1/2 ounces *each*) black-eyed peas, rinsed and drained

2-1/2 cups water

2 cups frozen okra, thawed

1 cup uncooked instant rice

Salt and pepper to taste

1 pound fully cooked kielbasa *or* Polish sausage, diced

1 can (14-1/2 ounces) diced tomatoes, undrained

In a Dutch oven, combine peas, water, okra, rice, salt and pepper. Bring to a boil. Reduce heat; cover and simmer for 10 minutes. Add sausage and tomatoes; cover and simmer 15 minutes longer or until liquid is absorbed. **Yield:** 6-8 servings.

These chicken roll-ups taste as though they came from a fancy French restaurant, but they're so simple to make in your own kitchen.

~Margaret Potten
GLENDALE, NEW YORK

Flavorful Chicken Roll-Ups

6 boneless skinless chicken breast halves

1 package (10 ounces) sliced mozzarella cheese

1/2 cup all-purpose flour

2 eggs, lightly beaten

2/3 cup seasoned bread crumbs

1/2 cup butter, melted

1/2 teaspoon dried oregano

Flatten chicken to 1/3-in. thickness. Place one cheese slice on each piece of chicken; roll up tightly. Secure with a toothpick.

Place the flour, beaten eggs and bread crumbs in separate shallow bowls. Coat chicken with flour. Dip in beaten eggs, then coat with bread crumbs.

Place seam side down in an ungreased 2-1/2-qt. baking dish. Combine the butter and oregano; drizzle over the chicken. Bake, uncovered, at 350° for 40-50 minutes or until chicken juices run clear. Discard toothpicks before serving. **Yield:** 6 servings.

I've been known to make this recipe twice a week—it's so delicious. I like to call it "sticky chicken" since the slightly sweet sauce of honey, lemon juice and herbs nicely coats the chicken thighs.

~Dorothy Reinhold
MALIBU, CALIFORNIA

Oregano-Lemon Chicken

6 chicken thighs (3 pounds)

3 tablespoons lemon juice

2 tablespoons honey

1 tablespoon olive oil

3 garlic cloves, minced

2 teaspoons dried oregano

Place the chicken in a greased 13-in. x 9-in. x 2-in. baking dish. Combine the lemon juice, honey, oil, garlic and oregano; pour over chicken.

Bake, uncovered, at 375° for 45 minutes or until a meat thermometer reads 180° and chicken juices run clear, basting occasionally with pan juices. **Yield:** 6 servings.

Rounding Up Lamb in *Wyoming*

WYOMING'S extensive grazing land makes it the third largest lamb-producing state, behind California and Texas.

Every year, U.S. producers sell 303 million pounds of lamb. Once thought of as a seasonal product, lamb is now available fresh year-round.

Lamb is naturally tender and mild-tasting. Traditionally served as an elegant entree for special occasions, lamb now runs the gamut from lunch and dinner fare to appetizers and snacks.

Lamb is a delicious alternative to beef or chicken. I got this recipe from my friend Wendy Smith—she and her husband raise about 4,000 lambs yearly.
~Bonnie Hiller
POWELL, WYOMING

Lamb Fajitas

    1 boneless leg of lamb *or* lamb shoulder
      (3 to 4 pounds)
1/2 cup vegetable oil
1/2 cup lemon juice
1/3 cup soy sauce
1/3 cup packed brown sugar
1/4 cup vinegar
    3 tablespoons Worcestershire sauce
    1 tablespoon ground mustard
1/2 teaspoon pepper
    1 large green pepper, sliced
    1 large sweet red pepper, sliced
    1 large onion, sliced
  16 flour tortillas (7 inches), warmed
Chopped tomato and cucumber, optional

Cut lamb into thin bite-size strips. Combine the next eight ingredients; pour into a large resealable plastic bag or shallow glass container. Add lamb; seal or cover and refrigerate for 3 hours, turning occasionally.

Place the lamb and marinade in a Dutch oven or large saucepan; bring to a boil. Reduce heat; cover and simmer for 8-10 minutes or until meat is tender. Add peppers and onion; cook until vegetables are crisp-tender, about 4 minutes.

Using a slotted spoon, place meat and vegetables on tortillas; top with tomato and cucumber if desired. Fold in sides of tortilla and serve immediately. **Yield:** 8 servings.

I first made this special main dish for a 4-H demonstration, and it won an award. Now it's a winner with my husband, Stan, and our family and friends.
~Pat Horton
RIVERTON, WYOMING

Cheesy Lamb Cups

1 envelope onion soup mix

1/3 cup dry bread crumbs

1 cup evaporated milk

2 pounds ground lamb

4 ounces cheddar cheese, cut into 12 cubes

1 can (10-3/4 ounces) condensed cheddar cheese soup, undiluted

1/2 cup milk

1 teaspoon Worcestershire sauce

In a bowl, combine soup mix, bread crumbs and evaporated milk. Add lamb and mix well. Press half of the mixture into 12 greased muffin cups, filling each half full. Press one cube of cheese into the center of each cup. Cover with the remaining lamb mixture, mounding each slightly. Bake at 375° for 20-25 minutes or until a meat thermometer reads 160°.

Meanwhile, combine soup, milk and Worcestershire sauce in a small saucepan; heat through, stirring until smooth. Serve over lamb cups. **Yield:** 6 servings.

This satisfying stew was recommended to me by Jackie Palm, whose area ranch ships out several thousand head of lambs. Even though my husband, Randy, and I are "empty nesters," I always make a big batch of this flavorful stew with its rich gravy. Since we have a busy cattle ranch and I also substitute-teach, leftovers always come in handy.
~Sandra Ramsey
ELK MOUNTAIN, WYOMING

Wyoming Lamb Stew

5 bacon strips, diced

1/4 cup all-purpose flour

1 teaspoon salt

1/2 teaspoon pepper

6 lamb shanks (about 6 pounds)

1 can (28 ounces) diced tomatoes, undrained

1 can (14-1/2 ounces) beef broth

1 can (8 ounces) tomato sauce

2 cans (4 ounces *each*) mushroom stems and pieces, undrained

2 medium onions, chopped

1 cup chopped celery

1/2 cup minced fresh parsley

2 tablespoons prepared horseradish

1 tablespoon cider vinegar

2 teaspoons Worcestershire sauce

1 garlic clove, minced

In a Dutch oven, cook bacon until crisp; remove and set aside. Combine flour, salt and pepper in a large resealable plastic bag; add lamb shanks and shake to coat. Brown shanks on all sides in the bacon drippings; drain. Add remaining ingredients. Bring to a simmer.

Cover and bake at 325° for 2 to 2-1/2 hours or until the meat is very tender; skim fat. Garnish with bacon. **Yield:** 6 servings.

Lamb Tips

Marinating lamb enhances the flavor, but isn't necessary to achieve tenderness. It's best not to overcook lamb—the internal temperature for fresh lamb should be 150° for medium-rare and 160° for medium.

Most lamb cuts have less than 200 calories per 3-ounce cooked serving. A single serving supplies 10% of the U.S. recommended daily allowance of iron, 30% of the zinc and 27% of the niacin. Lamb has little internal fat, and external fat can be easily trimmed.

This is one of my very favorite recipes. I've made it countless times in more than 45 years of marriage. Our children always asked for it on their birthdays, and it has a wonderful flavor!

~Vicky Reinhold
STURGIS, SOUTH DAKOTA

Super Swiss Steak

1/4 cup all-purpose flour
1 teaspoon salt, *divided*
1/2 teaspoon pepper
2-1/2 pounds boneless beef round steak (about 1 inch thick), cut into serving-size pieces
2 tablespoons vegetable oil
1 can (14-1/2 ounces) stewed tomatoes
1 can (10-3/4 ounces) condensed tomato soup, undiluted
1 large onion, sliced
1/4 teaspoon dried marjoram
1/4 teaspoon dried thyme
1/4 teaspoon paprika
1/8 teaspoon ground cloves, optional
1 bay leaf

In a large resealable plastic bag, combine the flour, 1/2 teaspoon salt and pepper. Add the beef, a few pieces at a time, and shake to coat. Remove steak from bag and flatten to 3/4-in. thickness.

In a large skillet, brown steak on both sides in oil over medium-high heat. In a bowl, combine tomatoes, tomato soup, onion, marjoram, thyme, paprika, cloves if desired, bay leaf and remaining salt; pour over beef.

Bring to a boil. Reduce heat; cover and simmer for 1-1/4 to 1-3/4 hours or until meat is tender. Discard bay leaf. **Yield:** 8-10 servings.

My husband taught me how to make these burger steaks using his mother's recipe. I also like to make them for family gatherings because they're so easy.

~Bonnie Taylor
HOHENWALD, TENNESSEE

Burgers and Veggies

☑ **Uses less fat, sugar or salt. Includes Nutrition Facts and Diabetic Exchanges.**

2 eggs
1/2 cup egg substitute
2 teaspoons hot pepper sauce
1/2 cup quick-cooking oats
1/2 teaspoon salt
1/2 teaspoon rubbed sage
1/4 teaspoon pepper
2 pounds lean ground beef
1 cup water
1/3 cup steak sauce
1 large onion, sliced
1 large green pepper, sliced
8 tomato slices
8 lettuce leaves
8 parsley sprigs

In a bowl, combine the first seven ingredients. Crumble beef over mixture; mix well. Shape into eight patties. In a large nonstick skillet, bring water to a simmer. Using a spatula, lower patties into simmering water; cover and cook for 8 minutes. Turn patties over; top with steak sauce. Cover and cook 3-4 minutes longer or until meat is no longer pink. Remove patties and keep warm.

Add onion and green pepper to the skillet; cover and cook over medium heat until tender. Using a slotted spoon, spoon vegetables over patties; garnish with tomato, lettuce and parsley. **Yield:** 8 servings.

Nutrition Facts: One serving equals 261 calories, 12 g fat (5 g saturated fat), 94 mg cholesterol, 425 mg sodium, 9 g carbohydrate, 2 g fiber, 28 g protein. **Diabetic Exchanges:** 3 lean meat, 1 fat, 1/2 starch.

Here's a satisfying dish for big appetites. The corn and apples make a tasty stuffing for the chops.
~Judith Smith
DES MOINES, IOWA

Stuffed Iowa Chops

4 bone-in pork loin chops (1-1/2 inches thick)
1 tablespoon vegetable oil
1 cup whole kernel corn
1 cup diced peeled apple
1 cup dry bread crumbs
1 tablespoon minced fresh parsley
1 tablespoon finely chopped onion
1 tablespoon milk
1/4 teaspoon salt
1/4 teaspoon rubbed sage
1/4 teaspoon pepper

SAUCE:
1/4 to 1/2 cup Dijon mustard
1/2 cup honey
1 teaspoon minced fresh rosemary
1/2 teaspoon salt
1/4 teaspoon pepper

Cut a large pocket in the side of each pork chop. In a large skillet, brown the chops in oil over medium heat. Remove from the heat.

In a bowl, combine the corn, apple, bread crumbs, parsley, onion, milk, salt, sage and pepper. Stuff into pork chops. Place in a greased 13-in. x 9-in. x 2-in. baking dish.

Combine sauce ingredients; pour half over the chops. Bake, uncovered, at 350° for 1 hour or until a meat thermometer reads 160°, basting occasionally with remaining sauce. **Yield:** 4 servings.

I often serve these meatballs as an appetizer at parties or over steamed rice as a main entree for dinner.
~Diana Thomas
SAN ANTONIO, TEXAS

Sweet 'n' Sour Meatballs

1 egg
1 medium onion, finely chopped
1 tablespoon cornstarch
1/2 teaspoon salt
1/2 teaspoon pepper
1 pound lean ground beef
2 tablespoons vegetable oil

SAUCE:
1 can (20 ounces) pineapple chunks, undrained
2 medium green peppers, julienned
1/2 cup sugar
3 tablespoons cider vinegar
1 tablespoon vegetable oil
1 tablespoon soy sauce
3 tablespoons cornstarch
1/3 cup cold water

In a bowl, combine the first five ingredients. Crumble beef over mixture and mix well. Shape into 1-in. balls.

In a large skillet, brown meatballs in oil, turning often. Remove with a slotted spoon and set aside; drain.

To skillet, add the pineapple, green peppers, sugar, vinegar, oil and soy sauce. Cover and simmer until tender, about 5 minutes. Return meatballs to skillet; simmer until the meat is no longer pink.

Combine cornstarch and water until smooth. Stir into skillet. Bring to a boil; cook and stir for 2 minutes or until thickened. **Yield:** about 3 dozen.

~Betsy Carrington
LAWRENCEBURG, TENNESSEE

Grilled Pork Tenderloins

1/3 cup honey

1/3 cup soy sauce

1/3 cup teriyaki sauce

3 tablespoons brown sugar

1 tablespoon minced fresh gingerroot

3 garlic cloves, minced

4 teaspoons ketchup

1/2 teaspoon onion powder

1/2 teaspoon ground cinnamon

1/4 teaspoon cayenne pepper

2 pork tenderloins (about 1 pound *each*)

Hot cooked rice

In a bowl, combine the first 10 ingredients; mix well. Pour half of the marinade into a large resealable plastic bag; add tenderloins. Seal bag and turn to coat; refrigerate for 8 hours, turning occasionally. Cover and refrigerate remaining marinade.

Drain and discard marinade from meat. Grill, uncovered, over indirect medium-hot heat for 8-10 minutes on each side, basting with reserved marinade, until a meat thermometer reads 160° and juices run clear. Let stand for 5 minutes. Serve with rice. **Yield:** 8-10 servings.

My family made this up as we went along one night. There are endless possibilities for it, but I wrote down this version because we all liked it so much.

~Penny Childs
FERNDALE, WASHINGTON

Lemony Salmon And Pasta

1 whole garlic bulb

1 tablespoon water

3 tablespoons olive oil, *divided*

5 tablespoons Cajun seasoning

3 tablespoons honey

1 salmon fillet (2 pounds), cut into 2-inch pieces

3 plum tomatoes, quartered

1 medium sweet red pepper, cut into 1/4-inch strips

1 medium sweet yellow pepper, cut into 1/4-inch strips

1 large red onion, sliced

8 ounces uncooked penne *or* medium tube pasta

LEMON SAUCE:

1/3 cup butter, cubed

1/4 cup olive oil

3 tablespoons lemon juice

1 to 2 garlic cloves, minced

2 teaspoons grated lemon peel

1 tablespoon minced fresh parsley

1/2 teaspoon salt

Dash dried tarragon

Dash cayenne pepper

1/3 cup pitted ripe olives

1/4 cup sunflower kernels, toasted

Cut top off garlic bulb, leaving root end intact. Place cut side up in a small ungreased baking dish; drizzle water around the garlic. Slowly drizzle 1 tablespoon oil into center of bulb. Cover and bake at 350° for 50-60 minutes or until garlic is very soft. Cool for 5 minutes. Squeeze softened garlic from skins; set aside.

Combine the Cajun seasoning, honey and remaining oil; spoon half over the salmon. In a bowl, combine tomatoes, peppers and onion; add remaining honey mixture and toss to coat. Place salmon and vegetables on a greased broiler pan. Broil 3-4 in. from the heat for 6-8 minutes or until fish flakes easily with a fork and vegetables are crisptender.

Meanwhile, cook pasta according to package directions. In a saucepan, combine the first nine sauce ingredients; cook and stir until butter is melted. Drain the pasta. In a large serving bowl, gently toss pasta, lemon sauce, softened garlic, salmon and vegetables. Sprinkle with olives and sunflower kernels. **Yield:** 8 servings.

The combination of chicken, pork sausage, potatoes and cheese makes this a hearty as well as a tasty meal.
~Roberta Ressler
SANDWICH, ILLINOIS

Irish Pie

3 cups cubed cooked chicken

2 cups (8 ounces) shredded Monterey Jack cheese

1 teaspoon garlic salt

2 cups seasoned stuffing croutons

1 pound bulk pork sausage, cooked and drained

2 cups peeled cooked diced potatoes

2 cups (8 ounces) shredded cheddar cheese

3 eggs

1-1/2 cups milk

In a greased 3-qt. baking dish, layer the first seven ingredients in the order given. Beat the eggs and milk; pour over the cheese.

Cover and bake at 325° for 55 minutes. Uncover; bake 10 minutes longer. Let stand for 10 minutes before serving. **Yield:** 6-8 servings.

These crispy steaks will earn raves when you serve them for dinner. My husband asks me to prepare this recipe regularly. I like it because it's so easy to make. ~Denice Louk
GARNETT, KANSAS

Chicken-Fried Steaks

2-1/4 cups all-purpose flour, *divided*

2 teaspoons baking powder

3/4 teaspoon *each* salt, onion powder, garlic powder, chili powder and pepper

2 eggs, lightly beaten

1-2/3 cups buttermilk, *divided*

4 beef cube steaks (1 pound)

Oil for frying

1-1/2 cups milk

In a shallow bowl, combine 2 cups flour, baking powder and seasonings. In another bowl, combine eggs and 1 cup buttermilk. Dip each cube steak in buttermilk mixture, then coat with flour mixture. Let stand for 5 minutes.

In a skillet, heat 1/2 in. of oil on medium-high. Fry steaks for 5-7 minutes. Turn carefully; cook 5 minutes longer or until coating is crisp and meat is no longer pink. Remove the steaks and keep warm.

Drain, reserving 1/3 cup drippings; stir remaining flour into drippings until smooth. Cook and stir over medium heat for 2 minutes. Gradually whisk in milk and remaining buttermilk. Bring to a boil; cook and stir for 2 minutes or until thickened. Serve with steaks. **Yield:** 4 servings (2 cups gravy).

This recipe couldn't be easier—layer pork roast, vegetables and seasonings in a roasting pan, put it in the oven and forget about it.

~Carol Brzezinski
FOND DU LAC, WISCONSIN

Sauerkraut Pork Supper

- 2 cans (one 27 ounces, one 14 ounces) sauerkraut, undrained
- 1 boneless rolled pork loin roast (4 to 5 pounds)
- 1 can (14-1/2 ounces) diced tomatoes, undrained
- 3 celery ribs, cut into 1-inch pieces
- 2 medium carrots, cut in half widthwise and quartered
- 1 medium onion, quartered
- 3 tablespoons brown sugar
- 1/4 cup minced fresh parsley
- 4 bay leaves
- 1/2 teaspoon dried oregano
- 1/4 teaspoon pepper

Place half of the sauerkraut in a large roasting pan. Place pork roast over sauerkraut; top with remaining sauerkraut. Spoon tomatoes over top. Arrange the celery, carrots and onion around roast. Sprinkle brown sugar over tomatoes and sauerkraut. Add the parsley, bay leaves, oregano and pepper.

Cover and bake at 325° for 3 to 3-1/2 hours or until a meat thermometer reads 160°, basting occasionally with pan juices. Discard bay leaves. Let stand for 15 minutes before slicing. **Yield:** 8-10 servings.

Since my kids, grandkids and guests of all ages request this casserole often and it takes only about 30 minutes to make, I have it at least once every other month!

~Linda Humphreys
BUCHANAN, MICHIGAN

Mexican Chicken Bake

- 1 medium onion, chopped
- 1 small green pepper, chopped
- 2 large jalapeno peppers, seeded and chopped
- 1/4 cup butter
- 2 cans (10-3/4 ounces *each*) condensed cream of chicken soup, undiluted
- 1 can (12 ounces) evaporated milk
- 4 cups cooked long grain rice
- 3 to 4 cups cubed cooked chicken
- 3 cups (12 ounces) Colby-Monterey Jack cheese, *divided*

In a skillet, saute the onion, green pepper and jalapeno peppers in butter until tender. In a bowl, combine soup and milk. Stir in the rice, chicken, 2 cups cheese and onion mixture.

Transfer to a greased 13-in. x 9-in. x 2-in. baking dish. Bake, uncovered, at 350° for 25 minutes. Sprinkle with the remaining cheese. Bake 5-10 minutes longer or until heated through and the cheese is melted. **Yield:** 8-10 servings.

Editor's Note: When cutting or seeding hot peppers, use rubber or plastic gloves to protect your hands. Avoid touching your face.

Helpful Hint

Leftover Rice

When preparing rice, make extra. Packaged in freezer containers or heavy-duty resealable plastic bags, cooked rice will keep in the freezer for up to 6 months. To reheat, add 2 tablespoons of liquid for each cup of rice; microwave or cook in a saucepan until heated through.

Wild Rice Jambalaya

- 1 cup uncooked wild rice
- 4 cups water, *divided*
- 1/2 cup *each* chopped celery, sweet red pepper and green pepper
- 1 medium onion, chopped
- 4 garlic cloves, minced
- 1 cup uncooked long grain rice
- 2 tablespoons olive oil
- 1 can (14-1/2 ounces) chicken broth
- 1 package (16 ounces) fully cooked kielbasa *or* Polish sausage, chopped
- 1 can (10 ounces) diced tomatoes and green chilies
- 1/2 teaspoon salt
- 1/2 teaspoon pepper
- 1/4 cup minced fresh parsley

In a large saucepan, combine wild rice and 3 cups water. Bring to a boil. Reduce heat; cover and simmer for 50-55 minutes or until rice is nearly tender. Drain. In a large skillet, saute the celery, peppers, onion, garlic and long grain rice in oil over medium-high heat for 10 minutes or until vegetables are tender and rice begins to brown.

Stir in the broth, sausage, tomatoes, wild rice, salt, pepper and remaining water. Bring to a boil. Reduce heat; cover and simmer for 20-25 minutes or until the liquid is absorbed and rice is tender. Stir in parsley. **Yield:** 8 servings.

Grilled Barbecued Chicken

- 1 large onion, chopped
- 2/3 cup butter, melted
- 6 tablespoons cider vinegar
- 4 teaspoons sugar
- 1 tablespoon chili powder
- 2 teaspoons salt
- 2 teaspoons Worcestershire sauce
- 1-1/2 teaspoons pepper
- 1-1/2 teaspoons ground mustard
- 1/2 teaspoon hot pepper sauce
- 2 garlic cloves, minced
- 6 bone-in chicken breast halves (4 to 5 pounds), skin removed

In a bowl, combine the first 11 ingredients. Cover and refrigerate 1/3 cup for basting. Place the chicken in a large resealable plastic bag; add remaining marinade. Refrigerate for at least 1 hour, turning occasionally.

Drain and discard marinade from chicken. Grill chicken, covered, over indirect medium heat for 20 minutes. Turn; grill 15-25 minutes longer or until juices run clear, basting occasionally with reserved marinade. **Yield:** 6 servings.

The sweetness of pineapple is delicious in the golden brown sauce that covers the chicken.

~LaVonne Hegland
ST. MICHAEL, MINNESOTA

Pineapple Chicken

☑ **Uses less fat, sugar or salt. Includes Nutrition Facts and Diabetic Exchanges.**

8 bone-in chicken thighs (6 ounces *each*), skin removed
1/2 cup sugar
7-1/2 teaspoons cornstarch
1/2 teaspoon salt
1/2 teaspoon garlic powder
1/2 teaspoon ground ginger
1/4 teaspoon pepper
1 can (20 ounces) unsweetened pineapple chunks, undrained
1/2 cup reduced-sodium soy sauce
1/4 cup white vinegar

Place the chicken in a 13-in. x 9-in. x 2-in. baking dish coated with nonstick cooking spray. Cover and bake at 350° for 20 minutes.

In a bowl, combine the sugar, cornstarch and seasonings. Stir in the pineapple, soy sauce and vinegar until blended. Pour over chicken. Bake, uncovered, 20-30 minutes longer or until juices run clear and sauce is thickened, basting occasionally. **Yield:** 8 servings.

Nutrition Facts: One serving equals 283 calories, 9 g fat (3 g saturated fat), 79 mg cholesterol, 831 mg sodium, 26 g carbohydrate, 1 g fiber, 23 g protein. **Diabetic Exchanges:** 3 lean meat, 1 starch, 1 fruit.

This is a tasty way to use up some of the extra zucchini and squash from your vegetable garden.

~Velma Pelletier
ALLENSTOWN, NEW HAMPSHIRE

Summer Squash Pie

1 unbaked pastry shell (9 inches)
1 egg, beaten
2-1/2 cups sliced zucchini (1/4-inch slices)
2-1/2 cups sliced yellow summer squash (1/4-inch slices)
1 teaspoon vegetable oil
1/2 teaspoon salt
1/4 to 1/2 teaspoon dried thyme
1/4 teaspoon garlic powder
1/4 teaspoon paprika
1/4 teaspoon pepper
2 large tomatoes, sliced
1 cup (4 ounces) shredded cheddar *or* mozzarella cheese
3/4 cup mayonnaise

Line unpricked pastry shell with a double thickness of heavy-duty foil. Bake at 450° for 5 minutes. Remove foil; brush lightly with some of the egg. (Discard remaining egg.) Bake 5 minutes longer. Remove to a wire rack; reduce heat to 350°.

In a nonstick skillet, saute zucchini and yellow squash in oil for 10 minutes or until very tender. Sprinkle with seasonings; spoon into pastry shell. Top with tomatoes. Combine the cheese and mayonnaise; spread over the top. Bake at 350° for 25 minutes or until golden brown. Refrigerate any leftovers. **Yield:** 6-8 servings.

Editor's Note: Reduced-fat or fat-free mayonnaise is not recommended for this recipe.

Turkey isn't just for Thanksgiving anymore. My family grills these tenderloins outside in summer and inside in winter. The friend who shared the recipe says the marinade is excellent with any poultry and game.
~Charlotte Casey
BARTON, VERMONT

Grilled Turkey Tenderloins

1-1/2 cups lemon-lime soda
3/4 cup vegetable oil
3/4 cup soy sauce
1 teaspoon prepared horseradish
1/4 teaspoon garlic powder
1/4 to 1/2 teaspoon Liquid Smoke, optional
2-1/2 pounds boneless skinless turkey breast tenderloins

In a large resealable plastic bag, combine the first five ingredients; add Liquid Smoke if desired. Add turkey; seal bag and turn to coat. Refrigerate for 8 hours or overnight, turning once.

Drain and discard marinade. Grill turkey, covered, over medium heat for 5-6 minutes on each side or until juices run clear. **Yield:** 10 servings.

The four different types of cheese make this lasagna a real crowd-pleaser. You can vary the amount of each to suit your preference.
~Clyda Conrad
YUMA, ARIZONA

Cheesy Lasagna

1 pound ground beef
1 large onion, chopped
1/2 cup chopped green pepper
3 cans (6 ounces *each*) tomato paste
3/4 cup water
2 tablespoons brown sugar
3 to 4 teaspoons dried oregano
1 tablespoon cider vinegar
1/4 teaspoon garlic powder
9 lasagna noodles, cooked and drained
2 cups (8 ounces) shredded mozzarella cheese
2 cups (8 ounces) shredded Monterey Jack cheese
8 ounces sliced provolone cheese
1/4 cup grated Parmesan cheese

In a large saucepan, cook beef, onion and green pepper over medium heat until meat is no longer pink; drain. Stir in tomato paste, water, brown sugar, oregano, vinegar and garlic powder.

In a greased 13-in. x 9-in. x 2-in. baking dish, spread 1 cup of meat sauce. Layer with three noodles, 1 cup meat sauce and mozzarella cheese; three noodles, 1 cup meat sauce and Monterey Jack cheese; three noodles, 1 cup meat sauce, provolone cheese and the Parmesan cheese.

Bake, uncovered, at 350° for 40-45 minutes or until cheese is melted. Let stand for 10 minutes before cutting. **Yield:** 12 servings.

Super Ways to Cook with *Sausage*

When you want family fare that's sure to be fast and filling, put these sizzling short-order sausage recipes to the test.

You can try different types of sausage for variety or to suit your family's tastes. More recipes and tips are on pages 70-71.

My family members all agree that this recipe's a keeper! For variety, you can try it with turkey sausage or spicy hot sausage.

~Elaine Anderson
ALIQUIPPA, PENNSYLVANIA

Italian Skillet Supper

(Pictured above)

> **3 cups uncooked spiral pasta**
> **1 pound bulk Italian sausage**
> **2 cans (14-1/2 ounces *each*) Italian diced tomatoes, undrained**
> **1 can (6 ounces) tomato paste**
> **2 cups (8 ounces) shredded mozzarella cheese**

Cook pasta according to package directions. Meanwhile, in a large skillet, cook sausage over medium heat until no longer pink; drain. Stir in the tomatoes and tomato paste. Bring to a boil. Reduce heat; cover and simmer for 5 minutes. Remove all but 1/2 cup meat sauce to a bowl.

Drain the pasta; place half over the sauce in skillet. Layer with half of the reserved meat sauce and 1 cup of the cheese. Repeat with the remaining pasta, meat sauce and cheese. Cover and cook over medium-low heat for 10 minutes or until heated through. **Yield:** 6-8 servings.

We love this combination of sauerkraut, bratwurst and salad dressing. It's a hearty meal that you can serve with or without the buns.

~Sharon Crider
ST. ROBERT, MISSOURI

Cheesy Kraut Bratwursts

> **3/4 cup shredded Swiss cheese**
> **1/3 cup sauerkraut, well drained**
> **4 fully cooked bratwursts**
> **2 to 3 tablespoons Thousand Island salad dressing**
> **4 bratwurst buns, split**

In a bowl, combine cheese and sauerkraut; set aside. Slice each bratwurst in half lengthwise but not all the way through; leave bottom attached. Spread cut sides with dressing; fill each with about 1/4 cup cheese mixture. Place on a broiler pan. Broil 4-6 in. from heat for 9-10 minutes or until cheese is melted and meat is heated through. Serve on buns. **Yield:** 4 servings.

I like to cook the potatoes and beans in the morning, and then I can just assemble and warm it up when I get home. If you like spicier flavor, add more seasoning.

~Marlene Melton
HOUSTON, TEXAS

Hearty Sausage and Potatoes

- 2 pounds small red potatoes
- 2 cups fresh *or* frozen cut green beans
- 1 pound fully cooked kielbasa *or* Polish sausage, cut lengthwise in half, then sliced
- 1 tablespoon olive oil
- 1 teaspoon Creole seasoning
- 1/4 teaspoon salt

Place potatoes in a Dutch oven or large kettle and cover with water. Bring to a boil. Reduce heat; cook, uncovered, over medium-high heat until almost tender, about 12-15 minutes. Add beans; cook 5-6 minutes longer or until vegetables are tender. Drain and set aside.

In the same pan, saute sausage until lightly browned. Add the oil, seasonings and potato mixture; stir gently to combine. Cover and cook on low heat until heated through, stirring occasionally. **Yield:** 4-6 servings.

Editor's Note: The following spices may be substituted for the Creole seasoning: 1/2 teaspoon *each* paprika and garlic powder, and a dash *each* cayenne pepper, dried thyme and ground cumin.

Mother always served this dish with coleslaw and homemade biscuits or corn bread.

~Patsye Yonce
OVID, NEW YORK

Sausage Jumble

- 1 pound bulk pork sausage
- 1/2 cup chopped onion
- 2 cups fresh *or* frozen whole kernel corn, thawed
- 1 can (28 ounces) chopped tomatoes, undrained
- 1 cup uncooked instant rice
- 3/4 cup water
- 1 teaspoon salt
- 1/2 teaspoon pepper
- 2/3 cup shredded cheddar cheese
- 1/3 cup shredded mozzarella cheese

In a large skillet, cook sausage and onion over medium heat until meat is no longer pink; drain. Add the corn, tomatoes, rice, water, salt and pepper. Bring to a boil.

Reduce heat; cover and simmer for 10 minutes or until rice is tender. Sprinkle with cheddar and mozzarella cheeses. Cook, uncovered, 5 minutes longer or until the cheese is melted. **Yield:** 4-6 servings.

This was created one night when I had little time to cook. It's so quick and satisfying, that many of my friends have adopted the recipe themselves.

~Linda Harris
WICHITA, KANSAS

O'Brien Sausage Skillet

- 1 package (28 ounces) frozen O'Brien hash brown potatoes
- 1 pound fully cooked kielbasa *or* Polish sausage, cut into 1/4-inch slices
- 2 medium tart apples, peeled and chopped
- 1 medium onion, chopped
- 1 tablespoon vegetable oil
- 1 cup (4 ounces) shredded cheddar cheese

Prepare potatoes according to package directions. Meanwhile, in a large skillet, saute the sausage, apples and onion in oil for 10 minutes or until apples and onion are tender; drain.

Spoon the sausage mixture over potatoes; sprinkle with cheese. Cover and cook for 3-5 minutes or until the cheese is melted. **Yield:** 6-8 servings.

For a different flavor, try using turkey sausage or spicy hot sausage in place of regular bulk sausage.

~Leisa Price-Storey
BROCKVILLE, ONTARIO

I prepare a skillet dish with sliced smoked sausage and vegetables. It's popular as an entree with seasoned rice and as the filling for a hot sandwich.

~Candace Shaw
VALPARAISO, INDIANA

Diced Italian sausage links add lots of zip to my tomato sauce. Sometimes I ladle it over pasta. Other times, I use it as a sauce for meatball subs.

~Rebecca Donahue
LINCOLN, CALIFORNIA

If you prefer spicy food, use just hot sausage—or combine regular and hot sausage for a milder taste.

~Evanell Havner
GRANT CITY, MISSOURI

My spaghetti sauce with Italian sausage doubles easily. I serve half the sauce for dinner and freeze the rest to use later.

~Loma Berndsen
WINFIELD, KANSAS

Want to add a tasty twist to a main dish? Substitute venison sausage for Italian sausage—it's great!

~Judy Stoddard
TULLY, NEW YORK

When grilling sausage, do not prick it before or during cooking. This will reduce the amount of fat that drips onto the coals and lessen the chances of a flare-up.

~Barbara Grabow
ALBUQUERQUE, NEW MEXICO

Try using sausage instead of your usual meat choice in your favorite meatball or meat loaf recipe.

~Adele Gustafson
MINOT, NORTH DAKOTA

I enjoy sharing this healthy, one-dish meal with family and friends whenever they request it. Much like jambalaya, it has a nice tang but is simpler to make. ~Shelley Wernlein
THORNTON, COLORADO

Black Bean Sausage Skillet

☑ **Uses less fat, sugar or salt. Includes Nutrition Facts and Diabetic Exchanges.**

- 4 celery ribs, sliced
- 1 medium sweet red pepper, cut into 1/2-inch pieces
- 12 ounces reduced-fat fully cooked kielbasa *or* Polish sausage, halved lengthwise and sliced
- 1/2 cup salsa
- 3 tablespoons lemon juice
- 1/4 to 1/2 teaspoon hot pepper sauce
- 1 can (15 ounces) black beans, rinsed and drained
- 2 cups hot cooked rice

Spray a large nonstick skillet with nonstick cooking spray. Add celery and pepper; saute over medium heat for 3-4 minutes or until crisp-tender. Add the kielbasa, salsa, lemon juice and hot pepper sauce. Cook for 8-10 minutes or until vegetables are tender, stirring occasionally.

Remove from the heat; stir in beans. Cover and let stand for 5 minutes or until heated through. Serve over rice. **Yield:** 4 servings.

Nutrition Facts: One serving (1 cup sausage mixture with 1/2 cup rice) equals 334 calories, 7 g fat (2 g saturated fat), 56 mg cholesterol, 1,135 mg sodium, 46 g carbohydrate, 6 g fiber, 21 g protein. **Diabetic Exchanges:** 2-1/2 starch, 2 lean meat, 1 vegetable.

This hearty stovetop entree has been a family favorite for years. The variety of vegetables makes this dish attractive. Cooking time is minimal.
~Ruby Williams
BOGALUSA, LOUISIANA

Sausage and Vegetable Skillet

1 pound fresh Italian sausage links, cut into 1/2-inch slices
2 tablespoons vegetable oil
2 cups cubed yellow summer squash
1 cup chopped green onions
3 to 4 garlic cloves, minced
3 cups chopped tomatoes
4 teaspoons Worcestershire sauce
1/8 teaspoon cayenne pepper

In a skillet over medium heat, cook sausage in oil until no longer pink; drain. Add squash, onions and garlic; cook for 3 minutes. Stir in tomatoes, Worcestershire sauce and cayenne pepper; heat through. **Yield:** 4 servings.

This plate-filling sausage dish appeals to most every appetite in my household, from basic meat-and-potatoes fans to gourmets.
~Lorraine Martin
LINCOLN, CALIFORNIA

Florentine Spaghetti Bake

8 ounces uncooked spaghetti
1 pound bulk Italian sausage
1 cup chopped onion
1 garlic clove, minced
1 jar (26 ounces) spaghetti sauce
1 can (4 ounces) mushroom stems and pieces, drained
1 egg, lightly beaten
2 cups (16 ounces) small-curd cottage cheese
1 package (10 ounces) frozen chopped spinach, thawed and squeezed dry
1/4 cup grated Parmesan cheese
1/2 teaspoon seasoned salt
1/4 teaspoon pepper
2 cups (8 ounces) shredded mozzarella cheese

Cook pasta according to package directions. In a large skillet, cook the sausage, onion and garlic over medium heat until sausage is no longer pink; drain. Stir in spaghetti sauce and mushrooms. Bring to a boil. Reduce heat; cover and cook for 15 minutes. Drain the pasta.

In a bowl, combine the egg, cottage cheese, spinach, Parmesan cheese, salt and pepper. Spread 1 cup sausage mixture in a greased 13-in. x 9-in. x 2-in. baking dish. Top with spaghetti and remaining sausage mixture. Layer with spinach mixture and mozzarella cheese.

Cover and bake at 375° for 45 minutes. Uncover; bake 15 minutes longer or until lightly browned and heated through. Let stand for 15 minutes before cutting. **Yield:** 9 servings.

Sides starring **fresh veggies** and colorful ingredients **add eye- and tummy-appeal** to the dinner table.

Side Dishes

SIMPLE DISHES. From left: Buttermilk Mac 'n' Cheese (p. 74) and Zesty Succotash (p. 75).

We enjoy parsnips here in the Northeast, and I've experimented with different ways of fixing them. This is by far my favorite.
~Robert Atwood
WEST WAREHAM, MASSACHUSETTS

Baked Parsnips

1-1/2 pounds parsnips, peeled and julienned
1/4 cup butter
1/4 cup water
1/2 teaspoon dried oregano
1/2 teaspoon dried parsley flakes
1/4 teaspoon salt
1/8 teaspoon pepper

Place parsnips in an ungreased 2-qt. baking dish; dot with butter. Add water to pan. Sprinkle the oregano, parsley, salt and pepper over parsnips. Cover and bake at 350° for 45 minutes or until tender. **Yield:** 4 servings.

Once you taste this version of an all-time favorite comfort food, you may never make the regular kind again. It's my most-requested recipe, and you can serve it with cooked sliced ham for a nice meal.
~Donna Fancher
LAWRENCE, INDIANA

Buttermilk Mac 'n' Cheese

(Pictured on page 73)

6 eggs
3-1/4 cups (13 ounces) shredded cheddar cheese
2-1/2 cups buttermilk
1/2 cup butter, melted
1 teaspoon salt
1 package (7 ounces) elbow macaroni, cooked and drained

In a large bowl, beat the eggs. Stir in the cheese, buttermilk, butter and salt. Add the macaroni and mix well.

Pour into a greased 13-in. x 9-in. x 2-in. baking dish. Bake, uncovered, at 350° for 45-50 minutes or until a thermometer reads 160°. **Yield:** 8-10 servings.

Unable to decide between topping pasta with tomato or Alfredo sauce, I combined them into one.
~Darlene Brenden
SALEM, OREGON

Tomato Alfredo Pasta

8 ounces uncooked ziti *or* small tube pasta
1 can (14-1/2 ounces) Italian stewed tomatoes, undrained
1/2 cup heavy whipping cream
1/4 cup chopped fresh basil *or* 1-1/2 teaspoons dried basil
1/2 cup grated Parmesan cheese

Cook pasta according to package directions. Meanwhile, in a large skillet, bring the tomatoes to a boil. Cook until most of the liquid is evaporated, about 5 minutes. Reduce heat.

Stir in the cream and basil; heat through (do not boil). Drain pasta. Add pasta and Parmesan cheese to sauce; toss. **Yield:** 4 servings.

This recipe is a staple at our neighborhood's annual barbecue. ~Mrs. J. Hindson
VICTORIA, BRITISH COLUMBIA

Baked Beans with Pineapple

- 1 pound sliced bacon, diced
- 1 large onion, chopped
- 3 cans (two 55 ounces, one 28 ounces) baked beans
- 2 cans (one 20 ounces, one 8 ounces) crushed pineapple, drained
- 1/2 cup packed brown sugar
- 1/2 cup ketchup

In a large skillet, cook bacon over medium heat until crisp. Remove with a slotted spoon to paper towels. Drain, reserving 2 tablespoons drippings. Saute onion in drippings until tender.

In a very large bowl, combine the beans, pineapple, bacon and onion. Combine brown sugar and ketchup; stir into the bean mixture.

Transfer to two greased 3-qt. or 13-in. x 9-in. x 2-in. baking dishes. Cover and bake at 350° for 20 minutes. Uncover; bake 25-35 minutes longer or until bubbly and beans reach desired thickness. **Yield:** 25-30 servings.

This dish is fun to serve because it's so colorful. The combination of corn, beans, peas and red pepper offers a nice texture contrast to the recipe, too. ~Sue Seymour
VALATIE, NEW YORK

Zesty Succotash

(Pictured on page 73)

- 2 cups fresh *or* frozen corn, thawed
- 1 can (16 ounces) kidney beans, rinsed and drained
- 1 cup frozen peas, thawed
- 1 small sweet red pepper, chopped
- 1/2 cup chopped onion
- 2 tablespoons butter
- 1 teaspoon chili powder
- 1/4 teaspoon salt

Dash hot pepper sauce, optional

In a large skillet, cook and stir the corn, beans, peas, red pepper and onion in butter over medium heat for 8-10 minutes. Sprinkle with chili powder, salt and hot pepper sauce if desired. **Yield:** 6 servings.

Our family enjoys this with chicken or ham. But sometimes we make a meal of it with warm bread and butter. ~Donna Cline
PENSACOLA, FLORIDA

🏅 Cider-Roasted Squash

- 4 cups cubed peeled butternut squash
- 1 medium onion, cut into thin wedges
- 2 tablespoons apple cider
- 1 tablespoon olive oil
- 1-1/2 teaspoons brown sugar
- 1/4 teaspoon salt
- 1/8 teaspoon pepper
- 1/8 teaspoon ground nutmeg

Place the squash and onion in a greased 13-in. x 9-in. x 2-in. baking dish. Combine remaining ingredients; pour over squash mixture.

Cover and bake at 450° for 35 minutes or until tender, stirring every 10 minutes. **Yield:** 4-6 servings.

You don't have to be from the South to savor this traditional treat—a wonderful way to use up unripened fall tomatoes. We start our tomato plants in early spring so we can enjoy their bounty for as long as possible.
~Gladys Gibbs
BRUSH CREEK, TENNESSEE

Zesty Fried Green Tomatoes

4 medium green tomatoes, sliced 1/4 inch thick
Salt
1/2 cup cornmeal
1/2 cup grated Parmesan cheese
3 tablespoons all-purpose flour
1/2 teaspoon garlic salt
1/2 teaspoon dried oregano
1/2 teaspoon ground ginger
1/8 teaspoon crushed red pepper flakes
2 eggs
1/4 to 1/2 cup olive oil

Sprinkle both sides of tomatoes with salt; let stand for 10 minutes. In a shallow bowl, combine the cornmeal, Parmesan cheese, flour and seasonings. In another shallow bowl, beat the eggs. Pat tomatoes dry. Dip into eggs, then coat with cornmeal mixture.

In a large skillet, heat 1/4 cup oil over medium heat. Fry tomatoes, a few at a time, for 3-4 minutes on each side or until golden brown, adding more oil as needed. Drain on paper towels. Serve warm. **Yield:** 6-8 servings.

Pineapple turns this hearty casserole into a side dish with a tropical twist. It's sure to be a big hit during the holidays when served along with roasted poultry or a festive baked ham.
~Ruth Beers
LARKSPUR, COLORADO

Sweet Potato Pineapple Bake

3 cups cooked mashed sweet potatoes
1/2 cup sugar
1/2 cup milk
1/4 cup butter, melted
2 eggs, lightly beaten
1 teaspoon vanilla extract
Dash salt

TOPPING:
1/4 cup sugar
1/4 cup all-purpose flour
1 can (8 ounces) crushed pineapple, undrained
1/4 cup butter, melted
2 eggs

In a large bowl, combine the first seven ingredients. Pour into a lightly greased 9-in. square baking dish. Combine the topping ingredients; pour over potato mixture.

Bake, uncovered, at 350° for 45-50 minutes or until a knife inserted near the center comes out clean. Refrigerate leftovers. **Yield:** 8-10 servings.

Helpful Hint
Add Flavor Add a little grated orange peel to your mashed sweet potatoes for refreshing citrus flavor. To save time and mess, just cut a 2- to 3-in. strip of orange peel and add it to the boiling potatoes. Then mash the softened peel with the potatoes for fresh, wonderful flavor.

If you like carrots and rutabagas, this colorful side dish is a winner. ~Esther Wachter
YAKIMA, WASHINGTON

🏵 Lemon-Glazed Carrots and Rutabaga

   5 medium carrots
   1 medium rutabaga
   1/2 cup chicken broth
   2 tablespoons butter
   1 tablespoon brown sugar
   1 tablespoon lemon juice
   1/2 teaspoon grated lemon peel
   1/4 teaspoon dill weed
Dash salt

Cut carrots and rutabaga into 3-in. x 1/4-in. strips. Place in a saucepan; add broth. Bring to a boil. Reduce heat; cover and cook for 13-15 minutes or until tender. Do not drain.

Meanwhile, in a small saucepan, combine the remaining ingredients; cook and stir for 3 minutes. Add to vegetables; cook, uncovered, 3-4 minutes longer or until vegetables are glazed, stirring gently. **Yield:** 6 servings.

I never have leftovers when I serve this attractive and deliciously creamy side dish. It's a snap to prepare, too. ~Barbara Groeb
ANN ARBOR, MICHIGAN

🏵 Asparagus in the Round

   3 cups cubed seasoned stuffing
   1/2 cup plus 2 tablespoons butter, melted, *divided*
   1/2 cup water
   2 tablespoons chopped onion
   2 tablespoons all-purpose flour
   1/2 teaspoon salt
   1/2 teaspoon ground mustard
Dash pepper
   1 cup half-and-half cream
   1 pound fresh asparagus, trimmed and cut into 1-inch pieces
   1 jar (4-1/2 ounces) sliced mushrooms, drained
   1/4 cup grated Parmesan cheese

In a bowl, combine stuffing mix with 1/2 cup butter and water. Let stand

for 5 minutes. Press onto the bottom and up the sides of a greased 9-in. pie plate.

In a saucepan, saute onion in remaining butter until tender. Stir in the flour, salt, mustard and pepper until blended. Gradually stir in cream. Bring to a boil; cook and stir 2 minutes or until thickened.

Remove from heat; add asparagus and mushrooms; mix well. Pour over crust. Sprinkle with Parmesan cheese. Cover and bake at 375° for 25-30 minutes or until lightly browned. **Yield:** 6-8 servings.

Three "Ears" for *Corn*

New York is one of the nation's biggest producers of sweet corn, where growers plant nearly 30,000 acres a year. Sweet corn provides protein and carbohydrates, but it's the flavor most folks savor.

When selecting corn, you'll find ripe ears of corn have silks that are brown and dried on the ends. To determine freshness, the husk should be crisp; avoid flimsy ones. Peel down the husk and poke a thumb into a kernel. Look for clear juice to squirt out. Milkier juices mean the corn is older and more starchy. To preserve freshness, refrigerate your corn as soon as possible.

Husband Walt and I love fresh corn on the cob and also corn I've frozen. This is a flavorfully different way to serve sweet corn.
~Donna Smith
VICTOR, NEW YORK

Herb-Buttered Corn

(Pictured above)

1/2 cup butter, softened
1 tablespoon minced fresh chives
1 tablespoon minced fresh dill
1 tablespoon minced fresh parsley
1/2 teaspoon dried thyme
1/4 teaspoon salt
Dash garlic powder
Dash cayenne pepper
10 ears fresh corn, husked and cooked

In a bowl, combine first eight ingredients; mix well. Spread over each ear of corn. **Yield:** 10 servings.

Corn is my three boys' favorite vegetable, so we eat a lot of it. My husband, Bob, and the boys really enjoy it.
~Marcia Hostetter
CANTON, NEW YORK

Corn and Bacon Casserole

6 bacon strips

1/2 cup chopped onion

2 tablespoons all-purpose flour

2 garlic cloves, minced

1/2 teaspoon salt

1/2 teaspoon pepper

1 cup (8 ounces) sour cream

3-1/2 cups fresh *or* frozen whole kernel corn

1 tablespoon chopped fresh parsley

1 tablespoon chopped fresh chives

In a large skillet, cook bacon until crisp. Drain, reserving 2 tablespoons of drippings. Crumble bacon; set aside. Saute onion in drippings until tender. Add flour, garlic, salt and pepper. Cook and stir until bubbly; cook and stir 1 minute more. Remove from the heat and stir in sour cream until smooth. Add corn, parsley and half of the bacon; mix well. Pour into a 1-qt. baking dish. Sprinkle with remaining bacon. Bake, uncovered, at 350° for 20-25 minutes or until heated through. Sprinkle with chives. **Yield:** 6-8 servings.

Nothing beats Grandma's corn pudding. I hope to one day pass the recipe to my granddaughter. This comforting dish was part of family meals for years and shared at gatherings.
~Paula Marchesi
ROCKY POINT, NEW YORK

Delicious Corn Pudding

4 eggs, *separated*

2 tablespoons butter, melted and cooled

1 tablespoon sugar

1 tablespoon brown sugar

1 teaspoon salt

1/2 teaspoon vanilla extract

Pinch ground cinnamon and nutmeg

2 cups fresh whole kernel corn (4 medium ears)

1 cup half-and-half cream

1 cup milk

In a mixing bowl, beat egg yolks until thick and lemon-colored, 5-8 minutes. Add butter, sugars, salt, vanilla, cinnamon and nutmeg; mix well. Add corn. Stir in cream and milk. Beat egg whites until stiff; fold into yolk mixture. Pour into a greased 1-1/2-qt. baking dish.

Bake, uncovered, at 350° for 35 minutes or until a knife inserted near the center comes out clean. Cover loosely during last 10 minutes of baking if necessary to prevent overbrowning. **Yield:** 8 servings.

This recipe is wonderful for a luncheon. The tomatoes, asparagus, garlic, olives, Italian seasoning and Romano cheese create a sensational taste combination.

~Joyce Speckman
HOLT, CALIFORNIA

Asparagus Pasta

- 1 pound fresh asparagus, cut into 1-inch pieces
- 8 ounces uncooked spiral pasta
- 1 cup sliced fresh mushrooms
- 1/2 cup chopped green onions
- 4 garlic cloves, minced
- 1/3 cup olive oil
- 2 cups chicken broth
- 1 cup diced fresh tomatoes
- 1/2 cup pitted ripe olives, quartered
- 3 tablespoons cornstarch
- 3 tablespoons cold water
- 1-1/2 to 2 teaspoons Italian seasoning
- 1 teaspoon salt
- 1/2 teaspoon pepper
- Grated Romano cheese

Place 1/2 in. of water in a saucepan; add asparagus. Bring to a boil; reduce heat. Cover and simmer for 3-5 minutes or until crisp-tender; drain and set aside.

Cook pasta according to package directions. Meanwhile, in a large skillet, saute the mushrooms, onions and garlic in oil until tender. Add the broth, tomatoes and olives. Combine cornstarch and cold water until smooth; stir into the mushroom mixture. Bring to a boil over medium heat; cook and stir for 2 minutes or until thickened.

Reduce heat. Add the asparagus, Italian seasoning, salt and pepper. Cook for 6-8 minutes or until heated through. Drain pasta; add to asparagus mixture and toss to coat. Sprinkle with Romano cheese. **Yield:** 6-8 servings.

As a pastor's wife, I often cook up contributions to church dinners using on-hand ingredients. This creamy bake was such a hit, I now take it to get-togethers as well. I make it up ahead, refrigerate it and bake it shortly before serving.

~Charlene Wells
COLORADO SPRINGS, COLORADO

Green Bean Potato Bake

- 6 cups cubed peeled cooked potatoes
- 2 cups frozen cut green beans, thawed
- 2 cups cubed fully cooked ham
- 2-1/2 cups (10 ounces) shredded Colby-Monterey Jack cheese, *divided*
- 2 tablespoons dried minced onion
- 1 can (10-3/4 ounces) condensed cream of mushroom soup, undiluted
- 1/2 cup milk
- 1/3 cup mayonnaise
- 1/3 cup sour cream

In a greased 13-in. x 9-in. x 2-in. baking dish, layer the potatoes, beans, ham, 2 cups cheese and onion. In a bowl, combine the soup, milk, mayonnaise and sour cream; pour over the top and gently stir to coat.

Cover and bake at 350° for 45 minutes. Uncover; sprinkle with remaining cheese. Bake 5-8 minutes longer or until cheese is melted. **Yield:** 8 servings.

🎗 Rice-Stuffed Tomatoes

4 medium tomatoes
1/8 teaspoon salt
1/2 cup chopped onion
3 tablespoons butter, *divided*
1-1/2 cups cooked rice
1/2 cup grated Parmesan cheese
2 tablespoons minced fresh parsley
1 tablespoon minced fresh basil *or* 1 teaspoon dried basil
1/2 teaspoon garlic salt

Cut a thin slice off the top of each tomato. Scoop out pulp, leaving 1/2-in. shells; discard seeds. Chop pulp and set aside. Sprinkle the insides of tomatoes with salt; invert onto paper towels to drain.

In a small skillet, saute onion in 2 tablespoons butter until tender. Add reserved tomato pulp; cook until most of the liquid has evaporated. Remove from the heat; stir in the rice, cheese, parsley, basil and garlic salt.

Stuff into tomato shells; dot with remaining butter. Place in a greased 9-in. square baking dish. Bake, uncovered, at 350° for 15-20 minutes or until heated through. **Yield:** 4 servings.

🎗 Broccoli with Yellow Pepper

4 cups fresh broccoli florets
4 teaspoons olive oil
1 medium sweet yellow pepper, cut into 2-inch thin strips
2 garlic cloves, minced
1 teaspoon minced fresh gingerroot
Salt and pepper to taste

In a wok or large skillet, stir-fry broccoli in oil until crisp-tender. Add the yellow pepper, garlic and ginger; stir-fry for 1-2 minutes or until heated though. Season with salt and pepper. **Yield:** 6 servings.

Roasted Vegetable Medley

2 medium onions, cut into 1-inch pieces
2 medium yellow summer squash, cut into 1-inch pieces
2 large sweet red *and/or* green peppers, cut into 1-inch pieces
1 teaspoon Italian seasoning
1/2 teaspoon salt
1/8 teaspoon pepper
1 tablespoon olive oil
3 garlic cloves, minced

In a bowl, combine the first six ingredients. Drizzle with oil; toss to coat. Place in a single layer in an ungreased 15-in. x 10-in. x 1-in. baking pan. Bake, uncovered, at 425° for 20 minutes. Stir; sprinkle with garlic. Bake 10-15 minutes longer or until vegetables are crisp-tender. **Yield:** 4 servings.

Kitchen aromas of freshly baking breads and rolls can't be beat!

Breads & Rolls

SAVORY GOODNESS. From left: Soft Bread Twists (p. 84) and Tomato Spice Muffins (p. 85).

Coming from the Sunflower State and the No. 1 wheat-producing state, I'm always looking for recipes that promote our agricultural products.
~Karen Ann Bland
GOVE, KANSAS

Sunflower Wheat Bread

1 cup warm milk (70° to 80°)
3/4 cup water
2 tablespoons salted sunflower kernels
2 tablespoons honey
1 tablespoon orange juice
4-1/2 teaspoons butter, softened
1 teaspoon salt
1/2 teaspoon grated orange peel
3 cups bread flour
1/2 cup whole wheat flour
1/3 cup old-fashioned oats
2 teaspoons active dry yeast

In bread machine pan, place all ingredients in order suggested by manufacturer. Select basic bread setting. Choose crust color and loaf size if available. Bake according to bread machine directions (check dough after 5 minutes of mixing; add 1 to 2 tablespoons of water or flour if needed). **Yield:** 1 loaf (2 pounds).

Editor's Note: If your bread machine has a time-delay feature, we recommend you do not use it for this recipe.

My family loves eating these zesty bread twists with a spaghetti supper. Soft and light as a feather, they have a perfect balance of garlic and oregano. Be sure to snatch one before passing them around the table.
~Kathy Ksyniuk
MACDOWALL, SASKATCHEWAN

Soft Bread Twists

(Pictured on page 83)

1 package (1/4 ounce) active dry yeast
2 teaspoons sugar
1 cup warm water (110° to 115°)
1 cup warm milk (110° to 115°)
1 egg, lightly beaten
1/2 cup vegetable oil
1-1/4 teaspoons salt, *divided*
5-1/2 to 6 cups all-purpose flour
1/4 cup cornmeal
1/2 teaspoon dried oregano
1/2 teaspoon garlic powder
1/4 cup butter, melted
Pizza sauce *or* salsa, optional

In a large mixing bowl, dissolve yeast and sugar in warm water; let stand for 5 minutes. Add the milk, egg, oil, 1 teaspoon salt and 4 cups flour; beat on low speed until smooth. Beat 5 minutes longer. Stir in enough remaining flour to form a soft dough.

Turn onto a lightly floured surface; knead until smooth and elastic, about 8-10 minutes (dough will be sticky). Place in a greased bowl, turning once to grease top. Cover and let rise in a warm place until doubled, about 1 hour.

Do not punch down. Divide dough into eight pieces. Combine cornmeal and oregano; sprinkle over work surface. Roll each piece of dough in cornmeal mixture and shape into a 15-in.-long rope. Cut each rope into three pieces. Twist each piece and place on greased baking sheets.

Bake at 400° for 8-12 minutes. Combine garlic powder and remaining salt. Immediately brush twists with melted butter, then sprinkle with garlic powder mixture. Serve with pizza sauce if desired. **Yield:** 2 dozen.

I'm always on the lookout for recipes using garden produce. Although I'm the only one in our family who likes tomatoes, my husband and daughter love these muffins. They have a yummy spice flavor, and the tomatoes keep them moist.
~Nancy Andrews
SALISBURY, NORTH CAROLINA

Tomato Spice Muffins

(Pictured on page 83)

4 cups all-purpose flour
2-1/2 cups sugar
2 teaspoons ground cinnamon
1-1/4 teaspoons baking soda
1 teaspoon baking powder
1 teaspoon salt
1 teaspoon ground cloves
1 teaspoon ground nutmeg
1/4 teaspoon pepper
2 eggs
1/2 cup butter, melted and cooled
2 teaspoons vanilla extract

5 cups seeded quartered tomatoes
  (about 6 medium)
1 cup raisins

In a large bowl, combine the first nine ingredients; set aside. In a food processor, combine the eggs, butter, vanilla and tomatoes; cover and process until tomatoes are finely chopped. Add to dry ingredients; stir just until moistened. Fold in raisins.

Fill greased or paper-lined muffin cups three-fourths full. Bake at 350° for 20-25 minutes or until a toothpick comes out clean. Cool for 5 minutes before removing from pans to wire racks. Serve warm. **Yield:** about 2 dozen.

If you have any of this bread leftover from dinner, you'll find it makes great sandwiches, too.
~Nancy Zimmerman
CAPE MAY COURT HOUSE, NEW JERSEY

Honey Beet Bread

2 packages (1/4 ounce *each*)
  active dry yeast
1-1/2 cups warm water (110° to 115°)
2 tablespoons honey
1-1/2 cups grated uncooked fresh
  beets, squeezed dry
1 cup warm milk (110° to 115°)
2 tablespoons butter, softened
2-1/2 teaspoons salt
6-1/4 to 6-3/4 cups all-purpose flour
1 egg white, beaten
Toasted sesame seeds

In a large mixing bowl, dissolve yeast in warm water. Add honey; let stand for 5 minutes. Add the beets, milk, butter, salt and 3 cups flour. Beat until smooth. Stir in enough remaining flour to form a soft dough.

Turn onto a floured surface; knead until smooth and elastic, about 6-8 minutes. Place in a greased bowl, turning once to grease top. Cover and let rise in a warm place until doubled, about 50 minutes.

Punch dough down. Turn onto a lightly floured surface; divide dough in half. Shape into two loaves. Place in two greased 9-in. x 5-in. x 3-in. loaf pans. Cover and let rise until doubled, about 40 minutes.

Brush with egg white; sprinkle with sesame seeds. Bake at 350° for 30-35 minutes or until top begins to brown. Remove from pans to wire racks to cool. **Yield:** 2 loaves.

Fresh mangos freeze well, so when they're in season, I dice and freeze them in 2-cup containers. That way, I always have some on hand for making these flavorful muffins.

~Nancy Leeds
DAVIE, FLORIDA

Mango Muffins

2 cups all-purpose flour
1 cup sugar
2 teaspoons baking soda
2 teaspoons ground cinnamon
1/2 teaspoon salt
3 eggs, lightly beaten
3/4 cup vegetable oil
1 tablespoon lime juice
2 cups diced ripe mango
1 medium ripe banana, mashed
1/2 cup raisins
1/2 cup chopped walnuts

In a large bowl, combine the first five ingredients. In another bowl, combine the eggs, oil and lime juice; add to the dry ingredients just until moistened. Stir in the mango, banana, raisins and nuts.

Fill paper-lined muffin cups two-thirds full. Bake at 350° for 20-25 minutes or until a toothpick comes out clean. Cool for 5 minutes before removing from pans to wire racks. **Yield:** about 1-1/2 dozen.

I've won prizes in several baking contests with this recipe. Since my granddaughters enjoy the rolls, I usually have a pan or two in the freezer for them to take home with them after a visit.

~Chris Litsey
ELWOOD, INDIANA

Yummy Yeast Rolls

2 packages (1/4 ounce *each*) active dry yeast
3/4 cup warm milk (110° to 115°)
3/4 cup lemon-lime soda
1/2 cup butter, cubed
4 eggs
3/4 cup sugar
1 teaspoon salt
5-3/4 to 6-1/2 cups all-purpose flour

In a large mixing bowl, dissolve yeast in warm milk. In a saucepan, heat soda and butter to 110°-115°. Add the warm soda mixture, eggs, sugar, salt and 2 cups flour to yeast mixture; beat until smooth. Stir in enough remaining flour to form a soft dough.

Turn onto a floured surface; knead until smooth and elastic, about 6-8 minutes. Place in a greased bowl, turning once to grease top. Cover and let rise in a warm place until doubled, about 1 hour.

Punch dough down. Turn onto a lightly floured surface; divide into four portions. Divide each portion into nine pieces. Shape each into a ball. Place on greased baking sheets. Cover and let rise until doubled, about 45 minutes. Bake at 350° for 18-20 minutes or until golden brown. Remove to wire racks to cool. **Yield:** 3 dozen.

This corn bread bakes to a deep golden color with flecks of sweet potato visible. It looks as good as it tastes.

~Judy Roland
MT. HOLLY, NORTH CAROLINA

Sweet Potato Corn Bread

2 cups all-purpose flour
2 cups cornmeal
1/2 cup sugar
7 teaspoons baking powder
2 teaspoons salt
4 eggs, beaten
3/4 cup milk
1/3 cup vegetable oil
2-2/3 cups mashed cooked
    sweet potatoes

In a large bowl, combine the first five ingredients. In a small bowl, combine the eggs, milk, oil and sweet potatoes. Stir into dry ingredients just until moistened. Pour into a greased 13-in. x 9-in. x 2-in. baking pan.

Bake at 425° for 30-35 minutes or until a toothpick inserted near the center comes out clean. Cut into squares. Serve warm. **Yield:** 12-16 servings.

Unlike many other baked goods, these muffins are surprisingly savory. I serve them with stew, soup and other entrees.

~Bernadette Colvin
HOUSTON, TEXAS

Cheddar Dill Muffins

3-1/2 cups all-purpose flour
1 cup (4 ounces) shredded
    cheddar cheese
3 tablespoons sugar
2 tablespoons baking powder
2 teaspoons dill weed
1 teaspoon salt
1-3/4 cups milk
2 eggs, lightly beaten
1/4 cup butter, melted

In a bowl, combine the first six ingredients. Combine milk, eggs and butter; stir into dry ingredients just until moistened. Fill greased or paper-lined muffin cups two-thirds full.

Bake at 400° for 25-30 minutes or until a toothpick comes out clean. Cool for 10 minutes; remove from pan to a wire rack. **Yield:** about 9 jumbo muffins or 1 dozen standard-size muffins.

Helpful Hint

On a Roll For crustier rolls, try this: In a blender, process 1/2 cup oats into a powder and lightly sprinkle them over your greased pan. Then add dough, bake...and enjoy each crunchy bite!

~Joyce Larson
NEW MARKET, IOWA

I make this recipe on a regular basis in the summer months when we're grilling up our favorite burgers.

~Loraine Thomas
KAMSACK, SASKATCHEWAN

Wholesome Burger Buns

☑ **Uses less fat, sugar or salt. Includes Nutrition Facts and Diabetic Exchanges.**

1-1/4 cups water (70° to 80°)
1/3 cup butter, softened
1 egg, lightly beaten
1 tablespoon unsalted sunflower kernels
1 tablespoon poppy seeds
1 teaspoon honey
1-1/2 teaspoons salt
2 cups all-purpose flour
2 cups whole wheat flour
1 tablespoon active dry yeast

In bread machine pan, place all ingredients in order suggested by manufacturer. Select the dough setting (check dough after 5 minutes of mixing; add 1 to 2 tablespoons of water or flour if needed).

When cycle is complete, turn dough onto a lightly floured surface. Divide into 16 portions; shape each into a ball.

Place 2 in. apart on baking sheets coated with nonstick cooking spray; flatten slightly. Cover and let rise in a warm place until doubled, about 30 minutes.

Bake at 350° for 15-20 minutes or until golden brown. Remove from pans to a wire rack to cool. **Yield:** 16 buns.

Nutrition Facts: One bun equals 158 calories, 5 g fat (3 g saturated fat), 23 mg cholesterol, 265 mg sodium, 24 g carbohydrate, 3 g fiber, 5 g protein. **Diabetic Exchanges:** 1-1/2 starch, 1 fat.

Now that our children are gone, I'm cooking for two most of the time. This recipe is good because we can enjoy fresh rolls for several days.

~Reba Erickson
EDWARDSVILLE, KANSAS

90-Minute Dinner Rolls

2 to 2-1/2 cups all-purpose flour
2 tablespoons sugar
1 package (1/4 ounce) quick-rise yeast
1/2 teaspoon salt
1/2 cup milk
1/4 cup water
2 tablespoons butter

In a large mixing bowl, combine 3/4 cup flour, sugar, yeast and salt. In a small saucepan, heat the milk, water and butter to 120°-130°. Add to dry ingredients; beat just until moistened. Stir in enough remaining flour to form a soft dough. Turn onto a floured surface; knead until smooth and elastic, about 6-8 minutes. Cover and let rest for 10 minutes.

Divide dough into 12 pieces; shape each piece into a roll. Arrange in a greased 9-in. round baking pan. Cover and let rise until doubled, about 35 minutes. Bake at 375° for 20-25 minutes or until golden brown. Remove from pan to a wire rack to cool. **Yield:** 1 dozen.

Anise Pumpkin Bread

2 eggs
1 cup packed brown sugar
1 cup canned pumpkin
1/3 cup vegetable oil
1 teaspoon vanilla extract
1-1/4 cups all-purpose flour
1/4 cup quick-cooking oats
2 teaspoons baking powder
1 teaspoon aniseed
1/2 teaspoon salt

GLAZE:

1/2 cup confectioners' sugar
2 to 3 teaspoons milk
1/4 teaspoon anise extract
1/4 teaspoon butter flavoring, optional

In a mixing bowl, combine the eggs, brown sugar, pumpkin, oil and vanilla. In another bowl, combine the flour, oats, baking powder, aniseed and salt; add to pumpkin mixture and stir until well blended. Pour into a greased and floured 8-in. x 4-in. x 2-in. loaf pan.

Bake at 350° for 45-50 minutes or until a toothpick inserted near the center comes out clean. Cool for 10 minutes before removing from pan to a wire rack to cool completely. Combine glaze ingredients; drizzle over bread. **Yield:** 1 loaf.

Cranberry Corn Bread

1/2 cup butter, softened
1 cup sugar
2 eggs
1-1/2 cups all-purpose flour
1 cup cornmeal
2 teaspoons baking powder
1/2 teaspoon salt
1-1/2 cups buttermilk
1 cup cranberries, halved

In a mixing bowl, cream butter and sugar. Add eggs; mix well. Combine the flour, cornmeal, baking powder and salt. Add to creamed mixture alternately with buttermilk. Fold in cranberries.

Transfer to a greased 9-in. square baking pan. Bake at 375° for 40-45 minutes or until a toothpick inserted near the center comes out clean. Serve warm. **Yield:** 9-12 servings.

If you like pizza, here's a tasty muffin recipe that combines many of the same ingredients that make pizza taste so good.

~Kathy Henson
ALICE, TEXAS

Pizza Muffins

1 can (14-1/2 ounces) diced tomatoes
2 cups all-purpose flour
3 teaspoons baking powder
1 teaspoon sugar
1 teaspoon dried oregano
1/2 teaspoon salt
1 egg
1/4 cup butter, melted
1/2 cup shredded mozzarella cheese, *divided*
2 tablespoons grated Parmesan cheese, *divided*

Drain tomatoes, reserving 1/4 cup liquid. In a bowl, combine the flour, baking powder, sugar, oregano and salt. Combine the egg, butter, tomatoes and reserved juice. Stir into dry ingredients just until moistened. Stir in 1/4 cup mozzarella cheese and 1 tablespoon Parmesan cheese.

Fill greased jumbo muffin cups two-thirds full. Sprinkle with the remaining cheeses. Bake at 350° for 20-25 minutes or until a toothpick comes out clean. Cool in pan for 5 minutes before removing to a wire rack. Serve warm. **Yield:** 6 servings.

It's no wonder my husband adores these pinwheels. I got the original recipe from his mother. They taste great warm or cold and freeze well in plastic bags. ~Wendy Mallard
STONY PLAIN, ALBERTA

Bacon-Cheese Pinwheel Rolls

2 packages (1/4 ounce *each*) active dry yeast
2 teaspoons plus 1/2 cup sugar, *divided*
2 cups warm water (110° to 115°), *divided*
1 cup warm milk (110° to 115°)
2/3 cup butter, melted
2 eggs, beaten
2 teaspoons salt
8-3/4 to 9-1/4 cups all-purpose flour
1 pound sliced bacon, diced
1/2 cup finely chopped onion
4 cups (16 ounces) shredded cheddar cheese

In a large mixing bowl, dissolve yeast and 2 teaspoons sugar in 1 cup warm water; let stand for 5 minutes. Add the milk, butter, eggs, salt, 7 cups flour and remaining water and sugar. Beat until smooth. Stir in enough remaining flour to form a soft dough.

Turn onto a floured surface; knead until smooth and elastic, about 6-8 minutes. Place in a greased bowl, turning once to grease top. Cover and let rise in a warm place until doubled, about 1 hour.

Meanwhile, in a skillet, cook bacon over medium heat until crisp. Remove to paper towels; drain, reserving 1 tablespoon drippings. Set bacon aside. Saute onion in drippings until tender; set aside.

Punch dough down. Turn onto a lightly floured surface; divide into fourths. Roll each portion into a 15-in. x 10-in. rectangle. Sprinkle each with a fourth of the cheese, about 1/3 cup bacon and about 2 tablespoons onion. Roll up jelly-roll style, starting with a long side; pinch seam to seal. Cut each into 12 slices.

Place cut side down 2 in. apart on ungreased baking sheets. Cover and let rise until doubled, about 30 minutes.

Bake at 350° for 25-30 minutes or until golden brown. Remove from pans to wire racks. Store in the refrigerator. **Yield:** 4 dozen.

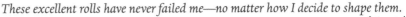

These excellent rolls have never failed me—no matter how I decide to shape them.
~Agnes Iveson
LITTLEFORK, MINNESOTA

Three-in-One Refrigerator Rolls

2 packages (1/4 ounce *each*) active dry yeast
1-1/2 cups warm water (110° to 115°)
1 cup warm mashed potatoes (110° to 115°, prepared without milk and butter)
2/3 cup sugar
2/3 cup shortening
1-1/2 teaspoons salt
2 eggs, lightly beaten
7 to 7-1/2 cups all-purpose flour
Melted butter

In a large bowl, dissolve yeast in warm water. Stir in potatoes, sugar, shortening, salt, eggs and 5 cups flour; beat until smooth. Stir in enough remaining flour to form a firm dough. Turn onto a floured surface; knead until smooth and elastic, about 5-7 minutes. Place in a large greased bowl, turning once to grease top. Cover and refrigerate for 8 hours or overnight. Punch dough down. Turn onto a lightly floured surface; divide dough into three portions.

For cloverleaf rolls, divide one portion into 48 pieces. Shape each piece into a 3/4-in. ball; place three balls each in greased muffin cups.

For four-leaf-clover rolls, divide one portion into 16 pieces. Shape each into a 1-1/2-in. ball; place in greased muffin cups. With scissors, cut each ball into quarters, but not all the way through, leaving dough attached at bottom.

For pan rolls, divide one portion into 16 pieces. Shape each piece into a 1-1/2-in. ball. Place in a greased 9-in. square baking pan.

Cover and let rise in a warm place until doubled, about 1-1/4 hours. Bake at 400° for 13-16 minutes or until golden brown. Brush with melted butter. **Yield:** 4 dozen.

I entered the corn recipe contest at the 1998 Iowa State Fair. I improvised with a banana nut bread recipe I had. I replaced the bananas with cream-style corn and used hazelnuts instead of pecans. It won both the blue ribbon and overall ribbon! ~Robin Carmen
DES MOINES, IOWA

Hazelnut-Raisin Corn Bread

3/4 cup raisins
1/2 cup boiling water
1/2 cup butter, softened
1 cup sugar
2 eggs
2-1/2 cups all-purpose flour
1 teaspoon baking soda
1/8 teaspoon salt
1 can (14-3/4 ounces) cream-style corn
1/2 cup finely crushed hazelnuts

Place the raisins in a bowl; add boiling water. Cover and let stand for 10 minutes; drain. In a large mixing bowl, cream butter and sugar; add eggs. Combine the flour, baking soda and salt; add to creamed mixture. Stir in the corn, nuts and raisins.

Pour into two greased 8-in. x 4-in. x 2-in. loaf pans. Bake at 350° for 60-70 minutes or until a toothpick inserted near the center comes out clean. Cool for 10 minutes before removing from pans to wire racks. **Yield:** 2 loaves.

These **handy treats** all make great entries into a **bake sale** or potluck and satisfy the **sweet tooth**.

Cookies, Bars & Candies

BAR NONE. Clockwise from top left: Swedish Butter Cookies (p. 94), Apple Pie Bars (p. 95) and Oatmeal Jumble Cookies (p. 96).

These moist bars have a great flavor. Everyone in my family loves them, and I get lots of requests for the recipe.

~Kim Gilliland
SIMI VALLEY, CALIFORNIA

Apricot Bars

2/3 cup dried apricots
1/2 cup water
1/2 cup butter, softened
1/4 cup confectioners' sugar
1-1/3 cups all-purpose flour, *divided*
2 eggs
1 cup packed brown sugar
1/2 teaspoon baking powder
1/4 teaspoon salt
1/2 teaspoon vanilla extract
1/2 cup chopped walnuts
Additional confectioners' sugar

In a small saucepan, cook apricots in water over medium heat for 10 minutes or until softened. Drain, cool and chop; set aside. In a mixing bowl, cream butter and confectioners' sugar. Add 1 cup flour; mix until smooth. Press into a greased 8-in. square baking dish. Bake at 350° for 20 minutes or until lightly browned.

Meanwhile, in a mixing bowl, beat eggs and brown sugar. Add the baking powder, salt, vanilla and remaining flour. Stir in apricots and nuts. Pour over crust.

Bake at 350° for 30 minutes or until set. Cool on wire rack. Dust with confectioners' sugar; cut into bars. **Yield:** 16 bars.

Among our large family's Christmas Eve traditions is enjoying these delectable cookies— one of the 20 varieties my sister bakes for the holiday. They have a pleasing pecan flavor and are so buttery and delicate, they almost melt in your mouth.

~Jo Chlopowicz
TUCSON, ARIZONA

Swedish Butter Cookies

(Also pictured on page 93)

1 cup butter, softened
1/2 cup sugar
1 egg, *separated*
1 tablespoon half-and-half cream
1 teaspoon vanilla extract
2 cups all-purpose flour
1/2 teaspoon baking powder
1/2 cup finely chopped pecans
Additional chopped pecans
Halved red maraschino cherries *or* red jelly of your choice

In a large mixing bowl, cream butter and sugar. Beat in egg yolk, cream and vanilla. Combine the flour and baking powder; gradually add to creamed mixture. Stir in finely chopped pecans. Roll into 3/4-in. balls.

In a small bowl, beat egg white. Dip balls in egg white, then roll in additional pecans. Place 2 in. apart on ungreased baking sheets.

Using the end of a wooden spoon handle, make an indentation in the center of each ball. Top each ball with a cherry half or fill with jelly. Bake at 350° for 12-15 minutes or until cookies are lightly browned. Carefully remove to wire racks to cool. **Yield:** about 5-1/2 dozen.

I use apples from our own apple trees to make this dessert. It's a big hit at potlucks as well as with my family.
~Debra Weiers
SILVER LAKE, MINNESOTA

Apple Pie Bars

(Also pictured on page 93)

2-1/2 cups all-purpose flour
    2 tablespoons sugar
    1/4 teaspoon salt
    1 cup shortening
    2 egg yolks, lightly beaten
    1/3 cup milk

FILLING:
    1 cup crisp rice cereal
    8 cups sliced peeled tart apples
      (about 9 medium)
    1 cup sugar
    1 teaspoon all-purpose flour
    1/2 teaspoon ground cinnamon
    2 egg whites, lightly beaten
    1 cup confectioners' sugar
    1 to 2 tablespoons milk

In a large mixing bowl, combine the flour, sugar and salt; cut in the shortening until the mixture is crumbly.

Combine egg yolks and milk; gradually add to the crumb mixture, tossing with a fork until dough forms a ball. Divide in half.

On a lightly floured surface, roll each portion into a 15-in. x 10-in. rectangle. Line a 15-in. x 10-in. x 1-in. baking pan with one rectangle; sprinkle with cereal.

Arrange apples over cereal. Combine the sugar, flour and cinnamon; sprinkle over apples. Top with remaining pastry; cut slits in top. Brush with egg whites.

Bake at 350° for 50-55 minutes or until golden brown. Cool completely on a wire rack. In a bowl, combine the confectioners' sugar and enough milk to achieve drizzling consistency. Drizzle over the bars. Store in the refrigerator. **Yield:** 3-4 dozen.

Cookies that melt in your mouth and are practically fat-free...is it any wonder crispy meringue morsels disappear as fast as I can whip them up? Friends and family love them.
~Jo Ann Blomquest
FREEPORT, ILLINOIS

Cherry Kisses

    4 egg whites
1-1/4 cups sugar
    1/3 cup chopped walnuts
    1/3 cup chopped pitted dates
    1/3 cup chopped candied cherries

Place egg whites in a mixing bowl; let stand at room temperature for 30 minutes. Beat on medium speed until soft peaks form.

Gradually beat in the sugar, 1 table-spoon at a time, on high until stiff glossy peaks form and the sugar is dissolved. Fold in the walnuts, dates and cherries.

Drop by teaspoonfuls 2 in. apart onto lightly greased baking sheets. Bake at 300° for 20-30 minutes or until lightly browned and firm to the touch. Remove to wire racks to cool. Store in an airtight container. **Yield:** 6 dozen.

I combined a favorite bar recipe and cookie recipe to come up with these classic cookies. They stay very chewy and keep well.
~Bobbi Conley
EDGEMONT, SOUTH DAKOTA

Oatmeal Jumble Cookies

(Pictured on page 93)

   1 cup butter, softened
1-1/2 cups packed brown sugar
   2 eggs
   1/3 cup molasses
   1 teaspoon vanilla extract
   4 cups quick-cooking oats
   2 cups all-purpose flour
   1 teaspoon baking powder
   1 teaspoon salt
   1/2 teaspoon ground cinnamon
   1 cup chopped walnuts

   1 cup semisweet chocolate chips
   1 cup butterscotch chips
   1 package (6 ounces) dried cranberries

In a large mixing bowl, cream butter and brown sugar. Add eggs, one at a time, beating well after each addition. Beat in molasses and vanilla. Combine the oats, flour, baking powder, salt and cinnamon; gradually add to the creamed mixture. Stir in walnuts, chips and cranberries.

Drop by tablespoonfuls 2 in. apart onto ungreased baking sheets. Bake at 375° for 10-12 minutes or until edges are lightly browned. Remove to wire racks to cool. **Yield:** 6 dozen.

To prepare these cute confections, our Test Kitchen staff shaped melted candies with cookie cutters. Then they piped royal icing in all sorts of fun designs.
~Taste of Home Test Kitchen

Candy Hearts

Satin ribbon
   1 package (7 ounces) watermelon-flavored hard candies

ROYAL ICING:
   3/4 cup confectioners' sugar
   4 teaspoons water
1-3/4 teaspoons meringue powder

Place heart-shaped cookie cutters on a piece of foil, leaving space above the top of each cookie cutter for placing the ribbon hanger later. Coat the foil and cutters with nonstick cooking spray.

Cut the satin ribbon into six 6-inch lengths. Place the ends of one ribbon piece together to form a loop. Position the ribbon loop at the top of one cookie cutter so the ends are touching the foil and the loop drapes over the top of the cookie cutter. In the same way, position a ribbon loop on each remaining cookie cutter. Set aside for now.

Unwrap the hard candies and place in a large resealable heavy-duty plastic bag. Crush the candies using a mallet or rolling pin. Transfer the candies to a large heavy skillet. Cook over medium heat until melted, stirring occasionally.

Fill each prepared cookie cutter with the melted candy to a 1/4-inch thickness, covering the ends of each ribbon loop at the same time. Let stand for 1-2 minutes. Carefully remove the cutters. Let stand until set, about 1 hour.

For royal icing, in a small mixing bowl, combine the confectioners' sugar, water and meringue powder. Beat on high speed for 6-8 minutes or until thickened.

Insert a pastry tip in one corner of a pastry or plastic bag and cut a hole in the bag. Place the icing in the pastry or plastic bag. Pipe the desired designs or Valentine phrases on each heart. **Yield:** 6 candy hearts.

Editor's Note: Meringue powder can be ordered by mail from Wilton Industries. Call 1-800/794-5866 or visit the Web site, *www.wilton.com.*

I've been making this recipe for over 35 years now, and it's still my family's all-time favorite cookie.
~Christine Harsh
KERENS, WEST VIRGINIA

Chocolate Island Cookies

1/2 cup shortening
1 cup packed brown sugar
1 egg
3 squares (1 ounce *each*) unsweetened chocolate, melted and cooled
1/4 cup strong brewed coffee
2 cups all-purpose flour
1/2 teaspoon baking soda
1/2 teaspoon salt
2/3 cup buttermilk
1/3 cup flaked coconut

FROSTING:
1-1/2 squares (1-1/2 ounces) unsweetened chocolate, melted and cooled
1/4 cup sour cream
1 tablespoon butter, softened
1 to 1-1/2 cups confectioners' sugar
2/3 cup flaked coconut

In a mixing bowl, cream shortening and sugar. Add egg, chocolate and coffee; mix well. Combine the flour, baking soda and salt; add to creamed mixture alternately with buttermilk. Stir in coconut.

Drop by tablespoonfuls 2 in. apart onto greased baking sheets. Bake at 375° for 12-15 minutes or until the edges are browned. Remove to wire racks to cool.

For frosting, combine the chocolate, sour cream and butter in a small mixing bowl. Add enough of the confectioners' sugar to achieve the desired spreading consistency. Frost cooled cookies. Sprinkle with coconut. **Yield:** about 4 dozen.

I baked these bars for a luncheon on a hot summer day. A gentleman made his way to the kitchen to compliment the cook who made them.
~Holly Wilkins
LAKE ELMORE, VERMONT

Lemon-Lime Bars

1 cup butter, softened
1/2 cup confectioners' sugar
2 teaspoons grated lime peel
1-3/4 cups all-purpose flour
1/4 teaspoon salt

FILLING:
4 eggs
1-1/2 cups sugar
1/4 cup all-purpose flour
1/2 teaspoon baking powder
1/3 cup lemon juice
2 teaspoons grated lemon peel
Confectioners' sugar

In a mixing bowl, cream butter and confectioners' sugar. Add lime peel; mix well. Combine flour and salt; gradually add to creamed mixture. Press into a greased 13-in. x 9-in. x 2-in. baking pan. Bake at 350° for 13-15 minutes or just until edges are lightly browned.

Meanwhile, in a mixing bowl, beat eggs and sugar. Combine the flour and baking powder. Add to egg mixture with lemon juice and peel; beat until frothy. Pour over hot crust.

Bake for 20-25 minutes or until light golden brown. Cool on a wire rack. Dust with confectioners' sugar. Cut into squares. Store in the refrigerator. **Yield:** 4 dozen.

Sugar Beats the *Sweet Tooth*

IN NORTH DAKOTA'S Red River Valley, about 3 million tons of sugar beets are produced in a year. These hardy roots are processed into the sugar many of us cook and bake with every day. Sugar will last almost indefinitely if stored in an airtight container in a cool, dry place. When making candy, test your candy thermometer before each use by bringing water to a boil; the thermometer should read 212°. Adjust your recipe temperature up or down based on your test.

My mother has made this brittle for years using several different kinds of nuts. When I married my husband, he raised sunflowers, so it seemed natural to use those. Now this crunchy golden brittle includes two great North Dakota products—sugar and sunflower seeds.

~Trish Gehlhar
YPSILANTI, NORTH DAKOTA

Sunflower Brittle

- 2 cups sugar
- 1 cup light corn syrup
- 1/2 cup water
- 1-1/2 cups raw *or* roasted sunflower kernels
- 1 tablespoon butter
- 1 teaspoon vanilla extract
- 1 teaspoon baking soda

Butter the sides of a large heavy saucepan. Add sugar, corn syrup and water; bring to a boil, stirring constantly. Cook and stir over medium-low heat until a candy thermometer reads 260° (hard-ball stage). Stir in sunflower kernels and butter. Cook on medium to 300° (hard-crack stage). Remove from the heat; vigorously stir in vanilla and baking soda. Pour into a buttered 15-in. x 10-in. x 1-in. baking pan; spread evenly to fill pan. Cool completely. Break into pieces. Store in an airtight container with waxed paper between layers. **Yield:** about 1-1/2 pounds.

This candy is a "must" at our house for Christmas. We raised our children on nutritious meals made of simple ingredients. Now I enjoy making special treats like this candy for our eight grandchildren.
~Darlene Edinger
TURTLE LAKE, NORTH DAKOTA

Soft 'n' Chewy Caramels

(Not pictured)

2 cups sugar
1 cup light corn syrup
2 cups half-and-half cream, *divided*
1 cup butter
1 teaspoon vanilla extract

Line a 13-in. x 9-in. x 2-in. pan with foil; butter the foil. Set aside. Combine sugar, corn syrup and 1 cup cream in a 5-qt. saucepan or Dutch oven; bring to a boil over medium heat, stirring constantly. Slowly stir in remaining cream. Cook over medium heat until a candy thermometer reads 250° (hard-ball stage), stirring frequently. Remove from the heat; stir in butter and vanilla until well mixed, about 5 minutes.

Pour into prepared pan. Cool. Remove foil from pan; cut candy into 1-in. squares. Wrap individually in waxed paper; twist ends. **Yield:** 9-10 dozen (2 pounds).

This recipe was passed down to me from my mother-in-law. These soft sugar cookies are a favorite with our four children.
~Karen Skowronek
MINOT, NORTH DAKOTA

Norwegian Cookies

1 cup butter, softened
1 cup sugar
1 egg
1/2 teaspoon vanilla extract
1/2 teaspoon almond extract
2 cups all-purpose flour
1/2 cup finely chopped walnuts
Red *and/or* green colored sugar

In a mixing bowl, cream butter and sugar. Add egg and extracts; beat until light and fluffy. Add flour and nuts; beat just until moistened. Cover and chill 1 hour or until firm enough to handle.

Shape into 1-in. balls; place 2 in. apart on greased baking sheets. Flatten to 1/4-in. thickness with a glass dipped in colored sugar. Sprinkle with additional sugar if desired. Bake at 350° for 10-12 minutes or until cookies are set. **Yield:** 3 dozen.

I love to bake treats like these brownies to share with co-workers. When I was growing up, I helped my mother make delicious, hearty meals and desserts like this for our farm family of eight.
~Judy Cunningham
MAX, NORTH DAKOTA

Fudgy Brownies

1-1/3 cups butter, softened
2-2/3 cups sugar
4 eggs
1 tablespoon vanilla extract
2 cups all-purpose flour
1 cup baking cocoa
1/2 teaspoon salt
Confectioners' sugar, optional

In a mixing bowl, cream butter and sugar. Add eggs and vanilla; mix well. Combine flour, cocoa and salt; add to the creamed mixture and mix well. Spread into a greased 13-in. x 9-in. x 2-in. baking pan. Bake at 350° for 25-30 minutes or until the top is dry and the center is set. Cool completely. Dust with confectioners' sugar if desired. **Yield:** 2-1/2 dozen.

Celebrate the Fourth of July or other patriotic holidays with a festive cookie display. Cut shapes from fast-to-fix homemade cookie dough, put wooden dowels between pairs of cutouts and arrange the baked cookies in a container. ~Taste of Home Test Kitchen

Patriotic Cookie Bouquets

3/4 cup butter, softened
1 cup sugar
1 egg
1 tablespoon milk
2-1/4 cups all-purpose flour
1 teaspoon baking powder
1/8 teaspoon salt
1 teaspoon apple pie spice
1 teaspoon vanilla extract

GLAZE:
4 cups confectioners' sugar
1/2 cup light corn syrup
2 to 4 tablespoons water
Red and blue gel food coloring

In a large mixing bowl, cream butter and sugar. Beat in egg and milk. Combine the flour, baking powder and salt, then gradually add to the creamed mixture. Beat in apple pie spice and vanilla. Cover and refrigerate dough for 2 hours or until easy to handle.

Roll out dough to a 1/4-in. thickness. With star cookie cutters, cut out shapes. Place only five or six shapes on an ungreased baking sheet. Place a dowel piece on top of each shape so that at least 1-1/2 in. of dowel is on top of shape, leaving the rest of dowel extended for handle. Top each dough shape with a matching shape. Press edges gently to seal. Place remaining shapes on another baking sheet.

Bake cookies at 375° for 7-9 minutes or until golden brown. Cool on wire racks, propping up each dowel handle so it remains parallel to the rack.

In a bowl, combine the confectioners' sugar, corn syrup and water until smooth. Place 1/3 cup of glaze in each of three bowls. Tint one portion red and one blue, leaving the remaining one white. Spread blue and red glaze over tops of some of the cookies. For a swirled design on remaining cookies, spread white glaze over the tops of cookies, immediately place three dots of each colored glaze on top of each cookie and swirl with a toothpick. Set cookies aside to dry.

Refer to the photo (above left) while assembling as directed in the instructions that follow. Using a serrated knife, cut floral foam to fit snugly inside a container for bouquet base. Insert the floral foam in the container. Cover the top of the foam with paper shred.

Insert the dowel handle of each cookie and the stick of each flag into the foam. Serve remaining cookies separately. **Yield:** about 1-1/2 dozen.

Holiday Cookies

Helpful Hint

Get a jump on holiday baking by making holiday cutout cookies ahead and freezing them without frosting (they keep better that way). Before a potluck, holiday party or other event, just thaw the cookies and frost them. They'll taste and look fresh-baked.

Whenever I'm invited to a potluck with family and friends, it's understood these scrumptious bars will come with me. Our grandchildren request them when they visit. Usually, I wait until they arrive, so we can make the treats together. ~Paula Marchesi
LENHARTSVILLE, PENNSYLVANIA

Best-Loved Chocolate Bars

- 1 package (18-1/4 ounces) chocolate cake mix
- 1 cup graham cracker crumbs (about 16 squares)
- 1/2 cup peanut butter
- 1 egg
- 3 tablespoons half-and-half cream
- 1 package (8 ounces) cream cheese, softened
- 1 jar (11-3/4 ounces) hot fudge ice cream topping
- 1 package (11-1/2 ounces) milk chocolate chips
- 1 cup salted peanuts

In a bowl, combine the dry cake mix and cracker crumbs. Cut in peanut butter until mixture resembles coarse crumbs. In a bowl, whisk the egg and cream. Add to the crumb mixture just until moistened. Set aside 3/4 cup for topping. Press the remaining crumb mixture into a greased 13-in. x 9-in. x 2-in. baking pan.

In a mixing bowl, beat cream cheese until smooth. Add fudge topping; mix well. Spread over the crust. Sprinkle with chocolate chips, peanuts and reserved crumb mixture. Bake at 350° for 25-30 minutes or until set. Cool on a wire rack. Cover and refrigerate at least 4 hours. Cut into bars. Refrigerate leftovers. **Yield:** 2 dozen.

Editor's Note: Reduced-fat or generic brands of peanut butter are not recommended for this recipe.

These sweet treats are one of my most requested recipes for special occasions. Maple flavor is prominent in both the dough and icing of these tasty twists. ~Doris Longman
HIGH SPRINGS, FLORIDA

Maple Pecan Twists

- 1/2 cup butter, softened
- 1/2 cup packed brown sugar
- 2 eggs
- 1 teaspoon maple flavoring
- 3 cups all-purpose flour
- 4 teaspoons baking powder
- 1/2 teaspoon salt
- 1/2 cup milk

FILLING:
- 1/4 cup butter, melted
- 1/2 cup finely chopped pecans

ICING:
- 1/4 cup butter, melted
- 2 cups confectioners' sugar
- 2 tablespoons milk
- 1/2 teaspoon maple flavoring

In a large mixing bowl, cream butter and brown sugar. Add eggs, one at a time, beating well after each addition. Beat in maple flavoring. Combine the flour, baking powder and salt; add to creamed mixture alternately with milk. Cover and refrigerate for 2 hours or until easy to handle.

On a lightly floured surface, roll the dough into an 18-in. x 9-in. rectangle. Brush with melted butter to within 1/2 in. of edges. Sprinkle with pecans. Fold one short side of dough a third of the way over filling; fold the other short side over the top, forming an 18-in. x 3-in. rectangle. Cut into 3/4-in. strips; twist each strip twice.

Place 2 in. apart on ungreased baking sheets. Bake at 350° for 20-22 minutes or until golden brown. Remove to wire racks to cool. In a small bowl, combine icing ingredients until smooth. Drizzle over twists. **Yield:** about 2 dozen.

These crispy treats are like a bread but more like a cookie! They're a tasty and delicious addition to a breakfast or brunch with coffee.

~Martha Nelson
ZUMBROTA, MINNESOTA

Danish Crispies

1 package (1/4 ounce) active dry yeast
1/2 teaspoon plus 3 tablespoons sugar, *divided*
1 cup warm water (110° to 115°), *divided*
3 egg yolks
4 cups all-purpose flour
1/3 cup nonfat dry milk powder
1 teaspoon salt
1 cup cold butter

FILLING:
6 tablespoons butter, softened
1/2 cup sugar
1 teaspoon ground cinnamon

TOPPING:
1-1/2 cups sugar
1 teaspoon ground cinnamon

In a large mixing bowl, dissolve yeast and 1/2 teaspoon sugar in 1/4 cup water; let stand for 5 minutes. Add egg yolks and remaining sugar and water; mix well.

Combine the flour, milk powder and salt; cut in butter until mixture resembles coarse crumbs. Gradually add to yeast mixture to make a soft dough. Place in a greased bowl, turning once to grease top; cover and refrigerate overnight.

Turn dough onto a lightly floured surface. Cover with a kitchen towel; let rest for 10 minutes. Roll into an 18-in. x 10-in. rectangle; spread with softened butter. Combine sugar and cinnamon; sprinkle over butter. Roll up jelly-roll style, starting with a long side. Pinch edges to seal. Cut into 3/4-in. slices.

Combine topping ingredients; sprinkle some on waxed paper. Place slices cut side down on cinnamon-sugar; roll each into a 5-in. circle, turning to coat both sides and adding cinnamon-sugar as needed. Place 2 in. apart on greased baking sheets. Sprinkle tops with leftover cinnamon-sugar if desired. Bake at 350° for 15-20 minutes or until golden brown. Remove from pans to cool on wire racks. **Yield:** about 2 dozen.

Since chocolate-mint is my favorite flavor combination, I sometimes eat these dainty shortbread-like treats by the dozen. But I manage to save some for guests because they make my cookie trays look so elegant.

~Anne Revers
OMAHA, NEBRASKA

Chocolate Mint Dreams

3/4 cup butter, softened
1 cup confectioners' sugar
2 squares (1 ounce *each*) unsweetened chocolate, melted and cooled
1/4 teaspoon peppermint extract
1-1/2 cups all-purpose flour
1 cup miniature semisweet chocolate chips

ICING:
2 tablespoons butter, softened
1 cup confectioners' sugar
1 tablespoon milk
1/4 teaspoon peppermint extract
1 to 2 drops green food coloring

DRIZZLE:
1/2 cup semisweet chocolate chips
1/2 teaspoon shortening

In a large mixing bowl, cream butter and confectioners' sugar. Beat in chocolate and mint extract. Gradually add flour. Stir in chocolate chips. (Dough will be soft.)

Drop by tablespoonfuls 2 in. apart on ungreased baking sheets. Bake at 375° for 6-8 minutes or until firm. Cool for 2 minutes before removing to wire racks to cool completely.

Meanwhile, combine icing ingredients; spread over cooled cookies. Let set. In a microwave, melt chocolate chips and shortening; stir until smooth. Drizzle over cookies. **Yield:** 4-1/2 dozen.

Snowmen Butter Cookies

1 cup butter, softened
1/2 cup sugar
1/4 teaspoon almond extract
2-1/2 cups all-purpose flour
1 teaspoon water
Red and green liquid *or* paste food coloring
Black and orange jimmies *or* sprinkles

In a mixing bowl, cream butter, sugar and extract. Gradually beat in flour and water. Place 1/3 cup each in two small bowls. Add red food coloring to one and green to the other; set aside. Shape remaining dough into twelve 1-in. balls and twelve 1-1/2-in. balls. Place one smaller ball above one larger ball on ungreased baking sheets; flatten slightly.

For each snowman, shape 2 teaspoons of colored dough into a hat; place above head. For scarf, shape 1/4 teaspoon of each color into a 3-in. rope; twist ropes together, leaving one end untwisted. Place scarf around snowman's neck. Insert jimmies for eyes and nose. Bake at 350° for 15-18 minutes or until set. Cool on baking sheets. **Yield:** 1 dozen.

Oatmeal Raisin Cookies

1 cup shortening
1 cup sugar
1 cup packed brown sugar
2 eggs
1 teaspoon vanilla extract
3 cups old-fashioned oats
1-1/2 cups all-purpose flour
1 teaspoon baking soda
1 teaspoon salt
1/2 cup chopped walnuts
1/2 cup golden raisins

In a large mixing bowl, cream shortening and sugars. Beat in eggs and vanilla. Combine the oats, flour, baking soda and salt; gradually add to creamed mixture. Stir in nuts and raisins.

Drop by tablespoonfuls 2 in. apart onto ungreased baking sheets. Bake at 375° for 10-12 minutes or until golden brown. Remove to wire racks to cool. **Yield:** 5 dozen.

Top your table with a **fabulous cake, pie** or **dessert**.

Cakes, Pies & Desserts

CAKE CREATIONS. From left: Luscious Lemon Cake Roll (p. 107) and Boston Cream Pie (p. 106).

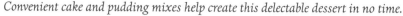

Convenient cake and pudding mixes help create this delectable dessert in no time.

~Edwina Olson
ENID, OKLAHOMA

Boston Cream Pie

(Also pictured on page 105)

> 1 package (18-1/4 ounces) yellow cake mix
> 1-1/2 cups cold milk
> 1 package (3.4 ounces) instant vanilla pudding mix
> 2 squares (1 ounce *each*) unsweetened chocolate
> 2 tablespoons butter
> 1 cup confectioners' sugar
> 1/2 teaspoon vanilla extract
> 2 to 3 tablespoons hot water

Prepare cake batter according to package directions. Divide between two greased and floured 9-in. round baking pans.

Bake at 350° for 28-33 minutes or until the cake springs back when lightly touched. Cool for 10 minutes before removing cake from pans to wire racks to cool completely.

In a bowl, whisk milk and pudding mix for 2 minutes. Cover and refrigerate. In a microwave, melt chocolate and butter; stir until smooth. Stir in confectioners' sugar, vanilla and enough water to achieve a thick glaze; set aside.

To assemble, place one cake layer on a serving plate; spread with pudding. Top with the second cake layer. Spoon chocolate glaze over the top, allowing it to drip down sides of cake. Refrigerate until serving. **Yield:** 6-8 servings.

I came up with this recipe when we had a bumper crop of raspberries, and a friend gave me some of the juiciest peaches we'd ever tasted.

~Jeanne Boelsma
BETHEL, MAINE

Raspberry Peach Pie

(Also pictured on front cover)

> 1-1/4 cups all-purpose flour
> 1/2 teaspoon salt
> 1/3 cup shortening
> 1/4 cup cold water

FILLING:
> 4 medium fresh peaches, peeled and sliced
> 1-1/3 cups sugar
> 5 teaspoons lemon juice
> 1/4 cup cornstarch
> 1/3 cup water
> 3 cups fresh raspberries

In a bowl, combine flour and salt. Cut in shortening until mixture resembles coarse crumbs. Stir in water until mixture forms a ball. Roll out pastry to fit a 9-in. pie plate. Transfer to pie plate; trim and flute edges. Line unpricked pastry shell with a double thickness of heavy-duty foil. Bake at 450° for 8 minutes. Remove foil; bake 5 minutes longer. Cool on a wire rack.

In a large saucepan, combine the peaches, sugar and juice. Combine cornstarch and water until smooth. Stir into peach mixture. Bring to a boil; cook and stir for 1 minute or until thickened. Remove from the heat; cool to room temperature. Fold in raspberries. Spoon into crust. Refrigerate for at least 4 hours or overnight. Refrigerate leftovers. **Yield:** 6-8 servings.

Plump berries from our strawberry patch turned into a real treat when I dipped them in chocolate! I like to make these before dinner and put them in the fridge, so they're ready when we're finished eating.
~Valerie Gee
DEPEW, NEW YORK

Chocolate-Dipped Strawberries

- 1 pint large strawberries
- 4 squares (1 ounce *each*) semisweet chocolate
- 1 tablespoon plus 1/2 teaspoon shortening, *divided*
- 1 square (1 ounce) white baking chocolate
- 4 drops red food coloring, optional

Wash strawberries and gently pat with paper towels until completely dry. In a microwave-safe bowl, melt semisweet chocolate and 1 tablespoon shortening at 50% power; stir until smooth. Dip strawberries and place on a waxed paper-lined baking sheet. Freeze strawberries for 5 minutes.

Meanwhile, microwave white chocolate and remaining shortening until melted; stir until smooth. Stir in food coloring if desired. Drizzle over strawberries. Refrigerate until serving. **Yield:** about 9 strawberries.

A co-worker shared the recipe for this elegant cake roll. It's perfect for rounding out a special meal.
~Darlene Brenden
SALEM, OREGON

Luscious Lemon Cake Roll

(Pictured on page 105)

- 4 eggs, *separated*
- 3/4 cup sugar, *divided*
- 1 tablespoon vegetable oil
- 1 teaspoon lemon extract
- 2/3 cup cake flour
- 1 teaspoon baking powder
- 1/4 teaspoon salt
- Confectioners' sugar

CREAMY LEMON FILLING:
- 1 can (14 ounces) sweetened condensed milk
- 1/3 cup lemon juice
- 2 teaspoons grated lemon peel
- 7 drops yellow liquid food coloring, *divided*
- 1-1/2 cups whipped topping
- 1/2 teaspoon water
- 1/2 cup flaked coconut

Line a greased 15-in. x 10-in. x 1-in. baking pan with waxed paper and grease the paper; set aside. In a large mixing bowl, beat egg yolks until lemon-colored. Gradually beat in 1/4 cup sugar. Stir in oil and lemon extract; set aside. In another mixing bowl, beat egg whites on medium speed until soft peaks form. Gradually add remaining sugar, 2 tablespoons at a time, beating until stiff glossy peaks form and sugar is dissolved. Fold into egg yolk mixture. Combine flour, baking powder and salt; fold into egg mixture.

Transfer to prepared pan. Bake at 375° for 10-12 minutes or until cake springs back when lightly touched. Cool for 5 minutes. Turn cake onto a kitchen towel dusted with confectioners' sugar. Gently peel off waxed paper. Roll up cake in towel, starting with a short side. Cool completely on a wire rack.

For filling, in a bowl, combine the milk, lemon juice, lemon peel and 5 drops of food coloring. Fold in whipped topping. Unroll cake; spread half of the filling over cake to within 1 in. of edges. Roll up again. Place seam side down on a platter. Spread remaining filling over cake.

In a large resealable plastic bag, combine water and remaining food coloring; add coconut. Seal bag and shake to tint. Sprinkle the coconut over cake. Refrigerate for at least 2 hours before serving. Refrigerate leftovers. **Yield:** 10 servings.

This rich and flavorful dessert is my cheesecake version of German chocolate cake. It makes an elegant ending to a special meal.

~Mary Bakken
NEW RICHLAND, MINNESOTA

German Chocolate Cheesecake

1-1/2 cups chocolate graham cracker crumbs (about 24 squares)
2 tablespoons brown sugar
1/4 cup butter, melted

FILLING:
2 packages (8 ounces *each*) cream cheese, softened
1 cup (6 ounces) semisweet chocolate chips, melted and cooled
2/3 cup packed brown sugar
2 tablespoons baking cocoa
5 eggs, lightly beaten
1 teaspoon vanilla extract
1 teaspoon almond extract

TOPPING:
3/4 cup flaked coconut
3/4 cup chopped walnuts
1/3 cup packed brown sugar
1/3 cup half-and-half cream
5 tablespoons butter

In a small bowl, combine the cracker crumbs and brown sugar; stir in butter. Press onto the bottom and 1 in. up the sides of a greased 9-in. springform pan. Place pan on a baking sheet. Bake at 350° for 10 minutes. Cool on a wire rack.

In a mixing bowl, beat cream cheese until smooth. Beat in the chocolate, brown sugar and cocoa. Add eggs; beat on low speed just until combined. Add extracts. Place pan on a double thickness of heavy-duty foil (about 16 in. square); securely wrap foil around pan. Pour the filling into crust.

Place pan in a large baking pan. Fill larger pan with 1 in. of hot water. Bake at 350° for 50-55 minutes or until center is just set. Remove springform pan from water bath. Cool on a wire rack for 10 minutes. Carefully run a knife around edge of pan to loosen; cool 1 hour longer. Refrigerate for 4 hours.

In a saucepan, combine topping ingredients. Bring to a boil over medium heat; boil and stir for 3 minutes. Cool. Remove sides of springform pan; spread topping over cheesecake. Refrigerate leftovers. **Yield:** 12 servings.

I always get recipe requests when I bring this pie to potlucks. Once, I got six requests after bringing it to a family reunion!

~Jane Allen
PROMISE CITY, IOWA

Candy Bar Cream Pie

1-2/3 cups finely crushed vanilla wafers (about 50 wafers)
1/3 cup butter, melted
16 large marshmallows, chopped
1/3 cup milk
1 carton (8 ounces) frozen whipped topping, thawed
3 Butterfinger candy bars (2.1 ounces *each*), crushed
1 teaspoon vanilla extract

In a small bowl, combine wafer crumbs and butter. Press onto the bottom and up the sides of a greased 9-in. pie dish. Bake at 375° for 6-8 minutes. Cool the crust completely.

In a small heavy saucepan, melt marshmallows with milk. Cool; transfer to a bowl. Add the whipped topping, crushed candy bars and vanilla. Pour into crust. Cover and refrigerate for 2-4 hours or until set. **Yield:** 8-10 servings.

Topped with sweetly seasoned pecans, this recipe is an apple pie lover's dream. My mother taught me to bake when I was young, and I've been heating up ovens with pies, cakes and cookies ever since.

~Joanna Patterson
MULBERRY, TENNESSEE

Nutty Sour Cream Apple Pie

- 3 tablespoons all-purpose flour
- 1/4 teaspoon salt
- 1/4 teaspoon ground nutmeg
- 1 egg
- 1/2 cup sour cream
- 1/3 cup honey
- 1/2 teaspoon vanilla extract
- 4 large tart apples, peeled and sliced
- 1 unbaked pastry shell (9 inches)

TOPPING:
- 1/2 cup coarsely chopped pecans
- 3 tablespoons brown sugar
- 1 teaspoon ground cinnamon

In a large bowl, combine the flour, salt and nutmeg. In another bowl, combine the egg, sour cream, honey and vanilla until smooth. Stir into dry ingredients. Fold in the apples. Spoon into pastry shell. Combine the topping ingredients; sprinkle over filling.

Bake at 425° for 25 minutes. Reduce heat to 325°; bake 25-30 minutes longer or until the apples are tender (cover pie edges loosely with foil if necessary to prevent overbrowning). Cool on a wire rack. Store in the refrigerator. **Yield:** 6-8 servings.

The peaches really complement the cake. It's been a favorite dessert for a long time in our family.

~Mrs. Kenneth Lundy
NAPA, CALIFORNIA

Peach-Filled Gingerbread

- 1/2 cup butter, softened
- 1/2 cup sugar
- 1 egg
- 1/2 cup molasses
- 1/2 teaspoon unsweetened instant tea
- 1/2 cup water
- 1-2/3 cups all-purpose flour
- 1 teaspoon baking soda
- 1 teaspoon ground ginger
- 1/4 teaspoon salt
- 2 teaspoons grated orange peel
- 4 medium fresh peaches, peeled and sliced
- Whipped cream

In a large mixing bowl, cream butter and sugar. Add egg and molasses; mix well. Dissolve tea in water. Combine flour, baking soda, ginger and salt; add to creamed mixture alternately with tea. Stir in peel. Pour into a greased 9-in. square baking pan. Bake at 350° for 30-35 minutes or until a toothpick inserted near the center comes out clean. Cool for 10 minutes before removing from pan to a wire rack to cool completely.

Just before serving, split cake horizontally into two layers. Spoon peaches over bottom layer; replace top layer. Cut into individual servings; top with whipped cream. **Yield:** 9 servings.

My mother used to make a simple peanut butter frosting for this cake when taking it to church suppers or family picnics. My husband's favorite way to eat it is warm from the oven with a glass of milk.

~Wanita Ann Aldrich
HINSDALE, NEW YORK

Chocolate Mayonnaise Cake

2 cups all-purpose flour
1 cup sugar
1/4 cup baking cocoa
2 teaspoons baking soda
Dash salt
1 cup water
1 cup mayonnaise
1 teaspoon vanilla extract
Confectioners' sugar

In a large mixing bowl, combine the dry ingredients. Add the water, mayonnaise and vanilla; beat on medium speed until well blended.

Pour into a greased 9-in. square baking pan. Bake at 350° for 30-35 minutes or until a toothpick inserted near the center comes out clean. Cool on a wire rack. Just before serving, sprinkle with confectioners' sugar. **Yield:** 9 servings.

Brighten up a dark winter day with this sunshiny peach pie! The mouth-watering dessert is yummy with a dollop of whipped cream. This was one of my father's favorites.

~Margaret Hanson-Maddox
MONTPELIER, INDIANA

Golden Peach Pie

Pastry for double-crust pie (9 inches)
2 cans (15 ounces *each*) sliced peaches
1/2 cup sugar
1/4 cup all-purpose flour
1 tablespoon lemon juice
1/4 teaspoon grated orange peel
Dash salt
2 tablespoons butter
1/8 teaspoon almond extract

Line a 9-in. pie plate with bottom crust; trim pastry even with edge. Drain peaches, reserving 1/3 cup juice. In a saucepan, combine the sugar, flour, lemon juice, orange peel, salt and reserved juice until blended. Bring to a boil; cook and stir for 2 minutes or until thickened.

Add the butter and almond extract; stir until butter is melted. Stir in peaches. Cool slightly. Transfer to crust. Roll out remaining pastry to fit top of pie. Place over filling. Trim, seal and flute edges. Cut slits in pastry.

Cover edges loosely with foil. Bake at 400° for 25 minutes. Remove foil and bake 15-20 minutes longer or until crust is golden brown and filling is bubbly. Cool on a wire rack. Store in the refrigerator. **Yield:** 6-8 servings.

This is such a simple way to say "I love you." Best of all, each fun little heart takes only minutes to assemble from purchased snack cakes.
~Tisha Cottman
BROKEN ARROW, OKLAHOMA

Raspberry Cake Hearts

2 cups fresh *or* frozen unsweetened raspberries, thawed
2 teaspoons sugar
4 individual cream-filled sponge cakes
1 carton (8 ounces) frozen whipped topping, thawed
Mint sprigs, optional

In a bowl, lightly toss together raspberries and sugar; set aside. Slice two sponge cakes diagonally widthwise in same direction. Slice remaining cakes diagonally in the opposite direction.

On each of four dessert plates, place two oppositely cut sponge cake wedges together to form a heart. Top hearts with whipped topping. Top with raspberry mixture and garnish with mint if desired. **Yield:** 4 servings.

Pretty and nutritious, these sweet berry-stuffed apples make a dessert packed with autumn appeal. Our Test Kitchen home economists are certain that even the pickiest of eaters will dig right into these tender treats.
~Taste of Home Test Kitchen

Cranberry-Stuffed Apples

1/3 cup dried cranberries *or* raisins
1/3 cup orange juice
4 large tart apples
1/4 cup chopped walnuts
2 tablespoons brown sugar
1/2 teaspoon ground cinnamon
Dash ground nutmeg
1 tablespoon butter
1-1/2 cups water

In a small bowl, combine cranberries and orange juice; let stand for 20 minutes. Core apples, leaving bottoms intact; peel tops of apples. Place each on a 12-in. square piece of foil. Drain cranberries; add the walnuts, brown sugar, cinnamon and nutmeg. Stuff into apples; dot with butter. Bring corners of foil up around each apple and twist to seal.

Place on a rack in a pressure cooker; add water. Close cover securely; place pressure regulator on vent pipe. Bring cooker to full pressure over high heat. Reduce heat to medium-high; cook for 10 minutes. (Pressure regulator should maintain a slow steady rocking motion; adjust heat if needed.)

Remove from the heat. Immediately cool according to manufacturer's directions until pressure is completely reduced. Remove apples from foil; serve warm or at room temperature. **Yield:** 4 servings.

Editor's Note: This recipe was tested at 15 pounds of pressure (psi).

This fudgy cake looked so stunning at our New Year's Day supper, I almost wished it wouldn't be eaten!

~Joyce Price
WHITEFISH, ONTARIO

Fudgy Pecan Cake

1-1/4 cups pecans, toasted
1 cup (6 ounces) semisweet chocolate chips
3/4 cup butter
4 eggs, *separated*
3/4 cup sugar, *divided*
2 tablespoons all-purpose flour
1/4 teaspoon cream of tartar

GLAZE:
1 cup (6 ounces) semisweet chocolate chips
1/2 cup heavy whipping cream

Place the pecans in a blender or food processor; cover and process until ground. Set aside 1 cup for cake (save any remaining ground nuts for another use). In a microwave, melt chocolate chips and butter; stir until smooth. Cool to room temperature.

In a large mixing bowl, beat egg yolks and 1/2 cup sugar until slightly thickened; stir in cooled chocolate mixture. Combine flour and reserved ground nuts; stir into egg yolk mixture. Set aside.

In another mixing bowl, beat egg whites and cream of tartar on medium speed until soft peaks form. Gradually beat in remaining sugar, 1 tablespoon at a time, on high until stiff glossy peaks form and sugar is dissolved. Fold a third of the egg whites into batter, then fold in remaining whites.

Spoon into a greased and waxed paper-lined 9-in. springform pan. Bake at 350° for 35-40 minutes or until a toothpick inserted near the center comes out with moist crumbs. Cool on a wire rack. (Cake top will puff, then fall during cooling.) Gently push down top and sides of cake to even surface. Run a knife around edge of cake to loosen. Remove sides of pan; invert cake onto a plate and gently peel off waxed paper.

For glaze, heat chocolate chips and cream in a microwave until melted; stir until smooth. Cool until slightly thickened. Spread a thin layer of glaze over top and sides of cake. Pour remaining glaze over cake; spread over top and sides, allowing glaze to drip down sides. Chill until glaze is set, about 30 minutes. Cut into wedges. **Yield:** 12 servings.

Editor's Note: This cake uses only 2 tablespoons of flour, so the texture is very dense.

This pretty pink cake is great for holidays or a little girl's birthday party. It turns out moist and tender with a nice flavor surprise from the cherries.

~Amy Kraemer
HUTCHINSON, MINNESOTA

Cherry Cake

1 package (18-1/4 ounces) yellow cake mix
1 can (21 ounces) cherry pie filling
3 eggs, beaten
1/2 cup packed brown sugar
2 teaspoons all-purpose flour
1 teaspoon ground cinnamon
2 teaspoons butter, softened
1/2 cup chopped pecans

In a large mixing bowl, beat the cake mix, pie filling and eggs until blended. Pour into a greased 13-in. x 9-in. x 2-in. baking pan. Combine the brown sugar, flour, cinnamon and butter; sprinkle over batter. Top with nuts.

Bake at 350° for 25-30 minutes or until a toothpick inserted near the center comes out clean. Cool on a wire rack. **Yield:** 15 servings.

Frosty Caterpillar Dessert

- **8 cream-filled chocolate sandwich cookies, crushed**
- **4 scoops raspberry orange sherbet** *or* **sherbet of your choice (about 1-1/3 cups)**
- **2 semisweet chocolate chips**
- **2 pieces red shoestring licorice (about 2 inches long)**
- **2 miniature marshmallows**
- **1 red-hot candy**
- **8 assorted colored Dots**
- **3 gummy worms**

Sprinkle cookie crumbs onto a serving platter. Arrange sherbet scoops in a zigzag pattern over crumbs, forming a caterpillar. For eyes, press chocolate chips into the first scoop.

Using a toothpick, make two small holes above eyes. For antennae, insert the end of a licorice piece into each marshmallow; insert the other end of licorice pieces into the holes. Add red-hot for nose. Press Dots onto the back of the caterpillar. Garnish with gummy worms. Serve immediately. **Yield:** 4 servings.

Strawberry Delight Torte

- **1 cup all-purpose flour**
- **1/2 cup packed brown sugar**
- **1/2 cup cold butter**
- **2/3 cup finely chopped pecans**
  - **1 jar (7 ounces) marshmallow creme**
  - **2 tablespoons lemon juice**
  - **1 package (16 ounces) frozen sliced sweetened strawberries, thawed**
  - **1 cup heavy whipping cream, whipped**
- **Fresh strawberries and mint sprigs, optional**

In a bowl, combine flour and brown sugar. Cut in butter until mixture resembles coarse crumbs. Stir in pecans.

Press onto the bottom of an ungreased 9-in. springform pan. Bake at 350° for 15-18 minutes or until lightly browned. Cool to room temperature.

In a mixing bowl, combine the marshmallow creme and lemon juice. Stir in strawberries. Fold in whipped cream. Pour over the crust. Cover and freeze overnight or until firm.

Remove from the freezer 20 minutes before serving. Garnish with strawberries and mint if desired. **Yield:** 12-14 servings.

I received this recipe from my sister-in-law many years ago, and it's been requested by my daughter for her birthday more than 20 times!

~Janet Akey
PRESQUE ISLE, WISCONSIN

Blueberry Pretzel Dessert

1-1/2 cups crushed pretzels
  1/2 cup sugar
  1/2 cup butter, melted
    1 package (8 ounces) cream cheese, softened
    1 cup confectioners' sugar
    1 carton (8 ounces) frozen whipped topping, thawed
    2 cans (21 ounces *each*) blueberry pie filling
Additional whipped topping, optional

In a bowl, combine the pretzels and sugar; stir in butter. Press into a 13-in. x 9-in. x 2-in. dish; set aside. In a large mixing bowl, beat the cream cheese and confectioners' sugar until smooth.

Fold in whipped topping. Spread over the crust. Top with pie filling. Cover and refrigerate for 30 minutes or until serving. Garnish with whipped topping if desired. **Yield:** 12-15 servings.

Here's a creamy dessert that is simply luscious. My husband loves it. I'm proud to serve it to company because it always draws raves. For convenience on busy summer days, I can make it ahead of time, then top with additional berries and chocolate curls just before serving.

~Jean Smalls
WEST BOOTHBAY HARBOR, MAINE

Two-Tone Cheesecake Pies

(Also pictured on page 116)

    1 cup fresh raspberries
  1/2 teaspoon sugar
    3 packages (8 ounces *each*) cream cheese, softened
    1 can (14 ounces) sweetened condensed milk
    1 teaspoon vanilla extract
    4 eggs, lightly beaten
    1 cup (6 ounces) semisweet chocolate chips, melted and cooled
    2 graham cracker crusts (9 inches)
Chocolate curls and additional raspberries, optional

In a small bowl, combine raspberries and sugar; set aside. In a mixing bowl, beat cream cheese until light and fluffy. Gradually beat in milk and vanilla; mix well. Add eggs; beat on low speed just until combined.

Divide cream cheese mixture in half. Add melted chocolate to one portion; beat on low just until blended. Pour half of the chocolate mixture into each crust. Stir reserved raspberry mixture into remaining cream cheese mixture; spoon over chocolate layer.

Bake at 350° for 25-30 minutes or until center is almost set. Cool on wire racks for 1 hour. Chill for 4 hours or overnight. Garnish with chocolate curls and raspberries if desired. **Yield:** 2 pies (6-8 servings each).

Good any time of year, cupcakes make a great get-up-and-go treat on busy summer days.
~Ellen Moore
SPRINGFIELD, NEW HAMPSHIRE

Buttermilk Chocolate Cupcakes

(Also pictured on page 117)

1/2 cup butter, softened
1-1/2 cups sugar
2 eggs
1 teaspoon vanilla extract
1-1/2 cups all-purpose flour
1/2 cup baking cocoa
1 teaspoon baking soda
1/4 teaspoon salt
1/2 cup buttermilk
1/2 cup water

FROSTING:
1/2 cup butter, softened
3-3/4 cups confectioners' sugar
2 squares (1 ounce *each*) unsweetened chocolate, melted
2 tablespoons evaporated milk
1 teaspoon vanilla extract
1/4 teaspoon salt
Chocolate sprinkles

In a mixing bowl, cream butter and sugar. Add eggs, one at a time, beating well after each addition. Beat in vanilla. Combine the flour, cocoa, baking soda and salt. Combine buttermilk and water. Add dry ingredients to creamed mixture alternately with buttermilk mixture.

Fill paper-lined muffin cups two-thirds full. Bake at 375° for 15-20 minutes or until a toothpick comes out clean. Cool for 10 minutes before removing from pans to wire racks to cool completely.

For frosting, in a small mixing bowl, beat butter and confectioners' sugar. Beat in melted chocolate, milk, vanilla and salt. Frost cupcakes; garnish with chocolate sprinkles. **Yield:** 2 dozen.

This refreshing ice cream cake roll is drizzled with a mouth-watering homemade chocolate sauce.
~Sonja Wilhau
GRUNDY CENTER, IOWA

Mint-Chip Ice Cream Roll

(Pictured on page 117)

3/4 cup all-purpose flour
1/4 cup baking cocoa
1/4 teaspoon salt
5 eggs, *separated*
1 cup sugar
1 tablespoon lemon juice
1 tablespoon confectioners' sugar
1-1/2 quarts mint chocolate chip ice cream, softened

CHOCOLATE SAUCE:
1 cup sugar
2 tablespoons baking cocoa
1/4 cup butter, cubed
2 tablespoons water
1 can (5 ounces) evaporated milk

Line a greased 15-in. x 10-in. x 1-in. baking pan with waxed paper; grease the paper and set aside. Sift together the flour, cocoa and salt; set aside. In a mixing bowl, beat the egg whites on medium speed until soft peaks form. Gradually beat in sugar, 2 tablespoons at a time, on high until stiff glossy peaks form.

In another bowl, beat egg yolks and lemon juice until thick and lemon-colored. Fold in egg whites. Fold in reserved dry ingredients just until blended. Spread batter evenly in prepared pan. Bake at 350° for 12-15 minutes or until cake springs back when lightly touched in center.

Cool for 5 minutes. Invert cake onto a kitchen towel dusted with confectioners' sugar. Gently peel off waxed paper. Roll up cake in the towel jelly-roll style, starting with a long side. Cool completely on a wire rack.

Unroll the cake; spread ice cream to within 1/2 in. of edges. Roll up again. Cover and freeze for at least 3 hours before serving.

In a saucepan over medium heat, bring the sugar, cocoa and butter to a boil. Add water; return to a boil. Stir in milk; boil 3 minutes longer. Cool to room temperature. Serve with ice cream roll. **Yield:** 15 servings.

Clockwise from top left: Two-Tone Cheesecake Pies (p. 114), Buttermilk Chocolate Cupcakes (p. 115), Mint-Chip Ice Cream Roll (p. 115) and Chocolate Chip Date Cake (p. 118).

Cakes, Pies & Desserts 117

I remember begging my mother to make this moist cake back in the '50s. Instead of sticky frosting, it's covered with a mixture of chocolate chips, sugar and nuts and is a wonderful treat to take along on picnics.

~Kathy Frees
FERGUS FALLS, MINNESOTA

Chocolate Chip Date Cake

(Pictured on page 116)

> 1 cup chopped dates
> 1-1/2 teaspoons baking soda, *divided*
> 1-1/2 cups boiling water
> 3/4 cup shortening
> 1-1/2 cups sugar, *divided*
> 1 egg
> 2 cups all-purpose flour
> 1/2 teaspoon salt
> 2 cups (**12** ounces) semisweet chocolate chips
> 1/2 cup chopped pecans

Place dates and 1 teaspoon baking soda in a bowl. Stir in boiling water; cool completely. In a mixing bowl, cream shortening and 1 cup sugar. Beat in egg. Combine the flour, salt and remaining baking soda; add to creamed mixture alternately with date mixture.

Pour into a greased 13-in. x 9-in. x 2-in. baking pan. Sprinkle with remaining sugar; top with chocolate chips and nuts. Bake at 350° for 30-35 minutes or until a toothpick inserted near the center comes out clean. Cool on a wire rack. **Yield:** 16-20 servings.

This is my favorite blueberry recipe, which I often make for family get-togethers.

~Cathy Medley
CLYDE, OHIO

Blueberry Swirl Cheesecake

> 1-1/2 cups fresh blueberries
> 1/4 cup sugar
> 1 tablespoon lemon juice
> 2 teaspoons cornstarch
> 1 tablespoon cold water

CRUST:
> 1 cup graham cracker crumbs (about **16** squares)
> 2 tablespoons sugar
> 2 tablespoons butter, melted

FILLING:
> 3 packages (**8** ounces *each*) cream cheese, softened
> 1 cup (**8** ounces) sour cream
> 2 teaspoons vanilla extract
> 1 cup sugar
> 2 tablespoons all-purpose flour
> 4 eggs, beaten

In a small saucepan, combine the blueberries, sugar and lemon juice. Cook and stir over medium heat for 5 minutes or until the berries are softened.

Combine cornstarch and water until smooth; stir into the blueberry mixture. Bring to a boil; cook and stir for 2 minutes or until thickened. Remove from the heat; cool to room temperature. Transfer to a blender; cover and process until smooth. Set aside. For crust, combine the crumbs and sugar in a small bowl; stir in the butter. Press onto the bottom of a greased 9-in. springform pan. Place pan on a baking sheet. Bake at 350° for 10 minutes. Cool on a wire rack.

In a large mixing bowl, beat cream cheese until smooth. Add sour cream and vanilla; mix well. Combine the sugar and flour; add to the creamed mixture, beating until smooth. Add eggs; beat on low speed just until combined. Pour into crust. Drizzle with blueberry mixture; cut through batter with a knife to swirl. Place pan on baking sheet.

Bake at 350° for 1 hour or until center is almost set. Cool on a wire rack for 10 minutes. Carefully run a knife around the edge of pan to loosen; cool 1 hour longer. Refrigerate overnight. Remove sides of the pan. Refrigerate leftovers. **Yield:** 12 servings.

This recipe is an old family favorite. My mother made it for us all the time, and now, I make it for my family. It tastes like a piece of sunshine.

~Danella McCall
PARADISE, CALIFORNIA

Sunshine Coconut Pineapple Cake

2 cups all-purpose flour
1-1/2 cups packed brown sugar
2 teaspoons baking soda
1 teaspoon salt
2 cups grated carrots
1 cup flaked coconut
1 cup chopped pecans
3/4 cup vegetable oil
2 tablespoons lemon juice
1 teaspoon vanilla extract
1 can (20 ounces) crushed pineapple

FROSTING:
1 package (8 ounces) cream cheese, softened
3 tablespoons confectioners' sugar
1 carton (12 ounces) frozen whipped topping, thawed
Flaked coconut, optional

In a large bowl, combine the first seven ingredients. Combine the oil, lemon juice and vanilla. Drain pineapple, reserving juice. If necessary, add enough water to juice to measure 3/4 cup. Add oil mixture and pineapple juice mixture to dry ingredients; stir just until moistened. Fold in pineapple.

Place in a greased 13-in. x 9-in. x 2-in. baking dish. Bake at 350° for 40-45 minutes or until toothpick inserted near the center comes out clean. Cool on a wire rack.

For the frosting, in a large mixing bowl, beat cream cheese and sugar until smooth. Fold in whipped topping. Spread over cake; sprinkle with coconut if desired. Store in the refrigerator. **Yield:** 12-16 servings.

The corn bread topping gives this old-fashioned fruit cobbler a brand-new taste. You can use most any combination of fruits to make it. A scoop of ice cream or a little whipped topping makes it extra special.

~Mary Kathryn Pitts
AMBIA, INDIANA

Mixed Fruit Cobbler

4 medium ripe apricots, peeled and sliced
2 large ripe nectarines, peeled and sliced
2 large ripe peaches, peeled and sliced
2/3 cup sugar, *divided*
2 tablespoons cornstarch
1 tablespoon cold butter, cut into small pieces
1 cup all-purpose flour
1/2 cup cornmeal
2 teaspoons baking powder
1/4 teaspoon ground cinnamon
1/8 teaspoon salt
1/2 cup milk
1/4 cup vegetable oil

In a bowl, combine the fruit, 1/3 cup sugar and cornstarch. Spoon into a greased 8-in. square baking dish. Dot with butter. In another bowl, combine the flour, cornmeal, baking powder, cinnamon, salt and remaining sugar. Stir in milk and oil just until moistened. Spread over fruit mixture. Bake at 375° for 35-40 minutes or until bubbly and top is golden brown. **Yield:** 9 servings.

By modifying a standard pudding recipe, I came up with this smooth and creamy indulgence.
~Ramona Hill
TWINING, MICHIGAN

Cinnamon Mocha Parfaits

1/3 cup sugar

3 tablespoons baking cocoa

2 tablespoons cornstarch

2 teaspoons instant coffee granules

Dash salt

Dash ground cinnamon

1-1/3 cups milk

1 tablespoon butter

1/2 teaspoon vanilla extract

1-1/4 cups whipped topping, *divided*

Chocolate curls

In a saucepan, combine first six ingredients; gradually stir in milk until smooth. Bring to a boil over medium-high heat; cook and stir for 2 minutes or until thickened. Remove from heat; stir in butter and vanilla.

Spoon 3 tablespoons into each of four parfait glasses. Pour the remaining pudding into a bowl; cover and refrigerate for 20 minutes. Fold in 1 cup whipped topping. Spoon into parfait glasses. Garnish with remaining whipped topping; top with chocolate curls. **Yield:** 4 servings.

My grandpa gave me many of my grandmother's and great-grandmother's recipes, including this one, along with many wonderful stories about them.
~Kate Murphy
UNION BAY, BRITISH COLUMBIA

Frozen Strawberry Dessert

1 cup all-purpose flour

1/4 cup packed brown sugar

1/2 cup butter, melted

1/2 cup chopped walnuts

2 egg whites

2/3 cup sugar, *divided*

2 teaspoons water

1/8 teaspoon cream of tartar

1 package (10 ounces) frozen sweetened sliced strawberries, thawed

2 tablespoons lemon juice

1 cup heavy whipping cream

Combine first four ingredients; mix well. Place in a 15-in. x 10-in. x 1-in. baking pan. Bake at 350° for 18-20 minutes, stirring occasionally, until golden brown; cool on a wire rack. Remove 1/3 cup for topping; sprinkle the remaining nut mixture into a lightly greased 13-in. x 9-in. x 2-in. dish.

In a saucepan, combine the egg whites, 1 tablespoon sugar, water and cream of tartar over low heat. With a portable mixer, beat on low speed for 1 minute. Continue beating on low speed until mixture reaches 160°. Pour into a large mixing bowl. Add strawberries, lemon juice and remaining sugar; beat on high for 8 minutes or until light and fluffy.

In another mixing bowl, beat cream until stiff peaks form. Fold into strawberry mixture. Transfer to the prepared dish; sprinkle with the reserved nut mixture. Cover and freeze for 6 hours or overnight. **Yield:** 8-10 servings.

The recipe for this flavorful cake has been handed down in my husband's family for four generations.
~Pauline Woodyard
HUMBLE, TEXAS

Moist Applesauce Fruitcake

- 1 cup chopped mixed candied fruit
- 1 cup finely chopped pecans
- 1 cup finely chopped walnuts
- 1 cup raisins
- 1/2 cup chopped dried apricots
- 1/2 cup chopped dried apples
- 2-1/2 cups all-purpose flour, *divided*
- 1 cup butter, softened
- 2 cups sugar
- 2 eggs
- 2 cups applesauce
- 2 teaspoons vanilla *or* rum extract
- 2 teaspoons baking soda
- 2 teaspoons ground cinnamon
- 1 teaspoon salt
- 1 teaspoon ground nutmeg
- 1 teaspoon ground cloves
- 1 teaspoon ground allspice

In a bowl, combine the first six ingredients; add 1 cup flour. Stir to coat. In a mixing bowl, cream butter and sugar; add eggs and mix well. Add the applesauce and vanilla extract. Combine the baking soda, cinnamon, salt, nutmeg, cloves, allspice and remaining flour; stir into applesauce mixture. Pour into a greased and floured 10-in. tube pan.

Bake at 325° for 60-65 minutes or until a toothpick inserted near the center comes out clean. Cool for 10 minutes before removing from pan to a wire rack to cool completely. **Yield:** 12-16 servings.

The wild blueberries on our property spark recipe ideas. Our 10 children, 19 grandkids and four great-grandchildren think this ice cream tastes great.
~Alma Mosher
MOHANNES, NEW BRUNSWICK

Blueberry Ice Cream

- 4 cups fresh *or* frozen blueberries
- 2 cups sugar
- 2 tablespoons water
- 4 cups half-and-half cream

In a large saucepan, combine blueberries, sugar and water. Bring to a boil. Reduce heat; simmer, uncovered, until sugar is dissolved and berries are softened. Strain mixture; discard seeds and skins. Stir in cream. Cover and refrigerate overnight.

Fill cylinder of ice cream freezer two-thirds full; freeze according to manufacturer's directions. Refrigerate remaining mixture until ready to freeze. Allow to ripen in ice cream freezer or firm up in the refrigerator freezer for 2-4 hours before serving. **Yield:** about 1-3/4 quarts.

~Vera Schreiner
AKRON, PENNSYLVANIA

Chocolate Oatmeal Cake

1 cup old-fashioned oats
1-1/2 cups boiling water
1/2 cup butter, softened
1-1/2 cups sugar
2 eggs
1-1/2 cups all-purpose flour
1/2 cup baking cocoa
1-1/2 teaspoons baking soda
1/2 teaspoon salt

TOPPING:
2/3 cup packed brown sugar
1/2 cup plus 1 tablespoon butter, melted
1-1/2 cups flaked coconut
3/4 cup chopped walnuts

6 tablespoons half-and-half cream
1-1/2 teaspoons vanilla extract

In a bowl, combine the oats and boiling water. Let stand for 15 minutes or until cooled. In a large mixing bowl, cream butter and sugar. Add eggs, one at a time, beating well after each addition. Add the oat mixture; mix well. Combine the flour, cocoa, baking soda and salt; add to creamed mixture.

Transfer to a greased 13-in. x 9-in. x 2-in. baking pan. Bake at 350° for 30-35 minutes or until a toothpick inserted near the center comes out clean. Combine the topping ingredients; spoon over top of warm cake; broil about 4 in. from heat for 3-4 minutes, or until top is lightly browned. **Yield:** 12-15 servings.

My mother-in-law makes this delicious dessert whenever our family gets together. It's especially good when prepared with a chocolate graham cracker crust. ~Michelle Gillum
SPRINGBORO, OHIO

Peanut Butter Cream Pie

3/4 cup plus 2 tablespoons
confectioners' sugar, *divided*
1/3 cup peanut butter
1 pastry shell (9 inches), baked
1 cup sugar
1/3 cup all-purpose flour
Dash salt
2 cups milk
2 eggs, lightly beaten
1 tablespoon butter
1 teaspoon vanilla extract
1-1/4 cups heavy whipping cream

Place 3/4 cup confectioners' sugar in a bowl. Cut in peanut butter until mixture resembles fine crumbs; set aside 3 tablespoons for garnish. Sprinkle the remaining mixture into the pastry shell; set aside.

In a saucepan, combine the sugar, flour and salt; gradually stir in the milk. Bring to a boil over medium heat; cook and stir for 2 minutes or until thickened. Remove from the heat. Stir a small amount into the eggs; return all to the pan. Bring to a gentle boil; cook and stir for 2 minutes.

Remove from heat; add butter and vanilla, stirring constantly. Pour into crust. Cool slightly; refrigerate 1-2 hours.

Meanwhile, in a mixing bowl, beat the cream until it begins to thicken. Add the remaining confectioners' sugar, 1 tablespoon at a time, beating until stiff peaks form. Spread over filling; sprinkle with reserved crumb mixture. Store in the refrigerator. **Yield:** 6-8 servings.

Mom and I have fun making this pie together, and I hope one day to be a great baker like she is.
~Sara West
BROKEN ARROW, OKLAHOMA

Blueberry Pie with Lemon Crust

2 cups all-purpose flour
1 teaspoon salt
1/2 teaspoon grated lemon peel
2/3 cup shortening
1 tablespoon lemon juice
4 to 6 tablespoons cold water

FILLING:
4 cups fresh blueberries
3/4 cup sugar
3 tablespoons all-purpose flour
1/2 teaspoon grated lemon peel
Dash salt
1 to 2 teaspoons lemon juice
1 tablespoon butter

In a bowl, combine the flour, salt and lemon peel. Cut in shortening until crumbly. Add lemon juice. Gradually add water, tossing with a fork until a ball forms. Cover and refrigerate for 1 hour. Divide dough in half. On a lightly floured surface, roll out one portion to fit a 9-in. pie plate. Transfer pastry to pie plate; trim to 1 in. beyond edge of plate.

In a large bowl, combine the blueberries, sugar, flour, lemon peel and salt; spoon into crust. Drizzle with lemon juice; dot with butter. Roll out remaining pastry; place over filling. Seal and flute edges. Cut slits in top crust. Bake at 400° for 40-45 minutes or until crust is golden and filling is bubbly. Cool on a wire rack. Store in refrigerator. **Yield:** 6-8 servings.

I served this bread pudding at the first Christmas dinner I made for my in-laws. Everyone loved it!
~Jennifer Dignin
MOSINEE, WISCONSIN

Christmas Bread Pudding

8 cups day-old bread cubes, crust removed
2 medium tart apples, peeled and chopped
1/2 cup dried cranberries *or* raisins
6 egg yolks
3 eggs
1 cup heavy whipping cream
1/2 cup milk
1 cup sugar

CREAM SAUCE:
1 cup heavy whipping cream
3 tablespoons sugar
1 to 2 teaspoons vanilla *or* rum extract
Dash ground cinnamon and nutmeg

In a bowl, combine bread cubes, apples and cranberries. Transfer to a greased 11-in. x 7-in. x 2-in. baking dish. In a bowl, combine egg yolks, eggs, cream, milk and sugar. Pour over bread mixture.

Place dish in a larger baking dish. Fill larger dish with boiling water halfway up the sides. Bake at 350° for 50-55 minutes or until a knife inserted near the center comes out clean. Remove from water bath. Cool 15 minutes.

For the cream sauce, in a saucepan, combine cream and sugar. Cook and stir until sugar is dissolved. Remove from the heat. Stir in the vanilla, cinnamon and nutmeg. Serve warm with pudding. **Yield:** 6-8 servings.

Everyone will be purring with delight when they see—and taste—this cat cake. Our Test Kitchen home economists used a store-bought cake mix for the body and head and purchased sponge cakes for the ears, paws and tail. Then they whipped up fluffy frosting to serve as "fur" and fashioned features from candy.

~Taste of Home Test Kitchen

Cat Cake

- 1 package (18-1/4 ounces) yellow cake mix
- 1 package (8 ounces) cream cheese, softened
- 1 jar (7 ounces) marshmallow creme
- 1/8 teaspoon almond extract
- 1 carton (8 ounces) frozen whipped topping, thawed
- 2 squares (1 ounce *each*) semisweet chocolate, melted and cooled
- 4 individual cream-filled sponge cakes
- 3 brown M&M's
- 2 pieces shoestring licorice, about 2 inches long
- 1 large pink candy heart

Prepare cake batter according to package directions. Grease and flour 3-cup and 2-qt. ovenproof bowls. Pour 1 cup of batter into the 3-cup bowl and remaining batter into the 2-qt. bowl.

Bake small cake at 350° for 30-35 minutes and large cake for 40-45 minutes or until a toothpick inserted near the center comes out clean. Cool each cake for 10 minutes before removing from bowl to wire rack to cool completely.

For frosting, in a mixing bowl, beat cream cheese until smooth. Add marshmallow creme and almond extract; mix well. Beat in whipped topping. Set aside 1/2 cup. Beat remaining the whipped topping mixture into the melted chocolate.

Place cakes domed side up on an 18-in. x 12-in. covered board. Cut one cream-filled sponge cake in half widthwise; place halves in front of large cake for front paws. Cut ends off another sponge cake; trim ends to form triangles. Set triangles aside for ears.

Arrange the remaining sponge cakes behind large cake to form the tail. Frost cat's face and ears with reserved white frosting. Frost rest of cat with chocolate frosting. Place the ears on head. Arrange M&M's, licorice and candy heart to form the face. **Yield:** 12-16 servings.

This dessert is easy to decorate for the holidays, and it's perfect for family reunions.

~Viorene Larson
SIOUX FALLS, SOUTH DAKOTA

Cherry Angel Dessert

☑ **Uses less fat, sugar or salt. Includes Nutrition Facts and Diabetic Exchanges.**

- 1 prepared angel food cake (16 ounces), cubed
- 1 can (20 ounces) reduced-sugar cherry pie filling
- 1-1/3 cups cold fat-free milk
- 1 package (1 ounce) sugar-free instant vanilla pudding mix
- 1/2 cup reduced-fat sour cream
- 1 carton (8 ounces) frozen reduced-fat whipped topping, thawed

Line the bottom of an ungreased 13-in. x 9-in. x 2-in. baking dish with cake cubes. Cover with pie filling. In a bowl, whisk milk and pudding mix for 2 minutes. Let stand for 2 minutes or until soft-set. Stir in sour cream. Carefully spread over pie filling; top with whipped topping. Cover and refrigerate for at least 24 hours before serving. Refrigerate leftovers. **Yield:** 15 servings.

Nutrition Facts: One serving equals 155 calories, 3 g fat (2 g saturated fat), 3 mg cholesterol, 233 mg sodium, 30 g carbohydrate, trace fiber, 3 g protein. **Diabetic Exchange:** 2 starch.

The peanut butter flavor comes through nicely in this pie, and it has a creamy consistency. My whole family loves it.

~Mary Ellen Friend
RAVENSWOOD, WEST VIRGINIA

Peanut Butter Praline Pie

1-1/2 cups vanilla wafer crumbs
   (about 40 wafers)
  6 tablespoons baking cocoa
1/3 cup confectioners' sugar
1/4 cup butter, melted

PRALINE LAYER:
1/4 cup packed brown sugar
  2 tablespoons sugar
  1 tablespoon cornstarch
1/3 cup butter, cubed
  2 tablespoons water
1/2 cup chopped pecans

FILLING:
  1 package (3 ounces) cook-and-
   serve vanilla pudding mix
  2 cups milk
  1 package (10 *or* 11 ounces)
   peanut butter chips
  1 cup whipped topping
Pecan halves and additional whipped
  topping

In a bowl, combine crumbs, cocoa and confectioners' sugar; stir in butter. Press into a 9-in. pie plate. Bake at 350° for 10 minutes. Cool on a wire rack.

In a saucepan, combine the sugars and cornstarch. Add butter and water. Bring to a boil over medium heat; cook and stir for 1 minute. Stir in pecans. Pour into crust; refrigerate.

Meanwhile, in a saucepan, combine pudding mix and milk until smooth. Cook and stir over medium heat until mixture comes to a boil. Remove from the heat. Stir in peanut butter chips until smooth. Cover and refrigerate for 1 hour.

Fold in whipped topping; spoon over praline layer. Refrigerate until set. Garnish with pecans and additional whipped topping. **Yield:** 6-8 servings.

This plum cobbler is pleasing to the eye and the taste buds.

~Mary Lou Thomason
MERLIN, OREGON

Deep-Dish Plum Cobbler

2-1/2 pounds plums, pitted and sliced
1-1/2 cups sugar
  1/4 cup quick-cooking tapioca
  1/4 teaspoon almond extract
  1/8 teaspoon salt
   2 tablespoons cold butter
Pastry for a single-crust pie (9 inches)
   1 egg white

Place plums in a large bowl. In another bowl, combine the sugar, tapioca, al-mond extract and salt. Cut in butter un-til crumbly; gently stir into plums. Let stand for 15 minutes.

Transfer to a greased 2-1/2-qt. bak-ing dish. Roll out pastry to 1/8-in. thickness; make a lattice crust. Place over filling. Trim edges. Beat egg white until foamy; brush over pastry. Bake at 425° for 40-45 minutes or until golden brown. **Yield:** 10-12 servings.

Bursting with Bountiful *Meringue*

Can you think of a sweeter way to use up leftover egg white? Still, some might avoid it, thinking the stuff is too much of a fuss to make.

Nothing could be farther from the truth! Whipping up meringue is simple, and the results are deliciously elegant. To ensure success, you'll want to use room-temperature egg whites and a clean glass or metal bowl. The rest is easy!

To prove it, we've gathered tried-and-true recipes for you. Not only will you be impressed at how effortless they are; you'll see how versatile meringue is as well.

Don't look for the meringue on top of this deep-dish chocolate pie—it's on the bottom!

~Florence Oblander
HILLSBORO, KANSAS

Chocolate Mocha Meringue Pie

(Pictured above)

> **3 egg whites**
> **1/4 teaspoon cream of tartar**
> **1/8 teaspoon salt**
> **3/4 cup sugar**

FILLING:
> **1 tablespoon unflavored gelatin**
> **1 cup cold water**
> **1 cup sugar**
> **3 tablespoons baking cocoa**
> **1 teaspoon instant coffee granules**
> **1/8 teaspoon salt**
> **1 cup milk**
> **1 cup heavy whipping cream, whipped**

Chocolate curls

Place egg whites in a mixing bowl; let stand at room temperature for 30 minutes. Add cream of tartar and salt; beat on medium speed until soft peaks form. Gradually beat in sugar, 1 tablespoon at a time, on high until stiff glossy peaks form and sugar is dissolved.

Spread onto the bottom and up the sides of a greased 9-in. deep-dish pie plate. Bake at 350° for 25-30 minutes or until meringue is lightly browned. Cool on a wire rack.

In a small bowl, sprinkle gelatin over water and let stand for 1 minute. In a saucepan, combine the sugar, cocoa, coffee granules, salt and milk until smooth. Bring to a boil, stirring constantly. Remove from the heat; stir in gelatin until dissolved.

Cool to room temperature; fold in the whipped cream. Pour into meringue shell. Refrigerate for 4 hours or until set. Garnish with chocolate curls. Refrigerate leftovers. **Yield:** 6-8 servings.

These yummy cupcakes are moist and tender and capped with swirls of golden brown meringue. I found the recipe in an old cookbook I picked up at an auction. My dad pronounced it a winner the first time I made it.
~Pam Good
WASHINGTON ISLAND, WISCONSIN

Meringue-Topped Spice Cupcakes

    2 eggs, *separated*
    1/2 cup butter, softened
      1 cup packed brown sugar
    2/3 cup milk
    1/2 teaspoon vanilla extract
1-1/2 cups cake flour
1-1/4 teaspoons pumpkin pie spice
    1/2 teaspoon baking soda
    1/4 teaspoon cream of tartar
    1/4 cup sugar
    1/4 cup ground pecans

Place egg whites in a mixing bowl; let stand at room temperature for 30 minutes. Meanwhile, in another mixing bowl, cream butter and brown sugar. Add the egg yolks, milk and vanilla; mix well.

Combine the flour, pumpkin pie spice and baking soda; add to the creamed mixture until combined. Fill paper-lined muffin cups half full. Bake at 350° for 20 minutes.

Add cream of tartar to egg whites; beat on medium speed until soft peaks form. Gradually beat in sugar, 1 tablespoon at a time, on high until stiff peaks form and sugar is dissolved. Fold in nuts. Spread about 2 tablespoons over each cupcake.

Bake 11-12 minutes longer or until golden brown and a toothpick inserted into cupcake comes out clean. Cool for 10 minutes before removing from pan to a wire rack to cool completely. **Yield:** 1 dozen.

I like to celebrate with something special from my oven, like this pretty dessert which has red strawberries cupped in fluffy white meringue!
~Judy Grimes
BRANDON, MISSISSIPPI

Strawberry Meringue Cups

      2 egg whites
    1/4 teaspoon cream of tartar
Dash salt
    1/2 cup sugar
      1 cup heavy whipping cream
      6 tablespoons confectioners' sugar
      1 pint fresh strawberries, sliced

Place egg whites in a mixing bowl; let stand at room temperature for 30 minutes. Add cream of tartar and salt; beat on medium speed until soft peaks form. Gradually beat in sugar, 1 tablespoon at a time, on high until stiff peaks form and sugar is dissolved.

Drop into four mounds on a parchment-lined baking sheet. Shape into 4-in. cups with the back of a spoon. Bake at 225° for 1-1/2 hours or until set and dry. Turn oven off; leave meringues in oven for 1-1/2 hours. Store in an airtight container.

In a small mixing bowl, beat cream until it begins to thicken. Add confectioners' sugar; beat until stiff peaks form. Just before serving, spoon into meringue shells. Top with strawberries. **Yield:** 4 servings.

This quick, make-ahead dessert looks high and impressive on a serving platter.

~Violet Davis
CROSSVILLE, ALABAMA

Blueberry Angel Torte

- 1 package (8 ounces) cream cheese, softened
- 1 cup sugar
- 1 cup confectioners' sugar
- 1 carton (16 ounces) frozen whipped topping, thawed
- 1 prepared angel food cake (16 ounces and 8 inches in diameter)
- 1 can (21 ounces) blueberry pie filling

In a large mixing bowl, beat the cream cheese and sugars until smooth; fold in whipped topping. Split cake into four horizontal layers. Place bottom layer on a serving plate; top with a fourth of the whipped topping mixture and a fourth of the pie filling. Repeat layers three times. Refrigerate until serving. **Yield:** 12-16 servings.

At our house, we celebrate George Washington's birthday with this cherry dessert.

~Verna Burkholder
DORCHESTER, WISCONSIN

Cherry Tarts

- 1-1/2 cups all-purpose flour
- 1/2 teaspoon salt
- 1/2 cup shortening
- 4 to 5 tablespoons cold water
- 3/4 cup sugar
- 3 tablespoons cornstarch
- 2 cans (14-1/2 ounces *each*) pitted tart cherries
- 1 tablespoon butter
- 1/4 teaspoon almond extract
- 4 to 5 drops red food coloring, optional

In a bowl, combine the flour and salt. Cut in shortening until mixture resembles coarse crumbs. Add enough water until dough forms a ball. Refrigerate for 30 minutes.

On a lightly floured surface, roll out dough to 1/8-in. thickness. Cut out eight 5-in. circles. Place each over an inverted custard cup on an ungreased 15-in. x 10-in. x 1-in. baking pan; flute edges. Bake at 450° for 10-11 minutes or until golden brown. Cool for 5 minutes before removing tart shells from custard cups; cool completely on wire racks.

For filling, in a saucepan, combine the sugar and cornstarch. Drain the cherries, reserving 1 cup juice. Set cherries aside. Stir reserved juice into the sugar mixture until smooth. Bring to a boil; cook and stir for 2 minutes or until thickened. Remove from the heat; stir in the cherries, butter, almond extract and food coloring if desired. Cool to room temperature. Spoon about 1/4 cup filling into each tart shell. **Yield:** 8 servings.

Butterscotch Lunchbox Cake

- 2 cups milk
- 1 package (3 ounces) cook-and-serve vanilla pudding mix
- 1 package (18-1/4 ounces) yellow cake mix
- 1 package (10 to 11 ounces) butterscotch chips
- 1/2 cup chopped pecans

In a large saucepan, combine milk and pudding mix. Bring to a boil over medium heat, stirring constantly. Remove from the heat; stir in cake mix (batter will be lumpy).

Pour into a greased 13-in. x 9-in. x 2-in. baking pan. Sprinkle with butterscotch chips and nuts. Bake at 350° for 30-35 minutes or until a toothpick inserted near the center comes out clean. Cool cake on a wire rack. **Yield:** 12-16 servings.

White Chocolate Banana Cake

- 1/2 cup shortening
- 2 cups sugar
- 2 eggs
- 1-1/2 cups mashed ripe bananas (about 3 medium)
- 3 teaspoons vanilla extract
- 3 cups all-purpose flour
- 1 teaspoon baking powder
- 1/2 teaspoon baking soda
- 1/2 teaspoon salt
- 1 cup buttermilk
- 4 squares (1 ounce *each*) white baking chocolate, melted and cooled

CREAM CHEESE FROSTING:
- 1 package (8 ounces) cream cheese, softened
- 3/4 cup butter, softened
- 1 teaspoon vanilla extract
- 5 cups confectioners' sugar
- 1/2 cup finely chopped pecans, toasted

In a large mixing bowl, cream shortening and sugar. Add eggs, one at a time, beating well after each addition. Beat in bananas and vanilla. Combine the flour, baking powder, baking soda and salt; add to creamed mixture alternately with buttermilk. Fold in chocolate.

Pour into three greased and floured 9-in. round baking pans. Bake at 350° for 25-30 minutes or until a toothpick inserted near the center comes out clean. Cool for 10 minutes before removing cake from pans to wire racks to cool completely.

For frosting, in a large mixing bowl, beat cream cheese, butter and vanilla until smooth. Beat in confectioners' sugar. Spread between layers and over top and sides of cake. Sprinkle with pecans. Store in refrigerator. **Yield:** 12-16 servings.

We serve this dessert at our house on special occasions. The topping on the cheesecake tastes like turtle candy.

~Amy Masson
CYPRESS, CALIFORNIA

Chocolate-Caramel Topped Cheesecake

1-1/3 cups shortbread cookie crumbs
1/4 cup butter, melted

FILLING:
3 packages (8 ounces *each*) cream cheese, softened
3/4 cup sugar
1/4 cup packed brown sugar
1 tablespoon vanilla extract
1/4 cup milk
2 tablespoons all-purpose flour
2 eggs
1 egg yolk

TOPPING:
1/2 cup semisweet chocolate chips
1-1/2 teaspoons shortening
1/2 cup coarsely chopped pecans, toasted
2 tablespoons caramel ice cream topping

In a bowl, combine the cookie crumbs and butter. Press onto the bottom of a greased 9-in. springform pan; set aside. In a large mixing bowl, beat cream cheese, sugars and vanilla until smooth. Beat in milk and flour. Add eggs and egg yolk, beating on low speed just until combined. Pour into crust. Place on a baking sheet.

Bake at 325° for 45-50 minutes or until center is almost set. Cool on wire rack for 10 minutes. Carefully run a knife around edge of pan to loosen; cool 1 hour longer. Cover and refrigerate for at least 6 hours or overnight.

Remove side of pan. In a microwave, melt chocolate chips and shortening; stir until smooth. Top the cheesecake with pecans; drizzle with chocolate mixture and caramel topping. Refrigerate leftovers. **Yield:** 12-14 servings.

Everyone who tries this declares it a hit! I also like to use strawberries or blackberries in place of the raspberries.

~Roberta Miller
DEMING, WASHINGTON

Frozen Raspberry Cream Squares

☑ Uses less fat, sugar or salt. Includes Nutrition Facts and Diabetic Exchanges.

2 cups finely crushed reduced-fat vanilla wafers (about 65 wafers)
1/4 cup butter, melted
2 cups frozen unsweetened raspberries
3/4 cup reduced-fat sour cream
1/2 cup sugar
1 cup fat-free half-and-half cream

In a bowl, combine the wafer crumbs and butter. Press half of the crumb mixture into the bottom of an 8-in. square baking dish coated with nonstick cooking spray.

Set remaining crumb mixture aside. Sprinkle berries over crust.

In a bowl, combine sour cream and sugar; gradually stir in half-and-half until smooth. Pour over berries. Sprinkle with remaining crumb mixture. Cover and freeze for 3 hours or until firm. Let stand at room temperature for 15-20 minutes before cutting. **Yield:** 9 servings.

Nutrition Facts: One piece equals 237 calories, 9 g fat (5 g saturated fat), 24 mg cholesterol, 171 mg sodium, 34 g carbohydrate, 1 g fiber, 3 g protein. **Diabetic Exchanges:** 1-1/2 starch, 1 fruit, 1 fat.

I earned a merit badge by dreaming up these cupcakes for a Cub Scouts meeting. You should have seen the grins when the kids bit into the chocolate kisses in the middle. My husband and grandkids say I don't make them often enough. ~Carol Hillebrenner
FOWLER, ILLINOIS

Secret Kiss Cupcakes

3-1/3 cups all-purpose flour
2 cups sugar
1 cup baking cocoa
2 teaspoons baking soda
1 teaspoon salt
2 cups buttermilk
1 cup butter, melted
2 eggs, lightly beaten
2 teaspoons vanilla extract
30 milk chocolate kisses
1 can (16 ounces) fudge frosting

In a bowl, combine the flour, sugar, cocoa, baking soda and salt; mix well. Combine the buttermilk, butter, eggs and vanilla. Add to the dry ingredients; mix well.

Fill paper-lined muffin cups two-thirds full. Press a chocolate kiss into the center of each cupcake until batter completely covers candy.

Bake at 375° for 20-25 minutes or until a toothpick inserted into the cake comes out clean. Cool for 10 minutes before removing from pans to wire racks to cool completely. Frost cupcakes. **Yield:** about 2-1/2 dozen.

Family gatherings wouldn't be the same without this wonderful pie my daughter-in-law first served years ago. ~Marion Krysiek
MILWAUKEE, WISCONSIN

Cranberry Nut Pie

Pastry for single-crust pie (9 inches)
1 package (12 ounces) fresh cranberries, halved
1/2 cup packed brown sugar
1/2 cup chopped walnuts
3 tablespoons butter, melted

TOPPING:
3/4 cup sugar
2 eggs
1/2 cup butter, melted
3/4 cup all-purpose flour
Whipped cream, optional

Line a 9-in. pie plate with pastry; trim and flute edges. Sprinkle cranberries into crust. Combine the brown sugar, walnuts and butter; sprinkle over the cranberries.

For topping, combine sugar, eggs and butter in a bowl. Gradually add flour. Pour over nut mixture. Bake at 350° for 40-45 minutes or until filling is bubbly and topping is golden brown. Cool on a wire rack. Garnish with whipped cream if desired. **Yield:** 6-8 servings.

This is a wonderful "jazzed-up" box cake. It's an easy way to make a rich cake for a special occasion without having to bake it from scratch.
~Miller Ferrie
HEBRON, NORTH DAKOTA

Candied Orange Chocolate Cake

(Also pictured on page 134)

1/3 cup sliced almonds
1 package (18-1/4 ounces) devil's food cake mix
1 package (3.9 ounces) instant chocolate pudding mix
3 eggs
1-1/4 cups milk
1/2 cup vegetable oil
1 teaspoon orange extract
1 cup chopped orange candy slices

ORANGE GLAZE:
3/4 cup confectioners' sugar
2 tablespoons butter
2 tablespoons orange juice

Sprinkle almonds into a greased 10-in. fluted tube pan; set aside. In a large mixing bowl, combine the cake mix, pudding mix, eggs, milk, oil and extract; beat on low speed for 30 seconds. Beat on medium for 2 minutes. Fold in orange slices.

Pour into prepared pan. Bake at 350° for 45-50 minutes or until a toothpick inserted near the center comes out clean. Cool for 10 minutes before removing the cake from pan to a wire rack to cool completely.

In a small saucepan, bring glaze ingredients to a boil. Boil for 1 minute, stirring frequently. Remove from the heat; cool for 5 minutes. Drizzle over cake. **Yield:** 12-16 servings.

Treat your whole family to this old-fashioned favorite. This dessert is suitable for Sunday dinner and everyday suppers, too.
~Liecha Collins
ONEONTA, NEW YORK

Blackberry Dumplings

1 quart fresh *or* frozen (loose-pack) blackberries
1 cup plus 1 tablespoon sugar, *divided*
3/4 teaspoon salt, *divided*
1/2 teaspoon lemon extract
1-1/2 cups all-purpose flour
2 teaspoons baking powder
1/4 teaspoon ground nutmeg
2/3 cup milk
Cream *or* whipped cream, optional

In a Dutch oven, combine the blackberries, 1 cup sugar, 1/4 teaspoon salt and extract; bring to a boil. Reduce heat and simmer for 5 minutes. Meanwhile, in a mixing bowl, combine flour, baking powder, nutmeg and remaining sugar and salt. Add milk; stir just until mixed (dough will be very thick).

Drop by tablespoonfuls into six mounds onto simmering blackberry mixture. Cover and simmer for 15 minutes or until a toothpick inserted into a dumpling comes out clean (do not lift cover while simmering). Spoon into serving dishes. Serve with cream or whipped cream if desired. **Yield:** 6-8 servings.

This fruity cake looks pretty on the plate and tastes like the kind Mom used to make. Try serving it warm from the oven with vanilla ice cream.
~Mary Wilhelm
SPARTA, WISCONSIN

🎗 Apricot Almond Upside-Down Cake

(Also pictured on page 135)

- 1 can (15-1/4 ounces) apricot halves in syrup
- 1/3 cup butter
- 1/2 cup packed brown sugar
- 1/2 cup slivered almonds
- 2 eggs
- 2/3 cup sugar
- 3/4 teaspoon almond extract
- 1 cup cake flour
- 1 teaspoon baking powder
- 1/4 teaspoon salt

Drain apricots, reserving 6 tablespoons syrup; set aside. In a small saucepan, melt butter over low heat; stir in brown sugar. Pour into a greased 9-in. square baking pan. Sprinkle with almonds. Arrange apricot halves cut side up in a single layer over almonds; set aside.

In a small mixing bowl, beat eggs on medium-high speed until lemon-colored. Gradually beat in sugar and reserved syrup. Stir in almond extract. Combine the flour, baking powder and salt; add to egg mixture, beating just until moistened. Spoon batter over apricots.

Bake at 350° for 35-40 minutes or until a toothpick inserted near the center comes out clean. Cool for 10 minutes before inverting onto a serving plate. **Yield:** 9 servings.

Rich, moist and cinnamony, this old-fashioned cake recipe was handed down from our beloved Grandma Kelly. It's a perfect way to use up a few carrots and an apple...and it's ideal for smaller families.
~Jackie Kohn
DULUTH, MINNESOTA

🎗 Grandma's Apple Carrot Cake

(Also pictured on page 135)

- 2 eggs
- 1/2 cup vegetable oil
- 1/2 cup sugar
- 1/2 cup packed brown sugar
- 1 cup all-purpose flour
- 2 teaspoons ground cinnamon
- 1/2 teaspoon baking powder
- 1/4 teaspoon baking soda
- 1/4 teaspoon salt
- 1-1/2 cups finely shredded carrots
- 1 cup finely shredded apple

CREAM CHEESE FROSTING:
- 1 package (3 ounces) cream cheese, softened
- 1 tablespoon butter, softened
- 1 teaspoon lemon juice
- 1/4 teaspoon vanilla extract
- 1-1/4 cups confectioners' sugar

In a large mixing bowl, beat the eggs, oil and sugars until smooth. Combine the flour, cinnamon, baking powder, baking soda and salt; add to egg mixture, beating until combined. Stir in carrots and apple.

Spoon into a greased 9-in. square baking pan. Bake at 350° for 25-30 minutes or until a toothpick inserted near the center comes out clean. Cool on a wire rack.

In a small mixing bowl, combine the frosting ingredients; beat until smooth. Spread over cake. Store in the refrigerator. **Yield:** 9 servings.

Clockwise from top left: Candied Orange Chocolate Cake (p. 132), Apricot Almond Upside-Down Cake (p. 133), Pumpkin Angel Cake (p. 136), Grandma's Apple Carrot Cake (p. 133) and Poppy Seed Bundt Cake (p. 136).

Since this moist cake keeps so well, you can make it the day before serving. It freezes beautifully, too, so you can pull it out for surprise guests. Flavored with almond extract and poppy seeds, it's great for taking to a picnic or potluck or to present as a hostess gift.

~Lois Schlickau
HAVEN, KANSAS

Poppy Seed Bundt Cake

(Pictured on page 134)

3 cups all-purpose flour
2-1/2 cups sugar
1-1/2 teaspoons baking powder
1/2 teaspoon salt
3 eggs
1-1/2 cups milk
1 cup vegetable oil
1 tablespoon poppy seeds
1-1/2 teaspoons almond extract
1-1/2 teaspoons vanilla extract
1 teaspoon butter flavoring

GLAZE:
3/4 cup confectioners' sugar
1/4 cup orange juice

1/2 teaspoon almond extract
1/2 teaspoon vanilla extract
1/2 teaspoon butter flavoring

In a large mixing bowl, combine the flour, sugar, baking powder and salt. Whisk eggs, milk, oil, poppy seeds, extracts and flavoring; add to dry ingredients. Beat on low speed for 30 seconds or just until moistened. Beat on medium for 2 minutes.

Pour into a greased and floured 10-in. fluted tube pan. Bake at 350° for 60-70 minutes or until a toothpick inserted near the center comes out clean. Cool for 10 minutes before removing from pan to a wire rack to cool completely.

In a small bowl, combine glaze ingredients until smooth. Pour over cooled cake. **Yield:** 12-14 servings.

I created this recipe one fall when I had a bumper crop of pumpkins. Many holiday desserts are high in fat and calories, but I like this cake because it's a healthier alternative.

~Judiann McNulty
NEWBERG, OREGON

Pumpkin Angel Cake

(Also pictured on page 134)

1-1/2 cups egg whites (about 12)
1 cup cake flour
1-1/4 cups sugar, *divided*
1 teaspoon ground cinnamon
1/2 teaspoon ground nutmeg
1-1/2 teaspoons cream of tartar
1 teaspoon vanilla extract
1/2 teaspoon salt
1/2 cup canned pumpkin
Confectioners' sugar

Let egg whites stand at room temperature for 30 minutes. Sift the flour, 1 cup sugar, cinnamon and nutmeg together twice; set aside.

In a large mixing bowl, beat the egg whites, cream of tartar, vanilla and salt on medium speed until soft peaks form. Gradually beat in remaining sugar, about 1 tablespoon at a time, on high until stiff glossy peaks form and sugar is dissolved. Gradually fold in flour mixture, about 1/2 cup at a time. Fold in pumpkin.

Gently spoon into an ungreased 10-in. tube pan. Cut through batter with a knife to remove air pockets. Bake on the lowest oven rack at 350° for 40-45 minutes or until lightly browned and entire top appears dry. Immediately invert pan; cool completely, about 1 hour.

Run a knife around the sides and center tube of pan. Remove to a serving plate. Sprinkle top of cake with confectioners' sugar. **Yield:** 12 servings.

My mother gave me this recipe more than 40 years ago, and it's withstood the test of time. The blueberry-filled cake has gone on to please four generations of our growing family.
~Joy McKibbin
CAMDEN, MICHIGAN

🎗 Blueberry Ripple Cake

3/4 cup all-purpose flour
3/4 cup packed brown sugar
1-1/4 teaspoons ground cinnamon
1/4 teaspoon salt
1/3 cup cold butter
1/2 cup chopped pecans
1 package (18-1/4 ounces) white cake mix
1-1/4 cups fresh *or* frozen blueberries

In a large bowl, combine the flour, brown sugar, cinnamon and salt; cut in butter until crumbly. Stir in pecans. Sprinkle half of the mixture into a greased 13-in. x 9-in. x 2-in. baking dish.

Prepare the cake batter according to package directions; spread over pecan mixture. Top with the blueberries and remaining pecan mixture; swirl with a knife. Bake at 350° for 45-50 minutes or until a toothpick inserted near the center comes out clean. Serve warm; or cool the cake on a wire rack and serve it at room temperature. **Yield:** 12-15 servings.

Editor's Note: If using frozen blueberries, do not thaw.

Baker's Secrets
Helpful Hint
Ice The Cake

When a chocolate cake calls for the pan to be greased and floured, I use baking cocoa instead of flour so there's no white powder on the bottom or edges of my cake. ~Melanie Harrington
OSWEGO, NEW YORK

Mom used to spread any leftover cake frosting between graham crackers for us when we were little. We loved those quick treats—and so does my daughter!
~Mabel Bond
SELLERSBURG, INDIANA

For no-fail cakes, I've learned to always use dry measures for dry ingredients and use glass measuring cups for liquids to ensure the most accurate amounts. Also, bring eggs to room temperature for higher, fluffier cakes. And always use the middle rack in a preheated oven when baking.
~Sharon Douthit
STERLING, ILLINOIS

For a lighter, more tender angel food cake, I always sift the flour and sugar mixture together several times, and I make sure not to overbeat the egg whites.
~Evelyn Smith
VOLANT, PENNSYLVANIA

Sometimes, I add 1 tablespoon of grated orange or lemon peel to a chocolate cake for a delicious flavor surprise. Also, to soften butter (or cream cheese) quickly, I place it in an oven-proof dish for 5 minutes in the oven as it is preheating. To melt the butter, I wait just a little longer. ~Corey Denton
DURHAM, NORTH CAROLINA

I use my potato masher to mash bananas for cakes and breads. It's fast, easy and produces the perfect texture.
~Tannis Claussen
SUNDRE, ALBERTA

Turn to this chapter for
suppers on a smaller scale.

Cooking for Two

PLEASING PORTION. From top: Tortellini Toss (p. 141) and Winter Pork Chop Bake (p. 140).

Pork has always been a family favorite, and this recipe is a winner. All the work is done in the preparation, so there is very little cleanup after the meal.

~Virginia Lynne Ricks
ROY, UTAH

Winter Pork Chop Bake

(Pictured on page 139)

     1 medium tart apple, diced
     1 small sweet red pepper, diced
     1 small onion, chopped
 1/4 cup golden raisins
 1/4 cup chopped walnuts
     1 tablespoon butter
     3 slices rye bread, toasted and cubed
 1/4 cup chicken broth
     3 tablespoons apple juice
 1/2 teaspoon rubbed sage
 1/4 teaspoon dried basil
     2 bone-in pork chops (1/2 inch thick)

     1 tablespoon vegetable oil
Salt and pepper to taste
     1 medium sweet potato, peeled and cut
       into 1/2-inch pieces

In a skillet, saute the first five ingredients in butter for 5 minutes or until red pepper and onion are tender. Remove from the heat; stir in the bread cubes, broth, juice, sage and basil.

Meanwhile, in a skillet, brown chops in oil. Place stuffing in a greased 11-in. x 7-in. x 2-in. baking dish. Place chops on top; sprinkle with salt and pepper. Arrange sweet potato around edges of the dish. Cover and bake at 350° for 35-40 minutes or until meat is no longer pink and sweet potato is tender. **Yield:** 2 servings.

I made up this recipe when I was looking for some good Chinese food in beautiful Oregon, and everyone liked it. Each time I make this, I change something slightly. Leftovers heat easily in the microwave or in a skillet.

~Annette Hemsath
SUTHERLIN, OREGON

Beef with Ramen Noodles

     1 tablespoon cornstarch
     1 cup beef broth, *divided*
     1 package (3 ounces) beef ramen
       noodles
 1/2 pound boneless beef sirloin
       steak, cut into thin strips
     1 tablespoon vegetable oil
     1 tablespoon soy sauce
     1 can (14 ounces) whole baby
       corn, rinsed and drained
     1 cup fresh broccoli florets
 1/2 cup diced sweet red pepper
 1/2 cup grated carrot
     2 green onions, cut into 1-inch
       pieces
 1/4 cup peanuts

In a small bowl, combine cornstarch and 2 tablespoons broth until smooth; set aside. Set aside seasoning packet from noodles. Cook noodles according to package directions.

In a skillet, stir-fry beef in oil. Add soy sauce; cook for 3-4 minutes or until liquid has evaporated. Drain noodles; add to beef.

Stir in the corn, broccoli, red pepper, carrot, onions and remaining broth. Sprinkle contents of seasoning packet over all.

Cook for 4-6 minutes or until vegetables are crisp-tender. Stir reserved cornstarch mixture and add to skillet. Bring to a boil; cook and stir for 2 minutes or until thickened. Sprinkle with peanuts. **Yield:** 2 servings.

This recipe is so delectable that I'm often asked to double it when family members visit over the holidays. I also suggest preparing it with shrimp for a quick convenient alternative that's also delicious.

~Janet Lebar
LITTLETON, COLORADO

Chicken Scampi

  4 ounces uncooked linguine
  2 green onions, thinly sliced
  2 garlic cloves, minced
  3 tablespoons butter
  2 tablespoons olive oil
  2 boneless skinless chicken breast
     halves
1/2 teaspoon salt
1/4 teaspoon coarsely ground
     pepper
1/2 cup chopped seeded tomato
  2 tablespoons lemon juice
  1 tablespoon minced fresh parsley
Grated Parmesan cheese

Cook linguine according to package directions. Meanwhile, in a skillet, saute the onions and garlic in butter and oil until garlic is tender. Sprinkle chicken with salt and pepper; add to skillet. Cook for 3 minutes on each side or until lightly browned.

Reduce heat; cover and cook 4 minutes longer or until juices run clear. Remove chicken and keep warm. Stir tomato, lemon juice and parsley into skillet; heat through. Drain linguine; toss with tomato mixture. Top with chicken and sprinkle with Parmesan cheese. **Yield:** 2 servings.

This hearty salad can serve as a main course or side dish. The creamy Italian dressing and marinated artichoke hearts create a tangy coating for the tortellini.

~Mary Ellen Pillatzhi
BUFFALO, MINNESOTA

Tortellini Toss

(Also pictured on page 139)

1-1/4 cups frozen cheese tortellini
    6 cherry tomatoes, halved
  1/4 cup sliced green onions
    1 jar (6-1/2 ounces) marinated
       artichoke hearts, drained and
       coarsely chopped
  1/4 cup creamy Italian salad
       dressing

Cook the tortellini according to package directions; drain and rinse with cold water. Place in a bowl. Add the tomatoes, onions, artichokes and salad dressing; toss to coat. Refrigerate until serving. **Yield:** 2-3 servings.

Quick Fix

When you have leftover cooked pasta, fry diced bacon. Then add the pasta, stewed tomatoes, green onions and a mixture of shredded cheeses for a delicious made-over meal.

I found this easy recipe for Cornish hens and prepare it often for my family. The glaze keeps the hens tender and moist, and the skin roasts to a golden glow. It's tasty, too. When the children are gone for the weekend, my husband and I enjoy this meal—perfect for two.

~Randi Ison
INDIO, CALIFORNIA

Apricot-Glazed Cornish Hens

1/2 teaspoon salt

1/4 teaspoon cayenne pepper

   2 Cornish game hens (20 ounces *each*)

   2 tablespoons butter, melted, *divided*

1/4 cup apricot preserves

   1 tablespoon honey

   1 tablespoon grated onion

1/8 teaspoon ground nutmeg

Combine salt and cayenne. Rub a third of mixture inside hens. Brush 1 tablespoon butter over hens; sprinkle with remaining salt mixture. Place on a rack in a shallow baking pan. Bake, uncovered, at 350° for 30 minutes.

Meanwhile, combine the preserves, honey, onion, nutmeg and remaining butter in a saucepan. Cook and stir until preserves are melted. Baste hens with apricot mixture. Bake 35-40 minutes longer or until golden brown and a meat thermometer reads 180°. Cover and let stand for 5-10 minutes before serving. **Yield:** 2 servings.

One day, I wanted to make my mashed potatoes more interesting, so I added a carrot and some onion. This delightful dish adds color to any entree and makes an attractive plate.

~Larry Stine
BROOKINGS, SOUTH DAKOTA

Mashed Potatoes with Carrot

2 medium potatoes, peeled and quartered
1 medium carrot, peeled and chopped
1/4 cup chopped onion
2 tablespoons heavy whipping cream
1 tablespoon butter
1/4 teaspoon salt
1/8 teaspoon pepper
Pinch sugar

Place the vegetables in a saucepan; cover with water. Bring to a boil. Reduce heat; cover and simmer for 12-15 minutes or until tender.

Drain and place vegetables in a mixing bowl; mash until smooth. Add the cream, butter, salt, pepper and sugar; mix well. **Yield:** 2 servings.

This rich and creamy dessert is especially nice for company. It's attractive and easy to serve, and much of it can be made ahead of time. The citrus flavor is refreshing after a full-course meal.

~Brian Barger
CHEVY CHASE, MARYLAND

Citrus Cream Tartlets

1/2 cup chopped macadamia nuts, toasted
3 tablespoons sugar
2 tablespoons all-purpose flour
2 tablespoons cold butter
2 packages (3 ounces *each*) cream cheese, softened
1/4 cup confectioners' sugar
2 teaspoons *each* orange, lemon and lime juice
1 teaspoon *each* grated orange, lemon and lime peel

In a blender or food processor, combine the nuts, sugar and flour; cover and process until blended. Add butter; blend until mixture forms coarse crumbs.

Press the nut mixture onto the bottom and up the sides of two greased 4-in. tartlet pans with removable bottoms. Bake at 350° for 13-15 minutes or until golden brown. Cool completely.

In a mixing bowl, beat cream cheese until fluffy. Add the confectioners' sugar, citrus juices and peels; beat until blended.

Spoon into crusts. Refrigerate for at least 1 hour. **Yield:** 2 servings.

About 25 years ago, after experimenting with recipes for a blue cheese dressing, I came up with this quick-to-make combination. I usually mix up a double batch because it never lasts long. It's also great as a dip for crackers, veggies or crusty breads, or instead of mayonnaise on sandwiches.

~Donna Cline
PENSACOLA, FLORIDA

Creamy Blue Cheese Salad Dressing

1/2 cup sour cream
1/2 cup mayonnaise
1 tablespoon lemon juice
1 tablespoon red wine vinegar
2 to 4 ounces crumbled blue cheese

In a bowl, combine all of the ingredients; mix well. Cover and refrigerate until serving. **Yield:** 1-1/4 cups.

I head south of the border for this stovetop dish that's easy to prepare.

~Edie Farm
FARMINGTON, NEW MEXICO

Mexican Steak and Beans

1 tablespoon all-purpose flour

1/2 to 1 teaspoon chili powder

1/4 teaspoon salt

1/8 teaspoon ground cumin

1/8 teaspoon pepper

1 boneless beef round steak (1/2 pound), cut into 1-inch cubes

1 tablespoon vegetable oil

3/4 cup thinly sliced celery

1 medium onion, chopped

1/2 cup water

1/4 cup chili sauce

1 medium carrot, cut into 1/2-inch slices

1 small green pepper, cut into 1-1/2-inch strips

3/4 cup kidney beans, rinsed and drained

Hot cooked rice, optional

In a resealable plastic bag, combine the first five ingredients. Add the steak; shake to coat. In a skillet, cook steak in oil until browned on all sides; drain. Add the celery, onion, water and chili sauce. Bring to a boil. Reduce heat; cover and simmer for 30 minutes. Add carrot; cover and simmer for 15 minutes.

Stir in green pepper and beans. Cover and simmer 10 minutes longer or until meat and vegetables are tender. Serve over rice if desired. **Yield:** 2 servings.

My wife and I are pasta lovers, and after we tried this dish at an Italian restaurant, I thought I could improve on it. I enjoy making pasta sauces, and this is one dish we like to serve to our pasta-loving friends.

~Robert Schieve
SEDONA, ARIZONA

Creamy Ham Fettuccine

4 ounces uncooked fettuccine

1/4 cup butter

1 tablespoon all-purpose flour

1 cup milk

1 egg yolk, beaten

3/4 cup shredded Swiss cheese

1/2 cup chopped fully cooked ham

1/2 cup frozen green peas

1 tablespoon grated Parmesan cheese

Cook fettuccine according to package directions. Meanwhile, in a heavy saucepan, melt butter; stir in flour until smooth. Gradually add milk. Bring to a boil; cook and stir for 1-2 minutes or until thickened. Remove from the heat.

Stir a small amount of hot mixture into egg yolk; return all to the pan, stirring constantly. Add Swiss cheese; cook and stir over low heat for 1 minute or until cheese is melted. Add ham and peas; cook 2 minutes longer or until heated through. Drain the fettuccine; top with ham mixture and Parmesan cheese. **Yield:** 2 servings.

It seemed like Mom was always standing at her old black stove, coming up with recipes. This was one of the old-time favorites. I love stuffed clams any time of the year. I buy them fresh when in season and save the shells. Then, when I can't buy them fresh, I use canned.

~Lillian Butler
STRATFORD, CONNECTICUT

Clam Stuffing Bake

2 tablespoons *each* chopped celery, green pepper and sweet red pepper
4-1/2 teaspoons chopped onion
2 tablespoons butter, *divided*
1/4 cup shredded carrot
1/2 cup chicken broth
1 cup seasoned stuffing mix
1 can (6-1/2 ounces) minced clams, drained
1/4 teaspoon lemon juice

In a saucepan, saute the celery, peppers and onion in 1 tablespoon butter until almost tender. Stir in carrot and broth. Bring to a boil. Stir in stuffing mix. Remove from the heat; cover and let stand for 5 minutes. Stir in clams.

Transfer to two 6-oz. ramekins or custard cups. Melt remaining butter; stir in lemon juice. Drizzle over the stuffing mixture. Bake, uncovered, at 350° for 15-20 minutes or until heated through and golden brown. **Yield:** 2 servings.

This mix is my all-time favorite to serve or bring to parties. The combination of popcorn and nuts is very satisfying, and even the kids can help make this treat.

~Shirley Nordblum
YOUNGSVILLE, PENNSYLVANIA

Nutty Seasoned Popcorn

1 package (3-1/2 ounces) butter-flavored microwave popcorn
1/2 teaspoon dried basil
1/2 teaspoon dried chervil
1/2 teaspoon dried thyme
3/4 cup mixed nuts

In a microwave, prepare popcorn according to package directions. Pour into a serving bowl. Add the basil, chervil and thyme; toss to coat. Add nuts; toss to combine. **Yield:** 2 servings.

Fruit, celery, nuts and cheese make a merry medley in this tangy twist on traditional Waldorf salad. And because it's sized for a pair, there are no leftovers to worry about.

~Valerie Belley
ST. LOUIS, MISSOURI

Cheesy Apple Salad

1/4 cup orange juice
3 tablespoons mayonnaise
1 teaspoon lemon juice
1/4 teaspoon grated orange peel
1 large apple, chopped
1/2 cup shredded cheddar cheese
2 tablespoons chopped celery
2 tablespoons chopped walnuts

In a small bowl, whisk the orange juice, mayonnaise, lemon juice and orange peel until combined. In another bowl, combine the apple, cheese, celery and walnuts. Add orange juice mixture and stir to coat. Cover and refrigerate for 15 minutes. **Yield:** 2 servings.

My guests often ask for this winning recipe and are surprised at how simple it is to prepare.

~Gloria Nerone
MENTOR, OHIO

Beef Steaks with Blue Cheese

- **2 beef tenderloin steaks, 1-1/2 inches thick**
- **2 ounces blue cheese, crumbled**
- **2 tablespoons butter, softened**
- **2 slices white bread, crusts removed and cut into cubes**
- **1 tablespoon olive oil**
- **2 tablespoons grated Parmesan cheese**

Place meat on broiler pan. Broil 4-6 in. from heat for 5-8 minutes on each side or until meat is cooked to desired

doneness (for medium-rare, a meat thermometer should read 145°; medium, 160°; well-done, 170°).

Meanwhile, in a bowl, combine blue cheese and butter; set aside. In a skillet, saute bread cubes in oil until golden. Sprinkle with Parmesan cheese. Top steaks with blue cheese mixture and sprinkle with croutons; broil 1 minute longer or until cheese is slightly melted. **Yield:** 2 servings.

A hint of ginger makes these peas special and one of my favorites.

~Suzanne Karsten
WINTER GARDEN, FLORIDA

Gingered Snow Peas

- 1/2 pound fresh snow peas, trimmed
- 1 tablespoon water
- 1 tablespoon butter, melted
- 1/4 teaspoon ground ginger
- 1/8 teaspoon salt

Place the peas and water in a 1-qt. microwave-safe dish. Cover and microwave on high for 3-4 minutes or until crisp-tender; drain. Combine the butter, ginger and salt. Drizzle over the peas; toss to coat. **Yield:** 2-3 servings.

Editor's Note: This recipe was tested in a 1,100-watt microwave.

This satisfying dish is nutritious and can be prepared a day ahead, refrigerated and baked before serving.

~Dominic Spano
COLONIE, NEW YORK

Twice-Baked Spuds

- 2 large baking potatoes
- 1 cup chopped peeled parsnips
- 1 garlic clove, peeled
- 2 tablespoons cream cheese, softened
- 2 tablespoons buttermilk
- 1/2 teaspoon salt
- Pinch pepper
- Dash hot pepper sauce
- 1/4 cup finely chopped green onions
- 1 tablespoon grated Parmesan cheese
- 1/8 teaspoon paprika

Bake potatoes at 375° for 1 hour or until tender. Allow to cool. Place parsnips and garlic in a small saucepan; cover with water. Bring to a boil over medium heat. Reduce heat; cover and simmer for 20 minutes or until tender. Drain and mash.

Cut a thin slice off the top of each potato; discard. Scoop out the pulp, leaving a thin shell. In a bowl, mash potato pulp with parsnips and garlic. Beat in next five ingredients, using a hand mixer.

Stir in green onions. Spoon into the potato shells. Combine the Parmesan cheese and paprika; sprinkle over top. Place on a baking sheet. Bake, uncovered, at 375° for 20-30 minutes or until heated through. **Yield:** 2 servings.

My aunt used to make this cheesecake for every party. Now I carry on her tradition.

~Karen Lacey
PARACHUTE, COLORADO

Miniature Lemon Cheesecake

- 1-1/4 cups graham cracker crumbs (20 squares)
- 1/3 cup butter, melted
- 1/4 cup sugar
- 2 packages (3 ounces *each*) cream cheese, softened
- 1 can (14 ounces) sweetened condensed milk
- 1/4 cup lemon juice
- 1 cup sour cream
- 1 cup heavy whipping cream, whipped
- Sliced strawberries, optional

In a bowl, combine crumbs, butter and sugar. Press onto the bottom and all the way up the sides of a greased 6-in. springform pan. Place on a baking sheet. Bake at 350° for 8-10 minutes. Cool completely on a wire rack. Set aside.

In a mixing bowl, beat cream cheese until fluffy. Beat in the sweetened condensed milk and lemon juice until blended. Fold in sour cream and whipped cream. Pour into crust (pan will be full). Refrigerate overnight.

Carefully run a knife around the edge of pan to loosen. Remove sides of pan. Garnish with strawberries if desired. Refrigerate leftovers. **Yield:** 4-6 servings.

My soup makes a very appetizing meal for two. I don't care for leftovers, and this recipe makes just enough. It's a hit at my house!
~Ruby Williams
BOGALUSA, LOUISIANA

Catfish Soup

1 large onion, chopped

1/4 cup chopped celery

4 garlic cloves, minced

2 teaspoons vegetable oil

1-1/2 cups chopped, seeded and peeled tomatoes

1 cup water

2 bay leaves

1 strip orange peel (about 2 inches x 1 inch)

1 tablespoon minced fresh parsley

3/4 to 1 teaspoon salt

1/4 teaspoon dried thyme

1/8 teaspoon coarsely ground pepper

Dash cayenne pepper

1 catfish fillet *or* firm whitefish of your choice (about 1/2 pound), cubed

In a saucepan, saute the onion, celery and garlic in oil for 3 minutes (some onion pieces will be lightly browned). Stir in the tomatoes, water, bay leaves, orange peel, parsley, salt, thyme, pepper and cayenne. Bring to a boil. Reduce heat; cover and simmer for 20 minutes.

Stir in catfish; return to a boil. Reduce heat; cover and simmer for 5 minutes or until fish is tender. Discard bay leaves and orange peel. **Yield:** 2 servings.

This is a great way to use leftover beef roast for a quick and easy meal during a busy week.
~Joan Baer
CANTON, OHIO

Mushroom Beef Skillet

2 to 3 tablespoons all-purpose flour

1 pound beef stew meat, cut into 1-inch cubes

2 tablespoons butter

1/2 cup chopped onion

3 garlic cloves, minced

1-1/2 cups beef broth

1/2 cup sliced fresh mushrooms

1 teaspoon dried basil

1/4 teaspoon salt

1/8 teaspoon pepper

Hot cooked rice

Place the flour in a large resealable plastic bag. Add beef, a few pieces at a time, and shake to coat. In a skillet, cook the beef in butter over medium heat until browned. Add onion and garlic; cook for 2-3 minutes or until onion is tender.

Add broth, mushrooms, basil, salt and pepper. Bring to a boil. Reduce heat; cover and simmer 1-1/2 hours or until meat is tender, stirring occasionally. Serve over rice. **Yield:** 2 servings.

My daughter's friend once brought this salad as a side dish for our dinner. It was so delicious. Since it's a good source of protein, it makes a great light lunch or dinner entree.
~Zelma McKinney
AMARILLO, TEXAS

Kidney Bean Salad

1 can (16 ounces) kidney beans, rinsed and drained
2 hard-cooked eggs, chopped
1/2 cup sliced celery
1 small onion, chopped
1/4 cup mayonnaise
1/4 cup dill pickle relish
1/2 teaspoon pepper
1/4 teaspoon salt
Lettuce leaf, optional

In a bowl, combine all of the ingredients; stir until coated. Refrigerate until serving. Serve in a lettuce-lined bowl if desired. **Yield:** 2 servings.

I wanted a quick and easy summer dessert to serve guests when we entertain outdoors. With just a few ingredients, there isn't a lot of preparation required. Topped with a strawberry and served in wine glasses, it looks pretty, too. ~Valerie Jones-Tollefsbol
ELIZABETHTOWN, PENNSYLVANIA

Strawberry Mallow Dessert

1 cup sliced fresh strawberries
1 teaspoon sugar
1/2 cup miniature marshmallows
1/4 cup sour cream

Place strawberries in a bowl and sprinkle with sugar; stir. Let stand for 5 minutes. Add marshmallows and sour cream; stir to coat. Spoon into dessert dishes. **Yield:** 2 servings.

Soy sauce adds a touch of Oriental flavor and paprika lends rich color to this moist, mouth-watering entree. It's super easy to double or triple the recipe for company, too. ~Karen Arthur
WAINFLEET, ONTARIO

Crusty Oven-Fried Chicken

1/4 cup soy sauce
1 tablespoon vegetable oil
1 garlic clove, minced
2 chicken legs with thighs
2 tablespoons dry bread crumbs
1 tablespoon minced fresh parsley
1 tablespoon sesame seeds
1/4 teaspoon paprika
1/4 teaspoon pepper

In a large resealable plastic bag, combine the soy sauce, oil and garlic; add chicken. Seal bag and turn to coat; let stand for 15 minutes, turning once.

In a shallow bowl, combine the remaining ingredients. Drain and discard marinade. Coat chicken in crumb mixture. Place in a greased 8-in. square baking dish. Bake, uncovered, at 350° for 50-55 minutes or until juices run clear. **Yield:** 2 servings.

I was delighted to find a healthy version of burgers with little fat but lots of flavorful ingredients.

~Margaret Pache
MESA, ARIZONA

Turkey Burgers

 1 egg, lightly beaten
 3 tablespoons toasted wheat germ
 3 tablespoons salsa
 2 tablespoons shredded carrot
 2 tablespoons finely chopped onion
 2 tablespoons shredded peeled apple
 1 garlic clove, minced
1/4 teaspoon salt

1/2 pound ground turkey *or* chicken
 2 hamburger buns, split

In a bowl, combine the first eight ingredients. Crumble turkey over mixture and mix well. Shape into two patties. Grill, broil or pan-fry for 7-8 minutes on each side or until no longer pink. Serve on buns. **Yield:** 2 servings.

This makes a nice side dish with dinner, but I often serve it as lunch for my husband and me.

~Eleanor Simon
OWATONNA, MINNESOTA

Cottage Cheese Salad

- **1 cup small-curd cottage cheese**
- **1 medium carrot, shredded**
- **1 medium red apple, diced**
- **2 tablespoons raisins**
- **2 tablespoons chopped walnuts**
- **1/8 teaspoon pepper, optional**

Lettuce leaves

In a bowl, combine the cottage cheese, carrot, apple, raisins, nuts and pepper if desired. Serve on lettuce. **Yield:** 2 servings.

My friend served this refreshing beverage when I was her guest one warm summer day.

~Romaine Wetzel
RONKS, PENNSYLVANIA

Ruby-Red Strawberry Burst

- **2 cups red grapefruit and strawberry juice drink**
- **1 medium firm banana, cut into chunks**
- **6 fresh strawberries**
- **1 cup ice cubes**
- **1 teaspoon sugar**

In a blender, combine all ingredients; cover and process until smooth. Serve immediately. **Yield:** 2 servings.

Sliced thin, these cookies are crispy and chewy; sliced thick, they have a cake-like texture.

~Kathryn Wilkins
NORFOLK, VIRGINIA

Date-Filled Pinwheels

- **3/4 cup firmly packed chopped dates**
- **1/3 cup sugar**
- **1/3 cup water**
- **1/3 cup chopped pecans**
- **1/3 cup shortening**
- **2/3 cup packed brown sugar**
- **1 egg**
- **1/4 teaspoon vanilla extract**
- **1-1/3 cups all-purpose flour**
- **1/4 teaspoon salt**
- **1/8 teaspoon baking soda**

In a large saucepan, combine dates, sugar and water. Cook and stir over medium heat for 10 minutes until very soft. Add pecans; cool. In a large mixing bowl, cream shortening and brown sugar. Beat in egg and vanilla. Combine flour, salt and baking soda; gradually add to creamed mixture. Cover and refrigerate for 1 hour or until easy to handle.

On a lightly floured surface, roll out dough into an 8-in. square. Spread with date mixture; roll up jelly-roll style. Wrap with plastic wrap. Refrigerate for 4 hours or until firm.

Unwrap and cut into 1/4-in. slices. Place 2 in. apart on lightly greased baking sheets. Bake at 400° for 8-10 minutes or until golden brown. Remove to wire racks to cool. **Yield:** about 2-1/2 dozen.

Even though I'm cooking for two, I'll still make a small pork roast sometimes and use the leftover meat for this recipe. If you don't have roast left over, this dish can be made with pork tenderloin cutlets, cooked before adding to the recipe. ~Nancy Nowaczek
GRAYSLAKE, ILLINOIS

Colorful Pineapple Pork

1 cup plus 3 tablespoons water, *divided*
2 tablespoons sugar
2 tablespoons cider vinegar
3/4 teaspoon salt
1/2 pound cubed cooked pork
1 small cucumber, peeled, halved and sliced
1 small carrot, sliced
1 can (8 ounces) pineapple chunks, drained
1 medium tomato, seeded and cut into 1-inch chunks
1/2 medium green pepper, thinly sliced

1 tablespoon soy sauce
2 tablespoons cornstarch
Hot cooked rice

In a skillet, combine 1 cup water, sugar, vinegar and salt. Bring to a boil. Reduce heat; add the pork, cucumber, carrot, pineapple, tomato, green pepper and soy sauce. Simmer, uncovered, for 5 minutes or until heated through.

Combine the cornstarch and remaining water until smooth. Stir into skillet. Bring to a boil; cook and stir for 2 minutes or until thickened. Serve over rice. **Yield:** 2 servings.

My husband was fond of fish, so I was always looking for new recipes. When we had this dish at an Italian friend's home, I got the recipe. It is a good choice for potluck suppers or picnics. ~Mary Dennis
BRYAN, OHIO

Italian Tuna Pasta Salad

1-1/2 cups cooked small shell pasta
1 cup shredded carrot
1 cup shredded zucchini
1 can (6 ounces) tuna, drained
6 tablespoons creamy Italian salad dressing
Lettuce leaf, optional

In a bowl, combine the pasta, carrot, zucchini, tuna and salad dressing. Cover and refrigerate for 2 hours or overnight. Serve in a lettuce-lined bowl if desired. **Yield:** 2 servings.

Helpful Hint

Pickle-icious

Save the leftover juice from bread-and-butter pickles. Then pour a little of the juice into the mayonnaise mixture when making tuna or macaroni salad for a little extra flavor.

I found this recipe in a cookbook over 30 years ago when I was newly married. It's tasty and simple to prepare—just right for a busy couple. It's also easy to double for a family of four.

~Barbara Kemmer
ROHNERT PARK, CALIFORNIA

Pizza Macaroni Bake

- 1/2 **pound bulk pork sausage**
- 1/4 **cup chopped green pepper**
- 2 **tablespoons chopped onion**
- 1/2 **cup elbow macaroni, cooked and drained**
- 1 **can (8 ounces) tomato sauce**
- 4 **tablespoons grated Parmesan cheese,** *divided*
- 2 **tablespoons water**
- 1/4 **teaspoon dried oregano**

Dash pepper

In a skillet, cook the sausage, green pepper and onion over medium heat until the meat is no longer pink; drain. Stir in the macaroni, tomato sauce, 2 tablespoons Parmesan cheese, water, oregano and pepper.

Transfer to a lightly greased 1-qt. baking dish; sprinkle with remaining cheese. Cover and bake at 350° for 25-30 minutes or until liquid is absorbed and casserole is heated through. **Yield:** 2 servings.

This tasty side dish makes my holiday meal complete. When I first tried the recipe, it was instantly a "keeper."

~Ruby Williams
BOGALUSA, LOUISIANA

Carrots 'n' Celery With Pecans

- 1-1/2 **cups sliced carrots**
- 3/4 **cup water**
- 1/4 **teaspoon salt**
- 1/2 **cup sliced celery**
- 1/4 **cup chopped pecans**
- 1/4 **teaspoon dill weed**
- 1 **tablespoon butter**

In a small saucepan, bring the carrots, water and salt to a boil. Reduce heat; cover and cook for 10 minutes. Add celery; cover and cook 5 minutes longer or until tender. Drain and keep warm.

In a small skillet, saute the pecans and dill in butter for 8 minutes or until golden brown. Add to carrot mixture; toss to coat. **Yield:** 2 servings.

This is one of my husband's favorite recipes, simple and delicious. The ingredients make it into a sort of Greek stew. Besides making it for my husband and myself, I like serving this impressive dish to company.

~Susan Orr Schwarz
SHERMAN OAKS, CALIFORNIA

Sea Bass with Shrimp and Tomatoes

2 sea bass *or* halibut steaks (8 to 10 ounces *each*)
6 to 8 large uncooked shrimp, peeled and deveined
1/2 small red *or* sweet onion, thinly sliced
1 can (14-1/2 ounces) Italian-style stewed tomatoes
1 package (4 ounces) crumbled feta cheese

Place the fish in a greased 8-in. square baking dish. Top with shrimp, onion, tomatoes and feta cheese. Bake, uncovered, at 325° for 45-50 minutes or until fish flakes easily with a fork. **Yield:** 2 servings.

I discovered this recipe while watching a cooking show some years ago. The first time I served it, my guests raved and were surprised when I told them it was brussels sprouts.
~Tangee Zayas-Thaler
SILVER LAKE, OHIO

Bacon-Mushroom Brussels Sprouts

2 cups fresh brussels sprouts, halved
3 bacon strips, cut into 1/2-inch pieces
1/2 cup finely chopped onion
1/2 cup sliced fresh mushrooms
1/4 cup chicken broth
1/4 teaspoon salt
1/8 teaspoon pepper

Place brussels sprouts in a saucepan; cover with water. Bring to a boil. Reduce heat; cover and simmer for 8 minutes or until crisp-tender. Drain and keep warm.

In a skillet, cook bacon over medium heat until crisp. Remove to paper towels; drain, reserving 2 tablespoons drippings. Saute onion and mushrooms in the drippings for 3-5 minutes or until tender.

Add the broth, salt and pepper; bring to a boil. Reduce heat; simmer, uncovered, for 3-4 minutes or until broth is reduced by half. Stir in brussels sprouts and bacon. **Yield:** 2-3 servings.

My dinner guests are impressed when they see these decorative flavorful butter pats on the table. I cut them in different shapes for variety. They're so easy to have on hand, stored in the freezer, and make an attractive complement to rolls, bread or fish.
~Pam Duncan
SUMMERS, ARKANSAS

Fine Herb Butter

1 cup butter, softened
2 tablespoons minced fresh parsley
2 tablespoons minced chives
1 tablespoon minced fresh tarragon
1 tablespoon lemon juice
1/4 teaspoon pepper

In a small mixing bowl, combine the butter, parsley, chives, tarragon, lemon juice and pepper; beat until well blended.

Spread on a baking sheet to 1/2-in. thickness. Freeze until firm. Cut into shapes with small cookie cutters. **Yield:** about 1 cup.

My Grandmother Addie made these bars for family picnics and enjoyed watching when all of her grandchildren try to resist them. But all it took was just one bite...then one bar didn't seem to satisfy. They disappeared in a flash. ~Marty Nickerson
ELLINGTON, CONNECTICUT

Raspberry Jam Bars

1 cup all-purpose flour
1 teaspoon baking powder
1/2 cup cold butter
1 egg, lightly beaten
1 tablespoon milk
1/3 cup seedless raspberry jam

TOPPING:
1 egg, lightly beaten
1 cup sugar
1 tablespoon butter, melted
2 cups flaked coconut

In a bowl, combine the flour and baking powder. Cut in butter until mixture resembles coarse crumbs. Combine egg and milk; stir into crumb mixture just until moistened.

Press into a greased 9-in. square baking pan. Bake at 350° for 15 minutes or until the crust is lightly browned. Spread jam over crust.

Combine topping ingredients; spoon over jam. Bake 25 minutes longer or until light golden brown. Cut into squares while warm. **Yield:** 9 servings.

Creamy veggie soup is really my specialty. A dash of Worcestershire sauce helps warm up the flavors and adds a bit of zip.

~Tina Dierking
SKOWHEGAN, MAINE

Cream of Vegetable Soup

1/3 cup cooked broccoli florets, *divided*
1/3 cup cooked cauliflowerets, *divided*
1/3 cup chopped cooked carrots, *divided*
3/4 cup chicken broth
  3 tablespoons finely chopped onion
  2 tablespoons butter
  2 tablespoons all-purpose flour
1/2 teaspoon salt
1/4 teaspoon dried basil
1/4 teaspoon dried thyme
1/8 teaspoon dill weed
1/8 teaspoon pepper
  1 cup half-and-half cream
1/8 teaspoon Worcestershire sauce, optional

Reserve 2 tablespoons each of broccoli, cauliflower and carrots; chop and set aside. In a blender, combine the chicken broth and remaining broccoli, cauliflower and carrots. Puree until smooth. In a saucepan, saute onion in butter until tender. Stir in the flour, salt, basil, thyme, dill weed and pepper until blended. Gradually whisk in cream.

Bring to a boil; cook and stir for 1-2 minutes or until thickened. Stir in chicken broth mixture; heat through. Stir in chopped broccoli, cauliflower and carrots, and Worcestershire sauce if desired; heat through. **Yield:** 2 servings.

On the lookout for time-saving but tasty dinner fare? This tangy pork dish is a real find! It makes a great quick meal. We love the blend of pineapple and green pepper.

~Sharon Ryzner
GIRARD, OHIO

Sweet-and-Sour Pork

  1 can (8 ounces) pineapple chunks
1/4 cup dark corn syrup
  3 tablespoons white vinegar
  1 tablespoon ketchup
  1 tablespoon soy sauce
1/2 pound boneless pork, cut into 1-inch cubes
  1 garlic clove, minced
  1 tablespoon vegetable oil
  1 small green pepper, cut into 3/4-inch chunks
  4 to 5 teaspoons cornstarch
  2 tablespoons cold water
Hot cooked rice

Drain pineapple, reserving juice; set pineapple aside. In a small bowl, combine the corn syrup, vinegar, ketchup, soy sauce and reserved juice; set aside.

In a small skillet, stir-fry the pork and garlic in oil for 4 minutes or until pork is browned. Add green pepper; stir-fry for 2 minutes or until crisp-tender. Stir in pineapple juice mixture; bring to a boil.

Combine the cornstarch and water until smooth; gradually stir into the skillet. Cook and stir for 1-2 minutes or until thickened. Stir in the reserved pineapple; heat through. Serve over rice. **Yield:** 2 servings.

Anytime is a good time to fire up the grill and toss on a steak that's soaked up this great marinade. One of our stock car racing buddies came up with the recipe, and we use it often.
~Betty Ann Ewert
ARLINGTON, MINNESOTA

Robust Marinated Steak

2 tablespoons red wine vinegar
2 tablespoons pineapple juice
4-1/2 teaspoons brown sugar
1 tablespoon Liquid Smoke
1-1/2 teaspoons soy sauce
1/2 teaspoon salt
1/4 teaspoon onion powder
1/8 teaspoon pepper
1 garlic clove, minced
3/4 pound boneless beef sirloin steak (1 inch thick)

In a large resealable plastic bag, combine the first nine ingredients; add steak. Seal bag and turn to coat; refrigerate overnight.

Drain and discard marinade. Grill steak, uncovered, over medium heat for 4-8 minutes on each side or until meat reaches desired doneness (for medium-rare, a meat thermometer should read 145°; medium, 160°; well-done, 170°). **Yield:** 2 servings.

Full of zesty flavor, this salad tastes especially good paired with grilled hamburgers. After my youngest daughter left for college, I adjusted the recipe to serve just two, and it still satisfies.
~Donna Adell
MCPHERSON, KANSAS

Floret Salad

(Pictured above with Robust Marinated Steak)

2/3 cup fresh cauliflowerets
2/3 cup fresh broccoli florets
2 tablespoons chopped red onion
2 tablespoons raisins
2 bacon strips, cooked and crumbled
3 tablespoons mayonnaise
5 teaspoons sugar

1/2 teaspoon white vinegar
2 tablespoons whole cashews

In a bowl, combine cauliflower, broccoli, onion, raisins and bacon. In a small bowl, whisk the mayonnaise, sugar and vinegar. Drizzle over salad and toss to coat. Cover and refrigerate the salad until serving. Sprinkle with cashews just before serving. **Yield:** 2 servings.

This simple, tasty spread is one I can quickly put together for unexpected company or for a snack.
~Bobbi Waller
ROANOKE, ALABAMA

Pineapple Spread

1 package (3 ounces) cream cheese, softened
2 tablespoons finely chopped green onions
1 medium fresh mushroom, finely chopped, optional
1 garlic clove, minced
Dash salt
Dash pepper
1/4 cup crushed pineapple, drained
Assorted crackers

In a small mixing bowl, beat cream cheese until fluffy. Stir in onions, mushroom if desired, garlic, salt and pepper. Fold in pineapple. Serve with crackers. **Yield:** 2/3 cup.

This flavorful skillet dinner has become a favorite. It's a great way to use chicken and makes a comforting meal for two.
~LaVonne Cunningham
COLFAX, ILLINOIS

Mediterranean-Style Chicken

2 bone-in skinless chicken thighs
1 teaspoon olive oil
2 garlic cloves, minced
1 can (14-1/2 ounces) stewed tomatoes, cut up
1 bay leaf
3/4 teaspoon sugar
3/4 teaspoon dried basil
1/4 teaspoon salt
Dash pepper
Hot cooked spaghetti
2 tablespoons sliced stuffed olives, optional

In a skillet, brown chicken in oil over medium-high heat for about 3 minutes on each side. Add garlic; cook and stir about 45 seconds. Stir in the tomatoes, bay leaf, sugar, basil, salt and pepper.

Bring to a boil. Reduce heat; cover and simmer for 20-25 minutes or until chicken juices run clear and chicken is tender. Simmer, uncovered, until sauce reaches desired thickness. Discard bay leaf. Serve over spaghetti. Garnish with olives if desired. **Yield:** 2 servings.

You'll reel in compliments with this colorful seafood salad. It makes a pretty side dish.
~Gail VanGundy
PARKER, COLORADO

Avocado Crabmeat Salad

1/2 cup flaked crabmeat, cartilage removed or imitation crabmeat
1/2 cup chopped lettuce
1/3 cup diced celery
1/2 teaspoon finely chopped onion
1/2 teaspoon lemon juice
1/8 teaspoon salt
1/8 teaspoon paprika

1 tablespoon mayonnaise
1 large ripe avocado, peeled, pitted and halved

In a bowl, combine the crab, lettuce, celery, onion, lemon juice, salt and paprika. Cover and refrigerate for 1 hour. Stir in mayonnaise until combined. Serve in avocado halves. **Yield:** 2 servings.

On warm Indian summer days, I like to prepare fast and fuss-free dishes that don't require heating up the kitchen. This tasty side dish makes the most of garden-fresh green beans.
~Sheryl Schmedeman
SPOKANE, WASHINGTON

Marinated Green Beans

1 cup cut fresh green beans
2 tablespoons French salad dressing
1 tablespoon finely chopped onion
2 lettuce leaves
2 tablespoons shredded cheddar cheese

Place beans in a saucepan and cover with water. Bring to a boil. Cook, uncovered, for 8-10 minutes or until crisp-tender. Rinse in cold water and drain.

In a small bowl, combine the beans, salad dressing and onion. Cover and refrigerate for several hours or overnight. Spoon onto lettuce leaves; sprinkle with cheese. **Yield:** 2 servings.

I came up with this dish by downsizing my recipe for a crowd. I experimented with amounts, adding and deleting until I got it just right. This is a great side dish that goes well with any meat.
~Ann Cargile
BIRMINGHAM, ALABAMA

Zucchini Casserole

1-1/3 cups sliced zucchini
  3/4 cup water
    1 medium onion, chopped
    1 tablespoon chopped green pepper
    1 egg
  1/2 cup mayonnaise
  1/3 cup grated Parmesan cheese
  1/4 teaspoon salt
  1/8 teaspoon pepper
  1/3 cup crushed butter-flavored crackers (about 8 crackers)

In a saucepan, combine the zucchini, water, onion and green pepper; bring to a boil. Reduce heat. Cover and simmer for 5 minutes or until vegetables are crisp-tender; drain.

In a bowl, beat the egg. Add mayonnaise, Parmesan cheese, salt and pepper; mix well. Stir into vegetable mixture. Transfer to a greased 1-qt. baking dish; sprinkle with cracker crumbs. Bake, uncovered, at 350° for 25-30 minutes or until golden brown. **Yield:** 2 servings.

Editor's Note: Reduced-fat or fat-free mayonnaise is not recommended for this recipe.

My mother often made this recipe and probably grew up with it in the Appalachian area of Tennessee. She usually served it on Monday, making use of leftover mashed potatoes from Sunday dinner. We used to eat this topped with brown gravy. ~Eva Molnar
PHILADELPHIA, PENNSYLVANIA

Mashed Potato Cakes

    1 medium onion, chopped
    2 tablespoons butter
    2 eggs
1-1/2 cups mashed potatoes
  1/4 cup all-purpose flour
  1/4 teaspoon salt
  1/8 teaspoon pepper
Dash hot pepper sauce, optional
    1 tablespoon water

In a skillet, saute onion in butter until tender. Remove from the heat. In a bowl, lightly beat one egg. Add the onion, potatoes, flour, salt, pepper and hot pepper sauce if desired.

Shape into four to six patties; place on a greased baking sheet. Lightly beat remaining egg; stir in water. Brush over potato cakes. Bake at 375° for 20-25 minutes or until heated through. **Yield:** 2 servings.

I especially like recipes that make just enough for the two of us, and these yummy sweet rolls fit the bill. Because these treats begin with a ready-made dough, they couldn't be easier or more convenient to whip up.

~Edna Hoffman
HEBRON, INDIANA

Jumbo Cinnamon Rolls

    4 frozen Texas-size dinner rolls
    2 tablespoons butter, melted
    1/4 cup coarsely chopped pecans
    2 tablespoons sugar
    3/4 teaspoon ground cinnamon

HONEY BUTTER:

    2 tablespoons butter, softened
    2 teaspoons honey

Let rolls rise in a warm place until doubled, about 45 minutes. Punch down. Roll each into a 12-in. rope; brush with butter. In a shallow bowl, combine the pecans, sugar and cinnamon; roll ropes in nut mixture.

Twist two ropes together; pinch ends to seal. Place in a greased 10-oz. custard cup. Repeat with remaining ropes. Cover and let rise for 30 minutes or until doubled. Bake at 375° for 15-20 minutes or until golden brown. Meanwhile, combine the honey butter ingredients. Serve with rolls. **Yield:** 2 servings.

These combined ingredients turn out a comforting flavorful combination. It seems like an unusual mix, but the fruit flavors and taste of citrus really enhance the oatmeal.

~Janice Hensley
OWINGSVILLE, KENTUCKY

Fruited Oatmeal

    3/4 cup water
    3/4 cup white grapefruit juice
    1/4 teaspoon ground cinnamon
    1/8 teaspoon salt
    3/4 cup old-fashioned oats
    2 tablespoons brown sugar, *divided*
    1 medium navel orange, peeled, sectioned and cut into chunks
    2 tablespoons chopped dates
    1 tablespoon sliced almonds, toasted

In a small saucepan, bring the water, grapefruit juice, cinnamon and salt to a boil. Stir in oats. Cook for 5 minutes, stirring occasionally. Remove from the heat. Stir in 1 tablespoon brown sugar. Cover and let stand for 5 minutes.

Spoon oatmeal into bowls. Sprinkle with orange, dates, almonds and remaining brown sugar. Serve immediately. **Yield:** 2 servings.

This is a combination of two different salads that my children liked when they were growing up. It probably originated when I was making one or the other of the salads and didn't have enough apples or bananas to make the amount of salad I needed.

~Bev Spain
BELLVILLE, OHIO

Peanut Banana Waldorf

1 small unpeeled red apple, cored and cut into bite-size pieces
1 small firm banana, halved lengthwise and sliced
2 tablespoons peanuts
2 tablespoons mayonnaise
1 tablespoon peanut butter

In a bowl, combine the apple, banana and peanuts. Combine the mayonnaise and peanut butter; add to the fruit mixture and toss to coat. Serve immediately. **Yield:** 2 servings.

I especially like this recipe because I can fix just one omelet that serves and completely satisfies the two of us. It also makes a fun, filling and colorful dish for holiday brunches.

~Cynthia Monachino Webb
KENMORE, NEW YORK

Mexicali Omelet

3 eggs
2 tablespoons water
1 flour tortilla (10 inches)
1/2 cup shredded Monterey Jack cheese
3/4 cup chopped deli turkey
1-1/2 cups shredded lettuce
1/4 cup salsa
2 tablespoons sliced ripe olives
2 tablespoons sour cream
1 tablespoon chopped red onion

In a bowl, beat the eggs and water. Pour into a nonstick 10-in. skillet coated with nonstick cooking spray. As eggs set, lift edges, letting uncooked portion flow underneath. When the eggs are completely set, top with the tortilla, cheese and turkey.

Fold omelet in half; cut in two. Serve on lettuce with salsa, olives, sour cream and onion. **Yield:** 2 servings.

This is a dish my wife had to learn to make in her high school home economics class. I've adapted and renamed it. To me, it has no equal and brings to mind those special days of the '40s.

~Richard Ramsey
EUGENE, OREGON

Goldenrod Eggs

2 hard-cooked eggs
2 tablespoons butter
2 tablespoons all-purpose flour
1/2 teaspoon salt
1/8 teaspoon white pepper
1 cup milk
2 slices bread, toasted and buttered

Cut eggs in half; remove yolks and set aside. Chop egg whites; set aside. In a small saucepan, melt butter. Stir in the flour, salt and pepper until smooth. Gradually stir in milk. Bring to a boil; cook and stir for 1-2 minutes or until thickened.

Stir in egg whites; heat through. Pour over toast. Force egg yolks through a sieve to break into small pieces; sprinkle over sauce. **Yield:** 2 servings.

This colorful entree makes dinner for two extra special. The subtle blend of flavors seasons the steaks just right.

~Arthur Baker
PITTSBURGH, PENNSYLVANIA

Cube Steak Dinner

2 beef cube steaks (**4 ounces** *each*)
2 tablespoons vegetable oil, *divided*
1/4 teaspoon dried oregano
1/8 teaspoon salt
1/8 teaspoon pepper
2 slices provolone cheese
1/2 cup sliced onion
1 garlic clove, minced
Green pepper rings
Sweet red pepper rings

In a skillet, cook the steaks in 1 tablespoon oil over medium heat until no longer pink. Sprinkle with oregano, salt and pepper. Top each with a slice of cheese; cover and cook for 1 minute or until melted.

Remove and keep warm. Drain drippings. In the same skillet, saute the onion, garlic and pepper rings in remaining oil until tender. Spoon over steaks. **Yield:** 2 servings.

This recipe came to me from a dear friend. I use these flavorful mushrooms as a side dish or to garnish an entree. They're always a big hit at potlucks.

~Sylvia Raynor
CORVALLIS, OREGON

Marinated Mushrooms

1/3 cup water
1/4 cup cider vinegar
  2 tablespoons vegetable oil
  2 tablespoons olive oil
  2 garlic cloves, peeled and cut into wedges
  1 bay leaf
  4 teaspoons minced fresh parsley
1/2 teaspoon dried basil
1/4 teaspoon dried oregano
1/4 teaspoon dried thyme

1/4 teaspoon pepper
1/8 to 1/4 teaspoon salt
1/2 pound fresh mushrooms

In a bowl, combine the water, vinegar, oils, garlic, bay leaf, parsley and seasonings. Add mushrooms; toss to coat. Cover and refrigerate for at least 6 hours. Discard bay leaf. Serve with a slotted spoon. **Yield:** 2 servings.

I've used this recipe since the early '50s, when I picked it up at a seminar. I like to serve these for dessert or as special treats for Halloween.

~Ella West
RICHMOND, VIRGINIA

Frosty Pumpkinettes

  1/4 cup canned pumpkin
    2 tablespoons sugar
1-1/2 teaspoons molasses
  1/8 teaspoon salt
  1/8 teaspoon ground cinnamon
  1/8 teaspoon ground ginger
  3/4 cup vanilla ice cream, softened
    4 individual graham cracker tart shells
    1 tablespoon chopped pecans

In a small mixing bowl, combine the pumpkin, sugar, molasses, salt, cinnamon and ginger; mix well. Fold in ice cream until smooth.

Spoon into tart shells; sprinkle with pecans. Freeze for 1 hour or until serving. Remove from the freezer 10 minutes before serving. **Yield:** 4 tarts.

These muffins are easy to make and can be mixed in just two bowls, making cleanup speedy. This is a pleasant-tasting date muffin with a nice texture, compatible with many meals.

~Deborah Ader
SULLIVAN, INDIANA

Nutty Date Muffins

3/4 cup all-purpose flour
1/4 cup sugar
  1 teaspoon baking powder
1/2 teaspoon ground cinnamon
1/8 teaspoon salt
1/8 teaspoon ground nutmeg
  1 egg
1/3 cup milk
1/4 cup butter, melted
1/4 cup chopped dates
1/4 cup chopped pecans

In a bowl, combine the flour, sugar, baking powder, cinnamon, salt and nutmeg. In another bowl, whisk the egg, milk and butter; stir into the dry ingredients just until moistened. Fold in the dates and pecans.

Fill greased or paper-lined muffin cups two-thirds full. Bake at 400° for 15-20 minutes or until a toothpick comes out clean. Cool for 5 minutes before removing to a wire rack. **Yield:** 6 muffins.

This is an easy method for turning simple pork chops into a hearty summer dish for two. The creamy sauce that tops the pork could not be simpler or more tasty. The chops and sauce make a satisfying entree when served over noodles or rice.

~Collette Conlan
BURLESON, TEXAS

Sesame Pork with Garlic Cream

      2 boneless pork loin chops
        (1/2 inch thick)
1-1/2 teaspoons sesame seeds,
        divided
      1 to 2 garlic cloves, minced
      2 teaspoons butter
  1/3 cup milk
      1 package (3 ounces) cream
        cheese, cubed
      1 tablespoon chopped green onion
Hot cooked pasta

Place pork chops on a broiler pan coated with nonstick cooking spray. Sprinkle with half of the sesame seeds. Broil 4-6 in. from the heat for 6 minutes. Turn over and sprinkle with the remaining sesame seeds. Broil 7-8 minutes longer or until meat juices run clear.

In a skillet, saute garlic in butter for 2 minutes or until tender. Reduce heat to medium-low. Add the milk and cream cheese; whisk until cheese is melted and mixture is smooth. Remove from the heat; stir in onion. Serve the pork chops and garlic cream over pasta. **Yield:** 2 servings.

This salad makes a colorful side dish when served with soup and sandwiches, but it's hearty enough to double as a meal in itself. The curry and chutney lend a nice zip to the dressing.

~Lethea Weber
MACOMB, ILLINOIS

Turkey Rice Salad

  2/3 cup frozen peas
1-1/4 cups cubed cooked turkey
  1/4 cup long grain rice, cooked
  1/4 cup finely chopped carrot
      2 tablespoons chopped onion
  1/3 cup sour cream
      1 tablespoon lemon juice
      1 tablespoon chutney
      1 tablespoon vegetable oil
  1/4 to 1/2 teaspoon curry powder
  1/4 teaspoon salt
  1/8 teaspoon pepper
Lettuce leaves and tomato wedges

Place 1 in. of water in a saucepan; bring to a boil. Add peas. Reduce heat; cover and simmer for 4-6 minutes or until tender. Drain.

In a large bowl, combine the peas, turkey, rice, carrot and onion. In a small bowl, whisk the sour cream, lemon juice, chutney, oil, curry powder, salt and pepper. Add to turkey mixture and toss to coat. Refrigerate for at least 2 hours. Serve over lettuce; top with tomato wedges. **Yield:** 2 servings.

This recipe came about as an experiment. I wanted to make a squash casserole but didn't have crackers, so I substituted instant stuffing mix. My family loved it. It's a good side dish and also serves as a welcomed potluck dish.

~Dot Morgan
MCMINNVILLE, TENNESSEE

Stuffing Squash Casserole

1-1/2 cups instant stuffing mix

3/4 cup boiling water

1 tablespoon butter

1 medium yellow summer squash, diced, cooked and drained

1 egg, beaten

2 tablespoons grated Parmesan cheese

In a bowl, combine the stuffing mix, water and butter; mix well. Let stand for 5 minutes. Add squash and egg. Transfer to greased 1-qt. baking dish; sprinkle with Parmesan cheese. Bake, uncovered, at 350° for 20-25 minutes or until golden brown. **Yield:** 2 servings.

When our friend served us this entree, I asked her for the recipe right away. It was so good, I thought I would share it with others. I cut the recipe down for a meal for two, but it can easily be doubled or tripled. It's great served as either a side dish or a main course.

~Jodee Harding
MT. VERNON, OHIO

Cheesy Chicken 'n' Shells

1-1/2 cups uncooked medium shell pasta

2 tablespoons all-purpose flour

1/4 cup water

1-1/4 cups chicken broth

1 can (10-3/4 ounces) condensed cream of chicken soup, undiluted

1/2 cup process cheese (Velveeta), diced

1/4 teaspoon salt

1/4 teaspoon pepper

1/4 teaspoon poultry seasoning

1/8 teaspoon paprika

1-1/2 cups cubed cooked chicken

3 tablespoons dry bread crumbs

1 tablespoon butter, melted

Cook pasta according to package directions. Meanwhile, in a saucepan, combine the flour and water until smooth. Gradually stir in broth.

Bring to a boil; cook and stir for 2 minutes or until thickened. Reduce heat; add the soup, cheese and seasonings. Cook and stir for 5 minutes or until cheese is melted.

Drain pasta; place in a bowl. Stir in soup mixture and chicken. Transfer to a greased 1-1/2-qt. baking dish. Toss bread crumbs and butter; sprinkle over the top. Bake, uncovered, at 350° for 30 minutes or until golden brown. **Yield:** 2-4 servings.

As the children were growing up, it was fun to try different recipes. If they ate what I served and liked it, I knew I could use it for an entree with company. If the dish passed the kids' palates, I knew others would enjoy it.
~Joi Freeman
OKLAHOMA CITY, OKLAHOMA

Chicken Marmalade

2 boneless skinless chicken breast halves
(about 6 ounces *each*)
1/2 teaspoon lemon-pepper seasoning, *divided*
1/4 teaspoon salt
1 large onion, thinly sliced
1 tablespoon olive oil
1 tablespoon butter
1/4 teaspoon garlic powder
2 tablespoons orange marmalade

Flatten chicken to 1/4-in. thickness. Sprinkle with 1/4 teaspoon lemon-pepper and salt; set aside.

In a large skillet, saute onion in oil and butter until tender. Sprinkle with the garlic powder and remaining lemon-pepper. Remove the onion and keep warm.

In the same skillet, cook chicken over medium heat for 3 minutes on each side or until browned. Spread marmalade over chicken. Return onion to the pan. Reduce heat; cover and simmer for 2-3 minutes or until the marmalade is melted and chicken juices run clear. **Yield:** 2 servings.

This colorful dish has a wonderful combination of flavors. The tarragon and lemon add zest and the honey sweetens the carrots in a perfect balance.

~Musette Colberg
STATEN ISLAND, NEW YORK

Honey Carrots

2 cups julienned carrots
1 thin lemon peel strip
4-1/2 teaspoons honey
1/8 teaspoon salt
1 tablespoon lemon juice
1 teaspoon minced fresh tarragon
   or 1/4 teaspoon dried tarragon
1/8 teaspoon ground nutmeg
1/8 teaspoon pepper

In a saucepan, combine the carrots, lemon peel, honey and salt; add just enough water to cover. Bring to a boil over medium heat.

Reduce heat; simmer, uncovered, for 12-15 minutes or until carrots are tender. Drain; discard lemon peel. Stir in the lemon juice and seasonings. **Yield:** 2 servings.

I've always loved my grandma's recipe for spinach-mandarin salad, so when I found this recipe, I knew it was one I had to try. It's easy to make and great for special occasions. I treasure this recipe and have passed it on to many family members and friends who have asked for it.

~Valerie Belley
ST. LOUIS, MISSOURI

Orange-Cucumber Lettuce Salad

5 cups torn Bibb lettuce
1 navel orange, peeled and sectioned
1/2 medium cucumber, sliced
1/4 cup orange juice
2 tablespoons honey
2 tablespoons olive oil
1/4 teaspoon cider vinegar

On two salad plates, arrange the Bibb lettuce, orange sections and sliced cucumber. In a small bowl, whisk together the orange juice, honey, oil and vinegar. Drizzle over salads. **Yield:** 2 servings.

I make lots of candies and I often add a few ingredients or leave some out. My great-nephew, Josh, is my taste-tester, and this recipe is among his favorites. It seems that my snack jar is always going on empty, but this gives me great joy.

~Marcille Groenke
MINNEAPOLIS, MINNESOTA

Caramel Pecan Clusters

30 pecan halves
6 caramels
6 squares milk chocolate candy bar

On a greased baking sheet, arrange pecans in six clusters of five pecans each. Place a caramel on each cluster. Bake at 300° for 4-5 minutes or until caramels are melted.

Top each with a chocolate square. Bake 1 minute longer or until chocolate is melted. Spread the chocolate over caramel until smooth. Remove clusters from pan to cool on a wire rack. **Yield:** 6 clusters.

Fresh-baked muffins topped with butter or fruity jam can make any meal special. These honey-wheat muffins bake up quick as a wink and are filled with flavor. The recipe makes four large or eight regular muffins. I serve them with a cool summer salad and call it supper!

~Edna Hoffman
HEBRON, INDIANA

Honey-Wheat Muffins

3/4 cup all-purpose flour
3/4 cup whole wheat flour
2 teaspoons baking powder
1/2 teaspoon salt
1 egg
1/2 cup milk
1/2 cup honey
1/4 cup butter, melted

In a bowl, combine the flours, baking powder and salt. In another bowl, combine the egg, milk, honey and butter. Stir mixture into the dry ingredients just until combined.

Fill greased or paper-lined muffin cups two-thirds full. Bake at 400° for 15-20 minutes or until a toothpick comes out clean. Cool for 5 minutes before removing from pan to a wire rack. **Yield:** 8 muffins.

Helpful Hint
Minute Muffins

To take fresh muffins to a gathering without last-minute fuss, make your batter ahead of time and freeze it in nonstick tins or paper muffin cups. Later, just bake as many as you need right from the freezer, adding about 10 additional minutes to the baking time.

We have always enjoyed scrambled eggs for any meal…breakfast, lunch or dinner. Maybe it was because this was one of the first dishes we taught the children in the family to cook and they especially liked to make it.

~Patrice Marlowe
HAVERTOWN, PENNSYLVANIA

Tomato-Egg Scramble

3 eggs
2 tablespoons milk
1/4 teaspoon salt
Dash pepper
3 tablespoons finely chopped onion
1 tablespoon butter
1 small fresh tomato, seeded and diced
2 slices bread, toasted and buttered

In a bowl, whisk together the eggs, milk, salt and pepper. Set aside. In a skillet, saute onion in butter until tender. Add egg mixture; cook and stir over medium heat until eggs are completely set. Stir in tomato. Spoon over toast. **Yield:** 2 servings.

My husband's grandmother came from Germany, so I was inspired to keep the German cooking traditions going in our family. This skillet dinner is one of the dishes she made.
~Lucy Bradshaw
NEW BERN, NORTH CAROLINA

Bratwurst Potato Skillet

2 teaspoons vegetable oil
2 medium red potatoes, cut into 1/4-inch slices
2 fully cooked bratwurst links, cut into 1-inch pieces
1 small onion, chopped
1/3 cup chopped green pepper
2 tablespoons soy sauce
1 tablespoon orange juice
1/2 teaspoon dried basil
1/4 teaspoon salt
Dash pepper

In a heavy skillet, heat oil over medium-high heat. Add the potatoes; cover and cook for 6 minutes or until browned and crisp-tender, stirring occasionally.

Add bratwurst, onion and green pepper. Cook and stir for 5 minutes or until meat is heated through and vegetables are crisp-tender.

Combine the soy sauce, orange juice, basil, salt and pepper; add to the skillet. Cook and stir 1-2 minutes longer or until meat and vegetables are evenly coated. **Yield:** 2 servings.

This is my favorite mainstay meal because it's fast, easy and very tasty. When I want to serve more than just my husband and me, I simply double or triple the recipe.
~Roxanne Kamberaj
WEST SENECA, NEW YORK

Pecan Chicken a la King

1/4 cup chopped celery
2 tablespoons butter
1 teaspoon chicken bouillon granules
2 tablespoons all-purpose flour
1/8 to 1/4 teaspoon salt
1/8 teaspoon poultry seasoning
1-1/4 cups milk
1 cup cubed cooked chicken
1 tablespoon diced pimientos
1 teaspoon lemon juice
1/4 cup chopped pecans, *divided*
Hot cooked rice

In a saucepan, saute celery in butter until tender. Add bouillon, stirring until dissolved. Stir in the flour, salt and poultry seasoning until blended. Gradually add milk, stirring until smooth. Bring to a boil over medium heat; cook and stir for 2 minutes or until thickened.

Add the chicken, pimientos, lemon juice and half of the pecans; cook until heated through. Serve over the rice. Sprinkle with remaining pecans. **Yield:** 2 servings.

A hot, **home-cooked meal** is just minutes away with these recipes that can be made in **half an hour** or less.

Meals in Minutes

TASTY TERIYAKI. Clockwise from left: Swiss Spinach Salad, Pink Lemonade Pie and Orange Beef Teriyaki (all recipes on p. 173).

Tasty *Teriyaki Meal*

This dish is my favorite anytime stir-fry. When my family comes to visit me, it satisfies them fast. My garden offers up a treasure trove of fresh vegetables to spark my imagination. When I toss my spinach with Swiss cheese and bacon, the salad tastes like quiche lorraine...without the effort. Plus, it's special enough to serve at patio parties with family and friends. A cool comfort food is Pink Lemonade Pie. On very hot days, I serve it straight from the freezer. That way, it's slightly frosty and extra refreshing.

~Nella Parker
HERSEY, MICHIGAN

Orange Beef Teriyaki

1 can (11 ounces) mandarin oranges
1 tablespoon cornstarch
1-1/2 pounds boneless beef sirloin steak, thinly sliced
2 tablespoons vegetable oil
1/2 cup soy sauce
2 tablespoons honey
1-1/2 teaspoons ground ginger
1 garlic clove, minced
Hot cooked rice
Green onion and orange peel curls, optional

Drain oranges, reserving juice; set oranges aside. In a small bowl, combine cornstarch and 2 tablespoons reserved juice until smooth; set aside.

In a large skillet or wok, stir-fry beef in oil. Add the soy sauce, honey, ginger, garlic and remaining juice. Cover and cook over medium heat for 5-10 minutes or until meat is tender.

Stir cornstarch mixture; stir into beef mixture. Bring to a boil; cook and stir for 2 minutes or until thickened. Stir in the oranges. Serve over rice. Garnish with curls if desired. **Yield:** 4-6 servings.

Swiss Spinach Salad

1 package (6 ounces) fresh baby spinach
1 cup (4 ounces) shredded Swiss cheese
3 tablespoons crumbled cooked bacon
1/2 cup Caesar salad dressing
Salad croutons

In a large bowl, combine spinach, cheese and bacon. Drizzle with dressing and toss to coat. Top with croutons. Serve immediately. **Yield:** 4-6 servings.

Pink Lemonade Pie

1 package (8 ounces) cream cheese, softened
3/4 cup pink lemonade concentrate
4 drops red food coloring, optional
1 carton (8 ounces) frozen whipped topping, thawed
1 shortbread pie crust (9 inches)
Lemon slices and additional whipped topping, optional

In a large mixing bowl, beat the cream cheese until smooth. Beat in lemonade and food coloring if desired. Fold in whipped topping. Spoon into pie crust. Freeze for 20 minutes. Refrigerate until serving. Garnish with lemon and additional whipped topping if desired. **Yield:** 6-8 servings.

Hawaiian *Crowd Pleaser*

Moist and tender, Aloha Chicken gets fruitful flavor from pineapple, peaches and a zesty lemon glaze. The main dish can be adapted to feature browned or precooked pork chops. You can also swap pineapple rings for tidbits. I quickly stir up the taste of curry when I serve Curried Confetti Corn in a glass bowl for our weekly family dinners. You can try 1-1/2 to 2 cups of fresh or frozen corn instead of canned kernels for the zesty side. As a finale, I bake syrup-soaked cakes called Baby Orange Babas. By using a muffin pan, I make individual-size servings of the citrusy dessert without putting a squeeze on my time. For an interesting flavor variation, drizzle your babas with syrup made from lemon or lime juice and grated peel. ~Gail Hutton*

BREMERTON, WASHINGTON

Aloha Chicken

- 4 boneless skinless chicken breast halves
- 4 tablespoons butter, *divided*
- 1 teaspoon cornstarch
- 1/3 cup pineapple juice
- 1/4 cup lemon juice
- 1 teaspoon grated lemon peel
- 1 teaspoon soy sauce
- 1/4 teaspoon dried thyme
- 2 tablespoons chopped onion
- 1 can (15-1/4 ounces) peach halves, drained
- 1 cup pineapple tidbits, drained

Hot cooked rice, optional

In a large skillet, brown chicken on both sides in 2 tablespoons butter. Transfer to a shallow microwave-safe dish. Cover and microwave on high for 4-5 minutes or until juices run clear.

In a small bowl, combine cornstarch and pineapple juice until smooth. Stir in the lemon juice, lemon peel, soy sauce and thyme. In the same skillet, saute onion in remaining butter until tender. Stir juice mixture and add to the skillet. Bring to a boil; cook and stir for 2 minutes or until thickened.

Arrange peaches and pineapple over chicken; baste with sauce. Cover and microwave for 1 minute or until sauce is bubbly. Serve over rice with remaining sauce if desired. **Yield:** 4 servings.

Editor's Note: This recipe was tested in a 1,100-watt microwave.

Curried Confetti Corn

- 3 tablespoons chopped onion
- 2 tablespoons chopped sweet red pepper
- 2 tablespoons chopped green pepper
- 3 tablespoons butter
- 2 cans (11 ounces *each*) Mexicorn, drained
- 3/4 teaspoon curry powder
- 1/2 teaspoon salt
- 1/4 teaspoon pepper
- 3/4 cup sour cream

In a small skillet, saute onion and peppers in butter. Add corn, curry powder, salt and pepper. Cook over low heat until vegetables are heated through. Stir in sour cream. Cook 1 minute longer or until heated through. **Yield:** 4 servings.

Baby Orange Babas

- 1 package (9 ounces) yellow cake mix
- 1/2 cup sugar
- 1/2 cup water
- 1/2 cup orange juice
- 2 teaspoons finely grated orange peel

Whipped topping and maraschino cherries

Prepare cake batter according to package directions. Fill greased muffin cups two-thirds full. Bake at 375° for 15 minutes or until a toothpick comes out clean. Cool for 10 minutes.

Meanwhile, in a saucepan, combine the sugar, water, orange juice and orange peel. Cook and stir for 5 minutes over medium heat until sugar is dissolved. Invert cupcakes onto a platter; immediately drizzle with hot orange syrup. Freeze for 10 minutes. Serve with whipped topping and cherries. **Yield:** 9 servings.

These golden baked fillets have the delicious crunch of batter-fried catfish without the extra calories or prep time. I often put the fish and crumb mixture into a plastic bag and shake on the coating without making a mess. A dash of lemon juice or salsa complements the mild fish nicely.

~Kay Bell
PALESTINE, TEXAS

Oven-Fried Catfish

1 cup crushed cornflakes
3/4 teaspoon celery salt
1/4 teaspoon onion powder
1/4 teaspoon paprika
1/8 teaspoon pepper
6 catfish fillets (6 ounces *each*)
1/3 cup butter, melted

In a shallow bowl, combine the cornflakes, celery salt, onion powder, paprika and pepper. Brush the fish fillets with butter; coat with crumb mixture.

Place in a greased 13-in. x 9-in. x 2-in. baking dish. Bake, uncovered, at 350° for 25 minutes or until fish flakes easily with a fork. **Yield:** 6 servings.

My broccoli side dish is an appealing partner for any entree. A buttery hint of citrus comes through deliciously in the sauce, and almonds add taste and texture.

~Tricia Moore
SOMERSWORTH, NEW HAMPSHIRE

Orange Broccoli

2 pounds fresh broccoli florets
5 tablespoons butter, cubed
1/4 cup orange juice
1 teaspoon grated orange peel
1/2 teaspoon salt
1/3 cup slivered almonds

Place 1 in. of water in a saucepan; add broccoli. Bring to a boil. Reduce heat; cover and simmer for 5-8 minutes or until crisp-tender. Drain and keep warm.

In the same pan, combine the butter, orange juice, orange peel and salt; heat until butter is melted. Return the broccoli to the saucepan; toss to coat. Transfer to a serving bowl; sprinkle with almonds. **Yield:** 6 servings.

I serve these treats as a snappy dessert or when sweet munchies are needed for company. The ladies in my card club rave about them, and I've even brought a fresh batch to a cookie exchange. These dressed-up graham crackers are an instant cure for the "hungries" any time of day. Try them as a late-night snack with a glass of ice-cold milk—delicious!

~Jean Komlos
PLYMOUTH, MICHIGAN

Praline Snackers

24 graham cracker squares
1/2 cup butter, cubed
1/2 cup packed brown sugar
1/2 teaspoon vanilla extract
1/2 cup chopped pecans
1 cup miniature marshmallows
1/4 cup chocolate syrup

Arrange graham crackers in a single layer in a foil-lined 15-in. x 10-in. x 1-in. baking pan. In a saucepan, bring butter and brown sugar to a boil; cook and stir just until sugar is dissolved. Remove from the heat; add vanilla. Pour evenly over crackers; sprinkle with nuts.

Bake at 350° for 5 minutes. Sprinkle with marshmallows; bake 3-5 minutes longer or until top is bubbly and marshmallows are lightly browned. Drizzle with chocolate syrup. Cool for 10 minutes. Break into squares. **Yield:** 2 dozen.

I rely on Stuffed Ham Rolls for weeknight meals with my husband, Joe, and as an entree for guests and potluck suppers. The rolls are ideal for a brunch, lunch or dinner served with fresh corn bread muffins. If you'd like, try garnishing the ham rolls with parsley, cherry tomatoes and fancy sandwich picks. You might substitute deli turkey slices and poultry-flavored stuffing as main ingredients also. I came up with a fuss-free Onion Cheese Sauce for the ham rolls. The recipe makes enough extra to use as a smooth, mild sauce on a side vegetable like cauliflower, broccoli or brussels sprouts. Instead of Onion Cheese Sauce, I recommend working warm honey-mustard barbecue sauce into my menu. Or, you could heat a half cup of either apple jelly or cranberry sauce and mix in a few plump raisins. My fruity Banana Delight Dessert saves me time twice. Not only is it a snap to assemble, it's so attractive, I don't need to make table decorations.

~Agnes Bucko
KUNKLETOWN, PENNSYLVANIA

Stuffed Ham Rolls

  1 package (6 ounces)
    pork-flavored stuffing mix
  8 slices deli ham
  1 cup Onion Cheese Sauce (recipe below)

Prepare stuffing mix according to package directions. Spread 1/4 cup stuffing lengthwise down the center of each slice of ham. (Save remaining stuffing for another use.)

Beginning with a long side, roll up. Place in a microwave-safe dish. Cover and microwave on high for 1-2 minutes or until heated through; serve with cheese sauce. **Yield:** 4 servings.

Editor's Note: This recipe was tested in an 1,100-watt microwave.

Onion Cheese Sauce

  1 small onion, chopped
  2 tablespoons butter
  2 tablespoons all-purpose flour
Salt and pepper to taste
1-1/4 cups milk
1-1/4 cups shredded cheddar cheese

In a saucepan, saute onion in butter. Stir in the flour, salt and pepper until blended. Gradually add the milk.

Bring to a boil; cook and stir for 1-2 minutes or until thickened. Reduce heat. Add the cheddar cheese; cook and stir until cheese is melted. **Yield:** 1-3/4 cups.

Banana Delight Dessert

  2 large ripe bananas, cut into quarters
  4 slices pineapple, cut into halves
1/2 cup whipped topping
  4 maraschino cherries

Place two banana quarters and two pineapple halves on each of four dessert or small plates. Top each with whipped topping and a cherry. **Yield:** 4 servings.

The egg noodles make a great crust and don't require the time it takes pizza dough to rise. Often, I use my food processor to chop up ingredients quickly. Or I'll buy presliced and shredded veggies and cheese. If your family likes pizza with every topping imaginable, you can add sausage, herbs, peppers and unique sauces to this casserole. Sometimes, I put different toppings on certain sections of the dish so each of us has a portion featuring our favorite pizza trimmings. ~C.C. Yeats
LEWISTON, IDAHO

Pepperoni Pizza Bake

    1 package (16 ounces) wide egg noodles
2-1/4 cups pizza sauce, *divided*
    1 cup sliced fresh mushrooms
    1 can (2-1/4 ounces) sliced ripe olives, drained
    1 package (3-1/2 ounces) sliced pepperoni
    2 cups (8 ounces) shredded mozzarella cheese

Cook the noodles according to package directions; drain. In a bowl, combine the noodles and 3/4 cup pizza sauce. Transfer to a greased 13-in. x 9-in. x 2-in. baking dish. Top with the remaining pizza sauce.

Layer with the mushrooms, olives and pepperoni. Sprinkle with cheese. Bake, uncovered, at 375° for 15-18 minutes or until heated through and cheese is melted. **Yield:** 8 servings.

I use a snappy recipe for my tossed salad that I can squeeze into any menu. Simple and colorful, it complements a casual lunch or a fancy holiday dinner. It's a little different from plain old iceberg lettuce and tomatoes. Canned kidney beans add protein and texture, and the pepperoni and other fixings give it a fresh, zesty taste. ~Gayle Parker
BELLVILLE, OHIO

Italian Tossed Salad

    1 package (12 ounces) ready-to-serve salad greens
    1 cup (4 ounces) shredded mozzarella cheese
    1 cup canned kidney beans, drained
    1 cup diced pepperoni
1/4 cup chopped onion

    2 medium tomatoes, diced
1/4 to 1/2 cup Italian salad dressing

In a salad bowl, combine the salad greens, cheese, beans, pepperoni, onion and diced tomatoes. Drizzle with dressing; toss to coat. **Yield:** 8 servings.

One of my favorite desserts comes together quick. It's made with only three ingredients that I always have on hand—ice cream, honey and nuts. Feel free to vary the measurements and use as much of each ingredient as you like. You could sprinkle on walnuts instead of almonds. And adding pecans will make you think you're eating pralines. This is such a pretty way to dress up a scoop of ice cream. It's a refreshing finishing touch. ~Tricia Moore
SOMERSWORTH, NEW HAMPSHIRE

Honey-Nut Ice Cream

1-1/2 quarts ice cream
    1/2 cup honey
    3 tablespoons slivered almonds, toasted

Scoop ice cream into serving dishes and drizzle with honey. Sprinkle with toasted almonds. **Yield:** 8 servings.

Among my creative morning offerings is the menu presented here. Like all beat-the-clock meals featured in this chapter, it can start waking up family taste buds in half an hour. Our grown children are big fans of ham and cheese. My Ham 'n' Swiss Rolls are perfect for families on the go. I started fixing Fluffy Scrambled Eggs years ago when we raised chickens and had fresh ingredients every morning. They're hard to beat when it comes to taste and texture. You can add zip and substance to the Fluffy Scrambled Eggs by mixing in bits of red or green pepper and diced sausages. My refreshing Strawberry Breakfast Shakes are so versatile, they can double as a fast snack. I make them when I baby-sit for our grandson, Jamie. The shakes can also be blended and frozen ahead of time and then taken to work. Pop one in the fridge and eat it with a spoon for lunch. Shake up the breakfast beverage by using fruits other than strawberries. Try raspberries, blackberries, blueberries or chunks of pineapple and banana instead.

~Marjorie Carey
FREEPORT, FLORIDA

Ham 'n' Swiss Rolls

1 tube (8 ounces) refrigerated crescent rolls
1 cup diced fully cooked ham
3/4 cup finely shredded Swiss cheese
1-1/2 teaspoons prepared mustard
1 teaspoon finely chopped onion

Separate crescent rolls into eight triangles. Combine the ham, cheese, mustard and onion; place 2 tablespoons in the center of each triangle. Fold points toward center and pinch edges to seal. Place on a lightly greased baking sheet. Bake at 375° for 11-13 minutes or until lightly browned. **Yield:** 4 servings (2 rolls each).

Fluffy Scrambled Eggs

8 eggs
1 can (5 ounces) evaporated milk
2 tablespoons butter
Salt and pepper to taste

In a bowl, whisk the eggs and milk until combined. In a skillet, heat butter until hot. Add egg mixture; cook and stir over medium-low heat until eggs are completely set. Season with salt and pepper. **Yield:** 4 servings.

Strawberry Breakfast Shakes

1-1/4 cups plain yogurt
1 package (10 ounces) frozen sweetened sliced strawberries
2/3 cup milk
2/3 cup crushed ice
1 tablespoon honey
4 whole strawberries

In a blender, combine the first five ingredients; cover and process mixture until smooth and thickened. Pour into chilled glasses. Garnish with whole strawberries. Serve immediately. **Yield:** 4 servings.

Helpful Hint
Hearty Scrambled Eggs

Like some add-ins for Fluffy Scrambled Eggs? In a large skillet, saute 1 cup cubed fully cooked ham and 1 cup sliced fresh mushrooms, 1/2 cup chopped sweet red pepper and 1/4 cup sliced green onions in 2 tablespoons butter until vegetables are tender. Remove vegetables and set aside. Whisk eggs with milk as directed in recipe above and add to skillet.

Cook and stir until eggs are slightly set. Add the ham mixture and continue to cook until eggs are completely set. Remove from the heat. If desired, sprinkle top with 1 cup (4 ounces) shredded cheddar cheese; cover and let stand for 1-2 minutes or until cheese is melted.

Comforting recipes still bring families together around the table.

Most Memorable Meals

UNFORGETTABLE FARE. From left: Jalapeno Corn Bread (p. 187), Southwestern Three-Meat Chili (p. 186), Italian Salad Dressing (p. 187) and Mexican Ice Cream Sundaes (p. 187).

When Mom came to live with me, I told her it was now my turn to cook. One goal was to enhance recipes of the Southwest, so I tried variations and developed several recipes. This chili is a favorite.

~Bob Wyatt
KANSAS CITY, MISSOURI

Southwestern Three-Meat Chili

3 pounds ground beef

1 pound pork tenderloin, cut into 1/2-inch cubes

1 pound bulk Italian sausage

2 large onions, chopped

2 celery ribs, diced

1 medium green pepper, diced

3 garlic cloves, minced

2 cans (28 ounces *each*) diced tomatoes, undrained

3 cans (15 ounces *each*) pinto beans, rinsed and drained

1 can (16 ounces) kidney beans, rinsed and drained

2 cans (4 ounces *each*) chopped green chilies

1 can (8 ounces) tomato sauce

1 cup beef broth

1 can (6 ounces) tomato paste

7-1/2 teaspoons chili powder

2 tablespoons ground cumin

2 tablespoons lemon juice

1 tablespoon all-purpose flour

1 tablespoon dried oregano

1 tablespoon brown sugar

1-1/2 teaspoons salt

1/2 teaspoon pepper

2 bay leaves

In a soup kettle or Dutch oven, cook the beef, pork and sausage over medium heat until no longer pink; drain. Add the onions, celery, green pepper and garlic; cook for 8-10 minutes or until vegetables are tender. Stir in the remaining ingredients. Bring to a boil. Reduce heat; simmer, uncovered, for 1-1/2 hours. Discard bay leaves before serving. **Yield:** 18-20 servings.

After many years of experimenting, I developed this recipe for corn bread. You can adjust the "heat" by the number of jalapeno peppers you use.

~Archie Timmons
MILWAUKIE, OREGON

Jalapeno Corn Bread

(Also pictured on front cover)

1-1/2 cups cornmeal
   1/2 cup all-purpose flour
   6 tablespoons sugar
   2 teaspoons baking powder
   1 teaspoon salt
1/2 teaspoon baking soda
   2 eggs
   1 cup buttermilk
1/4 cup olive oil
   3 jalapeno peppers, seeded and finely chopped

In a bowl, combine the first six ingredients. In another bowl, whisk the eggs, buttermilk and oil. Add to the dry ingredients and stir just until moistened. Stir in jalapenos. Pour into a greased 9-in. square baking pan.

Bake at 400° for 20-22 minutes or until a toothpick inserted near the center comes out clean. Cut into squares or wedges. Serve warm. **Yield:** 9 servings.

Editor's Note: When cutting or seeding hot peppers, use rubber or plastic gloves to protect your hands. Avoid touching your face.

I always have this dressing on hand since it yields a large jar. Italian salad dressing is very versatile.

~Maxine Johnson
FENTON, MICHIGAN

Italian Salad Dressing

1/3 cup sugar
   1 envelope Italian salad dressing mix
   3 garlic cloves, minced
3/4 cup cider vinegar
3/4 cup water
3/4 cup vegetable oil

In a small bowl, combine the sugar, salad dressing mix, garlic, vinegar and water; gradually whisk in oil. Store in the refrigerator. Stir before serving. **Yield:** about 2-1/3 cups.

This dessert makes an impressive presentation. The flour tortillas take on a subtle flavor sprinkled with cinnamon-sugar.

~Milbert Fichter
PITTSBURGH, PENNSYLVANIA

Mexican Ice Cream Sundaes

1/2 cup vegetable oil
   6 flour tortillas (6 inches), cut into 6 wedges *each*
   2 tablespoons sugar
1/2 teaspoon ground cinnamon
1/4 cup crushed cornflakes
   6 large scoops vanilla ice cream
Chocolate syrup, optional
Whipped cream in a can
   6 maraschino cherries with stems

In a large skillet, heat oil over medium heat. Fry tortilla wedges, a few at a time, for 1-2 minutes on each side or until crisp. Drain on paper towels. Combine the sugar and cinnamon; set aside 1 tablespoon. Sprinkle both sides of tortillas with remaining cinnamon-sugar.

In a shallow bowl, combine cornflake crumbs and reserved cinnamon-sugar. Roll ice cream in crumb mixture to coat. Freeze until serving.

Drizzle serving plates with chocolate syrup if desired. Place six tortilla wedges on each plate; top each with a scoop of ice cream. Pipe whipped cream around base and on top of ice cream. Garnish each with a cherry. **Yield:** 6 servings.

My mother got this recipe in the '40s, and I often requested this dish for my birthday meal.

~Peggy Lewis
MEAD, WASHINGTON

Short Ribs with Plums

    2 to 2-1/2 pounds beef short ribs
    1 tablespoon vegetable oil
    1/3 cup chopped onion
    1 teaspoon salt
    1 teaspoon browning sauce,
        optional
    1/4 teaspoon pepper
    1 cup water, *divided*
    15 pitted dried plums
    1 tablespoon cornstarch
Hot cooked rice

In a large skillet, brown the meat in oil over medium heat. Remove meat; keep warm. Add onion to the drippings. Saute onion until tender, scraping the pan to loosen browned bits; drain. Add the salt, browning sauce if desired, pepper, 3/4 cup water and dried plums. Bring to a boil; return meat to the pan. Reduce heat; cover and simmer for 1 hour or until meat is tender. Remove meat; keep warm.

Skim fat from the pan. Combine the cornstarch and the remaining water until smooth. Stir into pan drippings. Bring to a boil; cook and stir for 2 minutes or until thickened. Serve with ribs and rice. **Yield:** 4 servings.

This is a great salad that's worth trying. The combination of vegetables and a thick, creamy dressing make a perfect blend.
~Carl Anderson
LAKEVIEW, OHIO

Tasty Tossed Salad

8 cups torn leaf lettuce

1 cup sliced peeled cucumber

1 cup cauliflowerets

1 cup halved cherry tomatoes, optional

1 cup (4 ounces) shredded Mexican cheese blend

3 green onions, chopped

1/4 cup French onion dip

1/4 cup ranch salad dressing

In a large bowl, combine the lettuce, cucumber, cauliflower, tomatoes if desired, cheese and onions. In a small bowl, whisk together the dip and salad dressing. Serve with salad. **Yield:** 6-8 servings.

This is the only onion soup recipe I know of that is baked in a casserole, making it easy to serve to a crowd as a first course.
~Jeanne Robinson
CINNAMINSON, NEW JERSEY

Baked Beefy Onion Soup

1-1/2 pounds meaty beef soup bones

2 quarts water

1 medium carrot, quartered

4 black peppercorns

3 teaspoons beef bouillon granules

2 sprigs fresh parsley

2 large onions, thinly sliced

1/4 cup butter

6 slices French bread (1/2 inch thick)

6 slices Swiss cheese

In a soup kettle, combine the first six ingredients. Bring to a boil over medium-high heat. Reduce heat; cover and simmer for 3 hours. Strain the broth, discarding soup bones, carrot and seasonings; skim fat.

Meanwhile, in a large skillet, saute the onions in butter over medium heat for 30 minutes or until golden brown. Divide the onions among six ovenproof bowls. Ladle about 1 cup of broth into each. Top each with a slice of bread and Swiss cheese. Bake at 350° for 50-55 minutes or until golden brown. **Yield:** 6 servings.

I combined recipes to create these heart-shaped cookies for Valentine's Day, but you can enjoy them anytime. My children are grown, but I still bake the cookies for my husband and myself and for others.
~Sue Garrett
QULIN, MISSOURI

Valentine Cookies

1 cup butter, softened

1 cup sugar

1 egg

3 teaspoons vanilla extract

2 teaspoons almond extract

2-1/2 cups all-purpose flour

1 teaspoon baking powder

1/4 teaspoon salt

Prepared vanilla frosting and red colored sugar, optional

In a large mixing bowl, cream butter and sugar. Add egg, beating well. Add extracts; mix well. Combine the flour, baking powder and salt; add to the creamed mixture until combined. Cover and refrigerate for 3 hours or until easy to handle.

On a lightly floured surface, roll out dough to 1/8-in. thickness. Cut with a 3-in. heart-shaped cookie cutter dipped in flour. Place 1 in. apart on ungreased baking sheets.

Bake at 325° for 13-15 minutes or until lightly browned. Remove to wire racks to cool. Decorate with frosting and colored sugar if desired. **Yield:** 3 dozen.

During the '40s, Mother had a close group of friends whose husbands or sons were off to war. To ease their worries, the group frequently met for lunch. This was one of my mother's favorite lunch recipes.

~Marilyn Bagshaw
SAN RAFAEL, CALIFORNIA

Golden Shrimp Brunch Casserole

6 eggs

2-1/2 cups milk

2 tablespoons minced fresh parsley

3/4 teaspoon ground mustard

1/2 teaspoon salt

10 slices bread, crusts removed and cubed

2 cups frozen cooked salad shrimp, thawed

1 block (8 ounces) process cheese (Velveeta), cut into thin strips

In a large bowl, whisk eggs, milk, parsley, mustard and salt. In a greased 11-in. x 7-in. x 2-in. baking dish, layer bread cubes, shrimp and cheese; pour egg mixture over top.

Bake, uncovered, at 325° for 50-55 minutes or until mixture is set and top is puffed and golden. Let stand for 10 minutes before serving. **Yield:** 6 servings.

This very flavorful sausage ring is easy to prepare. It has a nice texture and holds its shape well...a warm, hearty meat dish that completes a brunch menu.

~Dorothy Elliott
DEKALB, ILLINOIS

Apple Sausage Ring

3 eggs
3/4 cup milk
2 cups crushed butter-flavored crackers (about 50 crackers)
1-1/2 cups chopped peeled tart apples
1/3 cup finely chopped onion
2 pounds bulk pork sausage

In a large bowl, beat eggs and milk. Stir in the cracker crumbs, apples and onion. Crumble sausage over mixture and mix well.

On a 15-in. x 10-in. x 1-in. baking pan coated with nonstick cooking spray, shape pork mixture into a 9-in. ring. Bake, uncovered, at 350° for 1 hour or until a meat thermometer reads 160°; drain. **Yield:** 12-14 servings.

I have been making this punch for over 40 years; my mother made it before I did. As soon as I see the first mint sprigs in my garden, I make my signature recipe.

~Janet Maulick
WHITE HAVEN, PENNSYLVANIA

Citrus Tea Punch

6 individual tea bags
6 cups boiling water
1-1/2 cups sugar
3 cups chilled club soda
2 cups orange juice
1 cup lemon juice
Crushed ice

Orange and lemon slices
Fresh mint sprigs, optional

Steep tea bags in boiling water for 15 minutes. Discard bags. Stir sugar into tea until dissolved.

Add the soda, orange juice and lemon juice; mix well. Refrigerate until chilled. Serve over ice. Garnish with orange and lemon slices and mint if desired. **Yield:** 3 quarts.

The lemon flavor in these yeast muffins makes them unique. My husband is a minister, and we're invited to many potlucks. People love these muffins.

~Marilyn Davis
ELLOREE, SOUTH CAROLINA

Lemon Yeast Puffs

1 package (1/4 ounce) active dry yeast
1/4 cup warm water (110° to 115°)
3/4 cup warm milk (110° to 115°)
1/3 cup sugar
1/3 cup shortening
1 tablespoon grated lemon peel
1 teaspoon salt
1 teaspoon lemon juice
2 eggs
3 cups all-purpose flour

TOPPING:
1 tablespoon sugar
1/2 teaspoon ground cinnamon

In a mixing bowl, dissolve yeast in warm water. Add milk, sugar, shortening, lemon peel, salt, lemon juice, eggs and 1-1/2 cups flour. Beat on low speed for 30 seconds. Beat on high for 3 minutes. Stir in remaining flour (batter will be thick). Do not knead. Cover; let rise in a warm place until doubled, about 1 hour.

Stir dough down. Fill greased muffin cups half full. Cover and let rise until doubled, about 30 minutes. Combine sugar and cinnamon; sprinkle over the dough. Bake at 375° for 15-20 minutes or until golden brown. Remove from pans to wire racks. Serve warm. **Yield:** 1-1/2 dozen.

When my mother was growing up, her mom made mince pies that contained meat. I created this recipe with my grandmother in mind.

~Candice Salazar
LOS ALAMOS, NEW MEXICO

Christmas Pork Pie

2 cups beef broth
3/4 cup chopped onion
1/2 cup diced dried apricots
1/2 cup raisins
1/2 cup whole-berry cranberry sauce
1/2 cup undrained crushed pineapple
1/2 teaspoon curry powder
1/4 teaspoon ground cinnamon
1 tablespoon cornstarch
1 tablespoon water
3 cups cubed cooked pork
1/2 cup chopped pecans
1/2 teaspoon salt
Pastry for double-crust pie (9 inches)
Milk and sugar

In a large saucepan, combine the first eight ingredients. Cook over medium heat for 20 minutes. Combine cornstarch and water until smooth; stir into fruit mixture. Bring to a boil; cook and stir for 2 minutes or until thickened. Remove from the heat; stir in pork, pecans and salt.

Line a 9-in. pie plate with bottom pastry; trim even with edge of plate. Fill with meat mixture. Roll out remaining pastry to fit the top of pie; make decorative cutouts in pastry. Set cutouts aside. Place top crust over filling; trim, seal and flute edges.

Brush pastry and cutouts with milk; place cutouts on top of pie. Sprinkle with sugar. Bake at 400° for 30-35 minutes or until golden brown. Cool for 10 minutes before serving. Refrigerate leftovers. **Yield:** 6 servings.

Cheese Potato Casserole

    5 tablespoons butter, *divided*
1/4 all-purpose flour
1/2 teaspoon salt
    2 cups milk
1/2 cup shredded cheddar cheese
1/2 cup shredded Romano cheese
    8 cups sliced cooked peeled potatoes
    1 tablespoon lemon juice
1/4 cup dry bread crumbs

In a large saucepan, melt 4 tablespoons butter. Stir in the flour and salt until smooth. Gradually add milk. Bring to a boil; cook and stir for 2 minutes or until thickened. Remove from the heat.

Stir in the cheeses until melted. Add potatoes; stir gently to coat. Transfer to a greased 2-1/2-qt. baking dish. Sprinkle with lemon juice.

In a small skillet, melt the remaining butter. Add bread crumbs; cook and stir over medium heat until lightly browned. Sprinkle over potato mixture. Bake, uncovered, at 350° for 40-45 minutes or until hot and bubbly. **Yield:** 6-8 servings.

Apple-Bacon Green Beans

6 bacon strips, diced
1 small onion, diced
1 package (16 ounces) frozen cut green beans
1 large tart apple, chopped
3 tablespoons brown sugar
3 tablespoons cider vinegar

2 tablespoons dried parsley flakes
Salt and pepper to taste

In a large skillet, cook bacon and onion over medium heat until bacon is crisp. Stir in the remaining ingredients. Reduce heat; cover and simmer until the apple and beans are tender. **Yield:** 5 servings.

Mint-Filled Brownies

1/3 cup shortening
    1 cup sugar
1/2 teaspoon vanilla extract
    2 eggs
    2 squares (1 ounce *each*) unsweetened chocolate, melted and cooled
    1 tablespoon half-and-half cream
2/3 cup all-purpose flour
1/4 teaspoon salt
1/3 cup chopped walnuts
1/4 cup chopped raisins

FILLING:
1-1/2 cups confectioners' sugar
    2 tablespoons hot milk
    1 teaspoon butter, melted

1/2 to 3/4 teaspoon peppermint extract
Green food coloring, optional

In a mixing bowl, cream the shortening, sugar and vanilla. Add eggs; mix well. Beat in chocolate and cream. Combine flour and salt; add to creamed mixture. Stir in walnuts and raisins.

Spread into two greased and floured 9-in. square baking pans. Bake at 350° for 15-20 minutes or until a toothpick inserted near the center comes out clean. Cool for 10 minutes before removing from pans to wire racks to cool completely.

Combine the filling ingredients; spread over one brownie layer. Top with second layer. Chill before cutting. **Yield:** about 2 dozen.

Comforting *Chicken Dinner*

There is no need for a special occasion to prepare this chicken recipe. It makes every occasion special!

~Lola Clifton
VINTON, VIRGINIA

Best-Ever Fried Chicken

(Also pictured on front cover)

1-1/2 to 2 cups all-purpose flour
2 teaspoons dried thyme
2 teaspoons paprika
1-1/2 teaspoons salt
1 egg, lightly beaten
1/3 cup milk
2 tablespoons lemon juice
1 broiler/fryer chicken (3 to 4 pounds), cut up
Oil for deep-fat frying

In a large resealable plastic bag, combine the first four ingredients. In a shallow bowl, combine the egg, milk and lemon juice. Place chicken pieces, one at a time, in the flour mixture; seal and shake to coat. Dip in the egg mixture and coat again with flour mixture.

In an electric skillet or deep-fat fryer, heat oil to 375°. Fry chicken, a few pieces at a time, for 6-10 minutes on each side or until chicken juices run clear. Drain on paper towels. **Yield:** 6-8 servings.

My guests rave about this salad. The big surprise is that there is no macaroni taste and it is not too sweet.   ~Ralph Beisel
ALLENTOWN, PENNSYLVANIA

Fruited Macaroni Salad

1/3 cup sugar
1 tablespoon all-purpose flour
Pinch salt
1 can (11 ounces) mandarin oranges, undrained
1 can (8 ounces) crushed pineapple, undrained
1 egg, lightly beaten
2 cups cooked elbow macaroni
1 cup whipped topping
1/4 cup chopped pecans, toasted

In a saucepan, combine the sugar, flour and salt. Drain juice from oranges and pineapple into a 1-cup measuring cup; cover and refrigerate fruit. Add enough water to the juice, if needed, to measure 1 cup; stir into the sugar mixture until smooth. Cook and stir over medium-high heat until thickened and bubbly.

Reduce heat; cook and stir 1 minute longer. Remove from the heat. Stir a small amount of hot mixture into egg; return all to pan, stirring constantly. Bring to a gentle boil; cook and stir 2 minutes longer. Remove from the heat.

In a bowl, combine the macaroni and cooked dressing. Cover and refrigerate for 8 hours or overnight. Just before serving, fold in whipped topping and reserved oranges and pineapple. Sprinkle with pecans. **Yield:** 6-8 servings.

This crunchy salad went so well with our chicken dinners. We always had a huge vegetable garden, and cabbage was plentiful.
~Jean Mahler
PERRINTON, MICHIGAN

Sweet-Sour Coleslaw

1/2 cup mayonnaise
1/3 cup sugar
1/4 cup buttermilk
2 tablespoons plus 1-1/2 teaspoons lemon juice
4-1/2 teaspoons cider vinegar
1/2 teaspoon salt
1/4 teaspoon pepper

1 medium head cabbage, shredded
1 medium carrot, shredded

In a small bowl, whisk together the first seven ingredients. Place the cabbage and carrot in a large bowl; add dressing and toss to coat. Cover and refrigerate for 1 hour or until serving. **Yield:** 10-12 servings.

This recipe was created years ago for church bridal and baby showers, the result of the hostess committee sharing ideas. We would use different flavored gelatins to color-coordinate with the decor of the occasion.
~Joy Bruce
WELCH, OKLAHOMA

Citrus Slush

2-1/2 cups sugar
1 package (3 ounces) lemon gelatin
1 package (3 ounces) pineapple gelatin
4 cups boiling water
1 can (12 ounces) frozen pineapple juice concentrate, thawed
1 cup lemon juice
1 envelope (0.23 ounce) unsweetened lemonade soft drink mix
10 cups cold water
2 liters ginger ale, chilled

In a large container, dissolve sugar and gelatins in boiling water. Stir in the pineapple juice concentrate, lemon juice, drink mix and cold water. If desired, place in smaller containers. Cover and freeze, stirring several times.

Remove from freezer at least 1 hour before serving. Stir until mixture becomes slushy. Just before serving, place 9 cups slush mixture in a punch bowl; stir in 1 liter ginger ale. Repeat with remaining slush and ginger ale. **Yield:** about 6 quarts (about 25 servings).

During the Depression, Mom's tasty salmon loaf was a welcome change from the usual meat loaf everyone made to stretch a meal. I still like a lot of the make-do meals of those days, but this loaf is one of my favorites.
~Dorothy Bateman
CARVER, MASSACHUSETTS

Salmon Loaf

1 small onion, finely chopped
1 can (14-3/4 ounces) salmon, drained, bones and skin removed
1/2 cup soft bread crumbs
1/4 cup butter, melted
3 eggs, *separated*
2 teaspoons lemon juice
1 teaspoon minced fresh parsley
1/2 teaspoon salt
1/8 teaspoon pepper

OLIVE CREAM SAUCE:
2 tablespoons butter
2 tablespoons all-purpose flour

1-1/2 cups milk
1/4 cup chopped stuffed olives

In a bowl, combine the first four ingredients. Stir in the egg yolks, lemon juice, parsley, salt and pepper. In a small mixing bowl, beat the egg whites on high speed until stiff peaks form. Fold into salmon mixture. Pour into a greased 8-in. x 4-in. x 2-in. loaf pan. Place loaf pan in a larger baking pan. Add 1 in. of hot water to larger pan.

Bake at 350° for 40-45 minutes or until a knife inserted near the center comes out clean. Let stand for 10 minutes before slicing.

Meanwhile, in a saucepan, melt the butter. Stir in flour until smooth; gradually add the milk. Bring to a boil; cook and stir for 1 minute or until thickened. Stir in olives. Serve over the salmon loaf. **Yield:** 4 servings.

This simple, refreshing salad suggests spring. The chopped dates complement the other ingredients, and slivered almonds give it a nice crunch.
~Katherine Clauson
PERHAM, MINNESOTA

Spinach Date Salad

6 cups torn fresh spinach

1 cup sliced fresh strawberries

1 cup chopped dates

1/4 cup slivered almonds

Raspberry *or* red wine vinaigrette

In a bowl, combine the spinach, strawberries, dates and almonds. Drizzle with vinaigrette; toss to coat. Serve immediately. **Yield:** 4-6 servings.

I've made this cake for my children, grandchildren and great-grandchildren. It is their favorite birthday cake…it's light and tasty, and lends itself beautifully to decorating. I often place a small arrangement of fresh flowers in the center.
~Grace Scowen
KELOWNA, BRITISH COLUMBIA

Daffodil Cake

6 egg whites

1/2 teaspoon cream of tartar

1/2 teaspoon vanilla extract

2/3 cup sugar

1/2 cup cake flour

1/2 teaspoon baking powder

1/2 teaspoon salt

YELLOW CAKE:

6 egg yolks

2 tablespoons warm water

1/2 cup cake flour

1/2 cup sugar

1 teaspoon baking powder

1/8 teaspoon salt

1/2 teaspoon vanilla extract

FROSTING:

1/2 cup sugar

4 teaspoons all-purpose flour

Pinch salt

1 cup pineapple juice

1 carton (8 ounces) frozen whipped topping, thawed

Place egg whites in a mixing bowl; let stand at room temperature for 30 minutes. Add cream of tartar and vanilla; beat on medium speed until foamy. Gradually beat in sugar, 1 tablespoon at a time, until soft peaks form. Combine the flour, baking powder and salt; fold into egg white mixture. Set aside.

In another large mixing bowl, beat egg yolks and water until thick and lemon-colored. Combine the flour, sugar, baking powder and salt; gradually beat into egg yolk mixture. Add vanilla. Alternately spoon yellow and white batters into an ungreased 10-in. tube pan. Bake at 350° for 35-40 minutes or until a toothpick inserted near the center comes out clean. Immediately invert pan.

For frosting, combine sugar, flour and salt in a saucepan. Stir in juice until blended. Bring to a boil; cook and stir for 2 minutes or until thickened. Cool. Fold in whipped topping. Remove cake from pan to a serving plate. Spread frosting over top and sides of cake. Store in the refrigerator. **Yield:** 12 servings.

This recipe was one of the first I tried from a new cookbook many years ago. I was intrigued by the variety of ingredients. It's been a favorite ever since, and whenever I take this dish somewhere, there are never any leftovers.
~Linda Stevens
MADISON, ALABAMA

Peas 'n' Bean Salad

1 package (10 ounces) frozen peas

1 package (10 ounces) frozen baby lima beans

1 package (9 ounces) frozen cut green beans

1 medium red onion, chopped

1 cup mayonnaise

1 tablespoon vegetable oil

1 to 2 teaspoons Worcestershire sauce

1/2 teaspoon salt

1/4 teaspoon pepper

Hard-cooked eggs, sliced

Sliced green onion, optional

Prepare the peas and beans according to package directions; drain and cool. Combine cooked vegetables in a 1-1/2-qt. clear glass bowl.

In a small bowl, combine red onion, mayonnaise, oil, Worcestershire sauce, salt and pepper; mix well. Spoon over vegetables; garnish with eggs and green onion if desired. Cover and refrigerate until serving. **Yield:** 6 servings.

General Recipe Index

☑ **Uses less fat, sugar or salt. Includes Nutrition Facts and Diabetic Exchanges.**

✓ **Uses less fat, sugar or salt. Includes Nutrition Facts and Diabetic Exchanges.**

✓ **Uses less fat, sugar or salt. Includes Nutrition Facts and Diabetic Exchanges.**

Alphabetical Index

✓ **Uses less fat, sugar or salt. Includes Nutrition Facts and Diabetic Exchanges.**